Final Cut® E[xpress] For Dumm[ies]

M000098760

File Menu Commands

Command	Keystroke Combination
New project	⌘+E
New sequence	⌘+N
New bin	⌘+B
Open	⌘+O
Save project	⌘+S
Save project as	Shift+⌘+S
Import files	⌘+I
Close active window	⌘+W
Close active tab	Control+W
Quit	⌘+Q

Edit Menu Commands

Command	Keystroke or Combination
Undo	⌘+Z
Redo	⌘+Y
Clear	Delete
Cut	⌘+X
Copy	⌘+C
Paste	⌘+V
Paste Insert	Shift+V
Find	⌘+F
Find Next	⌘+G
Selected Item Properties	⌘+9
Select All	⌘+A
Deselect All	⌘+D

Windows Menu Commands

Command	Keystroke Combination
Viewer	⌘+1
Canvas	⌘+2
Timeline	⌘+3
Browser	⌘+4
Audio Meters	Option+4
Effects	⌘+5
Trim edit	⌘+7
Log and Capture window	⌘+8
Standard window layout	Control+U

For Dummies: Bestselling Book Series for Beginners

Final Cut® Express For Dummies®

Editing Commands

Command	Keystroke or Combination
Mark in point	I
Mark out point	O
Clear in and out points	Option+X
Place marker	M
Delete marker	⌘+~
Mark clip	X
Select edit point	V
Insert edit (from Viewer)	F9
Overwrite edit (from Viewer)	F10
Fit to fill (from Viewer)	Shift+F11
Superimpose (from Viewer)	F12
Add edit	Control+V
Lift edit	Delete
Ripple delete	Shift+Delete
Make subclip (from Viewer)	⌘+U
Match frame	F
Snapping On/Off	N
Audio/Video linking On/Off	⌘+L
Default video transition	⌘+T
Set clip speed	⌘+J
Render selection	⌘+R
Sequence Settings	⌘+0

Navigation Controls

Command	Keystroke or Combination
Play forward: Fast-forward	L (repeat press for speed)
Play reverse: Fast-reverse	J (repeat press for speed)
Forward one frame	Right arrow (→)
Back one frame	Left arrow (←)
Forward one second	Shift+→
Back one second	Shift+←
Next edit	' or down arrow (↓)
Previous edit	; or up arrow (↑)
Next marker	Shift+↓
Previous marker	Shift+↑
Beginning of sequence	Home
End of sequence	End or Shift+Home
Zoom in	⌘++ (Note: That's the command key and the plus key together.)
Zoom out	⌘+-

The Tool Palette

- Selection tool
- Group tool
- Track tool
- Roll tool
- Slip tool
- Razor Blade tool
- Zoom tool
- Crop tool
- Pen tool

For Dummies: Bestselling Book Series for Beginners

Final Cut® Express

FOR

DUMMIES®

Final Cut® Express

FOR
DUMMIES®

by Helmut Kobler

WILEY

Wiley Publishing, Inc.

Final Cut® Express For Dummies®
Published by
Wiley Publishing, Inc.
909 Third Avenue
New York, NY 10022

www.wiley.com

Copyright © 2003 by Wiley Publishing, Inc., Indianapolis, Indiana

Published by Wiley Publishing, Inc., Indianapolis, Indiana

Published simultaneously in Canada

For general information on our other products and services or to obtain technical support, please contact
our Customer Care Department within the U.S. at 800-762-2974, outside the U.S. at 317-572-3993, or fax
317-572-4002.

Wiley also publishes its books in a variety of electronic formats. Some content that appears in print may
not be available in electronic books.

Library of Congress Control Number: 2003105405

ISBN: 0764541110

Manufactured in the United States of America

10 9 8 7 6 5 4 3 2 1

1B/SV/QU/QT/IN

About the Author

Helmut Kobler is a Los Angeles-based filmmaker who's putting the finishing touches on his latest project — a sci-fi action adventure entitled *Radius*. (You can see scenes from *Radius* in many of this book's figures.). Helmut's a confessed Mac addict (he writes a lot for *MacAddict* magazine, too) and has been using the Mac since 1987. In a past life, he directed and produced award-winning video games for PCs and the Sony Playstation.

If you want to know more about Helmut's film *Radius*, visit the Web site at www.radiusmovie.com.

Dedication

I'd like to dedicate this book to my father — a concentration camp survivor and self-made man who's always been an inspiration and a friend.

Author's Acknowledgments

At Wiley Publishing, I'd like to thank acquisition editor Tiffany Franklin for bringing me into this project and project editor Kala Schrager and copy editor Barb Terry for helping to hone my focus and prose to *For Dummies* standards. I'd also like to thank Cameron Craig and Jerry Hsu, from Apple, for their help in getting the project moving.

Publisher's Acknowledgments

We're proud of this book; please send us your comments through our online registration form located at www.dummies.com/register/.

Some of the people who helped bring this book to market include the following:

Acquisitions, Editorial, and Media Development

Project Editor: Kala Schrager

Acquisitions Editor: Tiffany Franklin

Copy Editor: Barbara Terry

Technical Editor: John Matson

Editorial Manager: Kevin Kirschner

Permissions Editor: Carmen Krikorian

Media Development Manager: Laura VanWinkle

Media Development Supervisor: Richard Graves

Editorial Assistant: Amanda Foxworth

Cartoons: Rich Tennant (www.the5thwave.com)

Production

Project Coordinator: Maridee Ennis

Layout and Graphics: Jennifer Click, Seth Conley, Lynsey Osborn, Jeremey Unger

Proofreaders: John Greenough, John Tyler Connoley

Indexer: TECHBooks Production Services

Publishing and Editorial for Technology Dummies

Richard Swadley, Vice President and Executive Group Publisher

Andy Cummings, Vice President and Publisher

Mary C. Corder, Editorial Director

Publishing for Consumer Dummies

Diane Graves Steele, Vice President and Publisher

Joyce Pepple, Acquisitions Director

Composition Services

Gerry Fahey, Vice President of Production Services

Debbie Stailey, Director of Composition Services

Contents at a Glance

Table of Contents

Introduction

Welcome to *Final Cut Express For Dummies!* Final Cut Express is a digital editing program that lets you capture raw video and audio (for example, dialogue, sound effects, and music) on your Macintosh and assemble these separate elements into polished movies ready for the Internet, CD-ROM, DVD, television, and even the big screen.

Final Cut Express is actually a spin-off of the Apple Computer Final Cut Pro software, which sells for about $1,000, and can do just about every last little thing a professional video editor could want (no wonder Pro has caught on like wildfire). But Apple realized that not every editor — professional or just arm-chair movie makers — needs all the Final Cut Pro features, let alone its hefty price tag, so voila: Final Cut Express was born! With its impressive features, bargain-basement price ($300!), and featherweight hardware requirements, Express is aimed at a new breed of digital filmmaker who are making their videos — from start to finish — right from their desktops. (By the way, I tend to refer to Final Cut Express as "Final Cut" or "Express" for short.)

About This Book

I wrote this book for two kinds of people: On one hand, it's for beginners who have no experience with Final Cut Express or digital video editing in general. On the other hand, the book is equally handy for those who've done digital editing with another program — maybe Adobe Premiere or Avid Media Composer — and who just need to know which button to press or menu item to choose in order to get things done.

Regardless of which camp you fall into, I think that you'll appreciate the book for its clear, down-to-earth, non-techy explanations. This book shows you what you're most likely to need without overwhelming you with every last nuance of every last obscure little feature. So when you turn to a chapter or a topic heading, I tell you what's most important to know about that topic right off the bat, and then I throw in some finer details to round off your grasp of it. End result? You'll be up and running with Final Cut Express in as little time as possible.

I admit: Final Cut Express can look a bit complicated and intimidating at first glance — especially if you're stepping up from a program like iMovie. When you load Express up, you're faced with lots of different windows, palettes, and extensive menu choices, but don't let them fool you!

Using Final Cut Express is like driving a car: Despite all the sophisticated gadgets and gizmos built into cars these days (environmental systems, GPS locators, night vision, and so on), all you really need in order to go anywhere is the gas, brake, and steering wheel. And so it goes with Final Cut Express: Despite all its features, you honestly can start editing with it very quickly by using just a few simple tools. (Just 20 to 30 minutes with this book should get you to this point.) After that, you can add to your skills at your own pace.

Take a quick look at some of the ground I cover in this book. You can find out how to do the following tasks is Final Cut Express:

- Equip your Macintosh so that it runs Final Cut Express smoothly
- Bring in media clips (pieces of video, audio, and still pictures) from different sources, such as DV videotape, microphones, music CD, or QuickTime media files
- Organize your media clips so that you can find them quickly and easily
- Arrange your video clips in time so that they tell the story you want to tell
- Add multiple audio tracks for dialogue, music, and sound effects
- Add text, such as opening titles and closing credits
- Use filters to stylize the look of your video and the sound of your audio
- Composite different video together to create montages or special effects (for example, placing an actor videoed against a blue screen in an entirely different setting)
- Record your final movie to DV videotape or save it as a QuickTime file (for DVD, CD-ROM, or Internet distribution)

In other words, you can be a movie-making machine in no time!

How to Use This Book

I don't expect you to read this book from cover to cover. For starters, you probably don't have the time to read all 384 pages, and even if you did, you'd suffer from information overload for sure!

Instead, I recommend this approach: Think about what you want to do with Final Cut Express, and then use this book to fill in whatever know-how you're missing. If you're completely new to digital video editing (or editing in general), you probably want to read closely, starting at Chapter 1, and continuing on until you've got your bearings. On the other hand, if you have digital editing experience, you're likely to hop and skip around, grabbing whatever you need and then moving on.

Adapt the book to your style of learning and your level of expertise. I wrote it with that kind of flexibility in mind, so you can get the most out of it with the least amount of effort or legwork.

One more thing: I recommend picking up the book every once in a while and browsing it for nothing in particular. You'd be surprised how much useful info you can pick up just by scanning headings and flipping through pages!

Foolish Assumptions

I made some (possibly foolish) assumptions about you as I wrote this book. I assume that you either don't have video editing experience, or that your experience is with a program other than Final Cut Express. (Maybe you've done some editing with other programs, such as Adobe Premiere or the Apple easy-does-it iMovie.) Either way, you'll feel right at home here.

Finally, I assume that you've mastered the basics of using a Mac, given whichever operating system you're running. Your expertise should include opening and saving files in the Mac standard dialog boxes, navigating your hard drive files with the Mac Finder, and so on — pretty straightforward stuff.

How This Book Is Organized

This book is organized to follow the basic workflow you'll use while editing. Part I gives you a bird's-eye-view of the entire editing process, so you understand each and every step you'll take to bring your projects to completion. Part II shows you how to import and organize the video and audio media your projects call for, while Part III shows how to edit all that media together into the story you want to tell. Part IV shows you how to add all sorts of pizzazz — such as titles, transitions, and special effects to your project — and Part V covers your options for saving your final movie to either tape or digital video files.

Here's a closer look at each part.

Part 1: First Things First

Part I is a quick introduction to the world of Final Cut Express and digital video in general. I explain how Express can help you make movies, commercials, documentaries, and all sorts of other video content, and I briefly cover how Express differs from its big brother, the esteemed Final Cut Pro. I also take you step by step through the Express workflow and give you a quick tour of its interface. Finally, I help you get up and running for the first time: I cover hardware requirements, show you how to connect all your hardware components together, advise you on locking in your general settings, and show you how to create and manage Express document files, called *projects*.

Part 11: Importing and Organizing Your Media

Part II shows you how to capture, import, and organize all the media you want to use in your Final Cut Express projects (that is, video, dialogue, music, sound effects, still pictures, titles, and so on). I show you how to capture (some say *digitize*) media from videotape by using a DV camera or deck that you've connected to your Mac. I also show you how to bring media into Express that's from sources other than videotape — video or audio files already on your hard drive, songs from a music CD, graphics from Photoshop, and so on.

Finally, I show you how to name, annotate, and organize all these different media clips in the Final Cut Browser window (the central repository for all your media), so you can easily find them when you need them.

Part 111: Editing Your Media

Part III is where the rubber meets the road, showing you how to take all your project media and arrange it in time so it tells the story you want to tell. I start with the basics of editing video and audio: that is, how to move clips to the Final Cut Express Timeline and then resize those clips, cut them up, or move them in time. I cover a lot of ground here, but by the time you reach the end of Chapter 6, you'll be able to edit most meat-and-potatoes projects. Later in Part III, I round out your new skills, giving you finer control over the Timeline, which is the heart of your editing universe, and I tackle the more-advanced editing features of Express. These advanced topics are things you don't need to know to accomplish most editing tasks, but they'll ultimately give you a lot more control over your work.

Part IV: Adding Pizzazz

Knowing how to edit media clips together is only half the fun in Final Cut Express. It offers tons of other tools and features that let you add real polish and pizzazz to your projects — things like slick transitions, moving titles, stylized image and sound effects, and more. In Part IV, I show you how to use many express video transitions, which let you smoothly blend one video clip to another. I also tackle how to create all sorts of titles in Express: everything from standard white-on-black text to typewriter effects to the scrolling credits you see at the end of a movie — plus plenty of other options.

Part V: Outputting Your Masterpiece

After you're finished editing and adding extra pizzazz (transitions, titles, filters, effects, and so on), you're ready for Part V, which focuses on outputting your movie to its final media destination. I've got all your bases covered: I show you how to record your finished masterpiece back to videotape (for tape duplication or broadcast) and how to save your finished movie to a QuickTime digital file, which you can later burn to a DVD or CD-ROM or broadcast over the Internet.

Part VI: The Part of Tens

What's a *For Dummies* book without The Part of Tens? I offer tips for managing projects in Final Cut Express. Finally, I serve up simple things you can do to become a more capable Final Cut Express editor, from honing your creative and technical know-how to upgrading your current Mac setup.

Icons Used in This Book

Tip icons provide extra information for a specific purpose. Tips can save you time and effort, so they're worth checking out.

Always read text marked with the Warning icon: These icons emphasize that dire consequences are ahead for the unwary.

This icon flags information and techniques that are a bit more techy than other sections of the book. The information here can be interesting and helpful, but you don't need to understand it to use the information in the book.

This icon is a sticky note of sorts, highlighting information that's worth committing to memory.

Contacting the Author

If you'd like to get in touch with me, Helmut Kobler, to say hello, ask a question not covered in this book, or offer feedback (which is very much appreciated), don't hesitate to drop an e-mail message at director@k2films.com.

Part I
First Things First

The 5th Wave   By Rich Tennant

"WELL! IT LOOKS LIKE SOMEONE FOUND THE 'LION'S ROAR' ON THE SOUND CONTROL PANEL."

In this part . . .

Part I is a quick introduction to the world of Final Cut Express and digital video in general, focusing on how Express can help you make movies, corporate and sales videos, commercials, documentaries, and all sorts of other video content. I take you step by step through the Express workflow and give you a tour of its interface. I discuss hardware and software requirements and show you how to connect all your major hardware components together. Then I tackle how to set the initial Express settings and conclude by showing you how to manage Express document files (called projects).

Chapter 1

Introducing Final Cut Express

*I*f you've watched your share of movies, you know that a good movie is made of many different elements, including photography, music, sound effects, and dialogue. However, these elements can only become a compelling story after they are woven seamlessly together. Final Cut Express can help with this task of making the end result greater than the sum of its parts.

Understanding the Purpose of Editing

Editing video or film is a bit like writing. When you write (or when *I* write, at least) you start by putting all your ideas on paper — good or bad — so that you can see what you're working with. Then you take the *best* ideas and arrange them in a logical order so that they say what you mean, as clearly and efficiently as possible.

It works the same way when you're editing digital video. (In this book, I refer to film as "video" from now on.) First, you scrutinize all the footage you shot on set (usually a lot). Slowly, you figure out which shots to keep and which ones to send to the proverbial cutting room floor. You may remove a shot for any number of reasons: weak acting, technical problems, or the fact that you can see a crew member's foot in frame. Next, you arrange your keeper shots, one by one, so that they begin to tell a story, and you bring in your dialogue, music, and sound effects to make the project complete.

Exploring the Capabilities of Final Cut Express

Final Cut Express lets you to do all this editing work on your Mac. To be a little more specific, when you're behind the wheel with Express, you can do the following:

- ✔ **Capture:** Capture video or audio from digital video (DV) cameras and video decks, CDs, microphones, and existing digital files onto your hard drive.

- ✔ **Organize:** Organize all your media files so that you can easily find them (a project might call for hundreds of different files).

- ✔ **Edit:** Edit your footage together, which is almost as easy as cutting and pasting text in a word processor.

- ✔ **Add audio:** Add audio to your movie — be it dialogue, voice narration, music, or sound effects — and control the volume for each.

- ✔ **Create transitions and add title:** Create transitions, such as fades and wipes, between shots and design title cards and credits.

- ✔ **Add effects:** Enhance video and audio with tons of custom effects filters.

- ✔ **Composite:** Create impressive visual montages by *compositing* (combining) multiple shots into one. This process is similar to the one in the popular Adobe After Effects program.

- ✔ **Create a final product:** Record your polished masterpiece to DV videotape, or export it to digital files destined for DVD, CD-ROM, or the Web.

Appreciating nondestructive editing

One of the great things about Final Cut Express is that it's a *nondestructive* editor, which means that no matter what you do to your video and audio inside the program, the original media files on your hard drive are never changed or erased. Say you have a bunch of video files on your hard drive, and you bring them into Express to edit together. Although it may seem as if you're cutting this media into different pieces, resizing it, and even deleting it, that's not the case. When you're editing, you're really just creating and moving a bunch of digital pointers to the media on your hard drive. The pointers tell Express what parts of the media you want to play in your final movie (in other words, play Clip A for three seconds, and then play part of Clip C for two seconds, and so on). Thanks to this approach, you can work and experiment knowing that you aren't hurting your precious media.

From the Stone Age to the Digital Age

You'll appreciate Final Cut Express even more when you consider how video editors worked in the days before digital media — it was slow and tedious, to say the least.

If you were a video editor in the dark ages, you edited with two video decks. On Deck A, you played through all your raw footage until you identified the shots you wanted to use in your edited story. Then you used Deck B to record those shots to a master tape (your show-in-progress), one shot after another. The process was entirely *linear* — you'd record the first shot you wanted in your show, and then the second, the third, fourth, and so on. And, later on, if you decided to insert or remove a shot in that sequence, you had to rewind the master tape to that point, record your change, and then *rere-cord* all the shots that followed your change — *ugh!*

By the way, that's why Apple calls Final Cut Express a *nonlinear editor.* Your footage isn't on a linear tape; it's on the hard drive and in the memory so that you can place it and rearrange it without negative repercussions. Express is to video editing what Microsoft Word is to that old Smith-Micro typewriter sitting in your garage.

Comparing Final Cut Express to the competition

Plenty of other editing programs are available these days: Premiere, Avid Media Composer, Avid Xpress DV, SpeedRazor, Final Cut Pro, and Apple's own iMovie all come to mind.

Several things make Final Cut Express special:

- ✔ **It's brimming with features:** Final Cut Express not only delivers the big power-features that sound great on the back of the box but also gets tons of details right — the little, thoughtful things that help you work smoothly, in a way that suits your personal style. Granted, Express can't do *everything,* but many editing jobs don't require *everything.* Some video editors — particularly those that work exclusively with footage in the digital video (DV) format — may never need another program.

- ✔ **Final Cut Express is relatively easy to use:** Okay, so it's not quite as easy as iMovie, but Express is streamlined enough that even casual, arm-chair editors can figure it out with a little homework (this book, of course, helps quite a bit). And iMovie can't do half the heavy lifting that Express can.

- ✔ **You don't need a super-computer or expensive, proprietary hardware to run Final Cut Express:** You can build your editing system around any Mac made within the last three or so years (including consumer iMacs and iBooks) and everyday peripherals, such as FireWire hard drives and inexpensive DV video cameras. (See Chapter 2 for more about system requirements.)

✔ **Final Cut Express is a steal at $300:** This price is about as inexpensive as professional video editing programs get — by a couple hundred dollars at least! Express is so cheap, in fact (and I mean cheap in a good way), that you don't even have to be a professional to afford it. It costs a little more than copy of Microsoft Word, and it's much more fun to use!

✔ **You can easily step up to Final Cut Pro:** Final Cut Express can handle many professional level editing jobs, but if your editing needs change, you can easily step up to Final Cut Pro from Apple, which can handle pretty much anything. Because Express and Pro use the same exact interface, and work with the same media files, and read the same project files, you won't skip a beat moving from Express to Pro. (See Chapter 18 for a rundown of what the Pro version gets you.)

Going with the Final Cut (Work) Flow

Final Cut Express starts to make sense when you take a look at the big picture by understanding how you'll use it from start to finish. So I've summarized its workflow in four easy steps:

1. **Capture and import all the media — that is, video, audio, and still pictures — that you want to use in your project.**

   This media can come from a camera, video deck, music CD, or other digital files already on your hard drive (or some other media, like a DVD-ROM disk, which is like a CD-ROM but it holds about 7 times as much information). The media shows up in the Final Cut Express Browser window, where you have easy access to it. Each piece of media you bring into the Browser by the way, is called a *clip*.

2. **Move your media clips to the all-important Final Cut Express Timeline.**

   You use the Timeline to place, move, and otherwise edit clips so that they tell the story you want to create.

3. **Add pizzazz in the form of titles, transitions (such as fades, dissolves, and wipes), and more advanced special effects.**

4. **Record your project to videotape or export it to a QuickTime digital file.**

   You'll make QuickTime digital files if you're aiming for digital distribution, such as the Internet, CD-ROM, or DVD.

Final Cut Express brims with many windows, dialog boxes, menus, and check boxes, but all this *apparent* complexity really boils down to the four easy preceding steps. Keep that in mind, and you'll see that using Express isn't rocket science.

Taking a Grand Tour of the Interface

After you've gotten a grasp of the Final Cut Express workflow, you can expand your expertise by taking a tour of the Express interface — namely its toolbar and the Browser, Viewer, Canvas, and Timeline windows, as shown in Figure 1-1. Keeping track of all these elements can seem daunting, but they don't have much to them, and they work together in an intuitive way. *Trust me*.

By the way, the Final Cut Express windows may be arranged differently on your screen than the way they're arranged in Figure 1-1. To get your screen to look like my screen shot, choose Window➪Arrange➪Standard from the menu bar at the top.

Viewer window   Canvas window

Figure 1-1:
The Final
Cut Express
interface.

Browser window   Timeline window   Tool palette

The Browser

The Browser is the central storage depot for all the media clips used by your Final Cut Express project. Just think of the Browser as a big file cabinet. When you want to work with a file (that is, a clip of media), you open the cabinet (or the Browser window) and grab whatever you need.

Although the Browser is powerful, you really need to know only these basics: When you import a piece of media into your project (either from your hard drive or by capturing it from videotape), the media automatically appears in the Browser as a *clip,* as shown in Figure 1-2. Within the Browser window, you can also create *bins,* which store groups of related media clips and help you keep your media well organized. (Bins work a lot like folders on your hard drive.)

Bin icons

Figure 1-2:
You can
view items
in the
Browser in
Icon view or
List view
(just like
your Mac's
Finder).

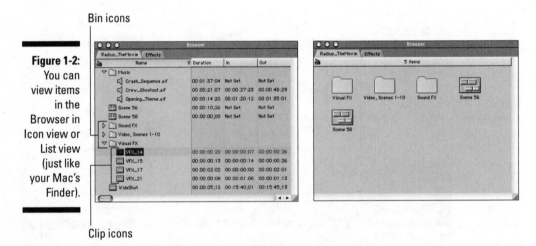

Clip icons

Besides clips and bins, the Browser window is also the home of any sequences you create for your movie. A *sequence* is a collection of clips that you've edited together in the Final Cut Express Timeline window. You might edit your movie into a single sequence, or for longer-running projects, such as a two-hour feature, you could create each major scene in its own sequence because shorter sequences are be a bit easier to navigate and work with.

The Viewer

The Viewer window lets you look at and listen to your media clips before you move them to the Final Cut Express Timeline. You can also use the Viewer to modify your media clips by using a variety of the Express effects filters, superimposed titles, and animation effects. To open a clip in the Viewer, just double-click its name or icon in the Browser window.

Playing with play controls

The Viewer sports an assortment of buttons and other gizmos, but focus for now on its play controls, shown in Figure 1-3. You can click the Play button to play your clip forward (another click pauses your clip), or use the Viewer Jog and Shuttle controls to move forward and in reverse at different speeds, also shown in Figure 1-3. As a clip plays, you see the Viewer playhead move across what's called the *scrubber bar,* frame by frame. You can click anywhere in the scrubber bar to move the playhead to that point, or click and drag the playhead anywhere as well.

Figure 1-3:
The Viewer lets you preview either video or audio clips (shown as waveforms) before bringing them to the Timeline.

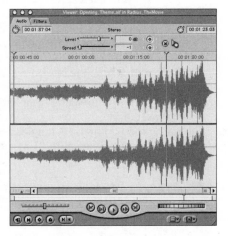

Shuttle   The Play/Pause button   Jog

The ins and outs of ins and outs

Besides playing clips, you use the Viewer to edit clips in a very basic way by setting *In* and *Out points.* (In fact, you also use these points in other Final Cut Express windows, but they're "regulars" in the Viewer.) As shown in Figure 1-4, In and Out points let you isolate only the part of a clip that you're interested in, before bringing it to the Timeline. Say you have a great clip, except that the first four seconds suffer from a shaky camera and the last five seconds prominently feature the leg of a crew member. Because you don't want to bring the entire clip to the Timeline, you can use the Viewer to set an In point at the clip's first good frame (right after the camera shake) and an Out point at the last good frame (before the leg shows up). Then Express knows to use only the frames between those points. (See Chapters 3 and 6 for more.)

In point   Out point

Figure 1-4:
In and Out
points.

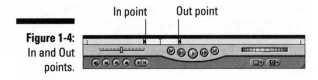

The Timeline

The Final Cut Express Timeline lets you arrange *when* your media clips play.
To better understand the Timeline, think of it as a sheet of music. Rather than
place musical notes one after another on the page, you place clips of video
and audio, and you tell Express how long to play each one — for example,
show a black screen for two seconds, play video Clip A for four seconds, then
play Clip B for three seconds, and so on.

So how does the Timeline work? I talk about plenty of nuances throughout the
book, but check out Figure 1-5 to take in the basics. Stretching across the top
of the Timeline is a bar with notches and numbers, which looks like a ruler.
But those numbers aren't measurements of distance, they're measurements
of time, increasing from left to right (for example, 5 seconds, 10 seconds, 15
seconds, and so on). As you edit, you move your media clips to the Timeline
(solid-colored rectangles represent clips on the Timeline) and position them
under a time value. That's exactly where, in time, the clips play in your story.

Figure 1-5:
Clips on the
Timeline,
playing at
0 seconds,
4 seconds,
and
8 seconds
into this
movie-in-
progress.

Video (V1) track   Clips on the Timeline   Ruler

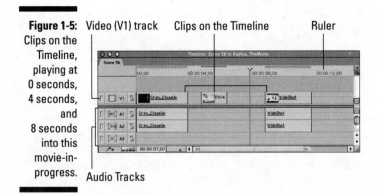

Audio Tracks

In Figure 1-5, you can also see that video clips appear in row V1 of the Timeline,
while audio clips (such as dialogue) go in rows A1 and A2 below it. (Final Cut
Express calls these rows *tracks,* but more on these later.) Some of your media
clips come with video and audio linked together in the same clip, in which
case, Express shows the clip in both the video and audio tracks. Other clips

carry just video or audio; for example, you can see in the figure that the video clip labeled FX14 has no audio along with it.

The Tool palette

After you move media clips to the Timeline, you can edit them, that is, make them last longer or shorter in time, cut them into smaller pieces, and rearrange them until they tell your story. Enter the Final Cut Express Tool palette, shown in Figure 1-6, which offers a host of tools that you can select (just click 'em) and use to edit your clips in all sorts of ways. The tool you'll find yourself using the most is the standard Selection tool (the plain arrow at the top of the palette), which you use to select and move media clips on the Timeline. To be honest, you can edit an entire movie with this tool alone, but the other palette tools make that work much easier. Some of the handy ones let you select huge groups of clips at once, cut clips in two, or quickly magnify your view of the Timeline so that you can better see what you're doing. You get to know all these tools soon enough.

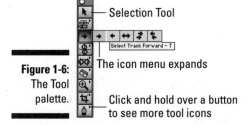

Selection Tool

Select Track Forward – T

The icon menu expands

Click and hold over a button
to see more tool icons

Figure 1-6:
The Tool
palette.

When you see a little black triangle in the upper-right corner of a tool icon, more tool icons are hidden underneath it. These additional tools are all related but do slightly different things. Just click and hold down the mouse button on such an icon, and the hidden tools pop up for you to choose.

The Canvas

After you've edited your video and audio clips on the Timeline and want to see (and hear) how they all play together, turn your attention to the Final Cut Express Canvas window. The Canvas is where you watch your movie-in-progress as you've arranged it on the Timeline.

As you can see in Figure 1-7, the Canvas looks a lot like the Viewer. You *do* have the same play controls, but the Canvas has some differences. (For instance, you can perform some basic edits on the Canvas instead of the

Timeline.) For now, all you need to know is that the Canvas lets you play, move forward, pause, and rewind through your Final Cut Express movie.

Figure 1-7:
The Canvas window plays the clips you've arranged on the Timeline.

Play / Pause button

Audio meters

The Final Cut Express Audio meters, shown in Figure 1-8, are supporting cast members, but they are really handy when you're tweaking your audio to sound as good as possible. In a nutshell, the meters visually show you the decibel (dB) range of an audio clip. (*Decibel* is a fancy way of saying *loudness.*) Using the meters as a guide, you can set the volume levels of all the audio clips in your movie so that they don't overpower one another. Also, the meters show you when a clip of audio is playing so loud that it's in danger of distorting.

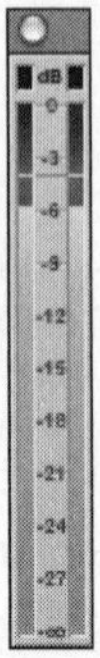

Figure 1-8:
The Audio meters can tell you when your audio is distorting.

Keyboard shortcuts

Final Cut Express sports tons of keyboard shortcuts to make you a faster editor. The shortcuts are extensive, letting you do everything from editing clips and navigating the Timeline to playing back video and selecting any tool in the Tool palette.

I point out keyboard shortcuts as I come to them, but if you're wondering whether the program has a shortcut for something you're doing, you can check out the Cheat Sheet at the front of this book, which is a reference card for handy shortcuts.

Chapter 2

Getting Started

*B*efore you can get into the fun of capturing and editing your media in Final Cut Express, you have to get a few preliminaries out of the way. For instance, you have to figure out what hardware you need to accomplish your editing goals. You also have to configure the Express settings to work with your particular hardware setup. Finally, you have to create a new project, which is where the editing magic begins.

Hardware Requirements

If you already have your Final Cut Express system assembled, you may want to skip to the "Getting Started" section, later in this chapter. But if you're still deciding what you need in order to build a workable Express system, or if you have questions about how you can expand the system you already have, read on.

QuickTime, compression codecs, and DV

QuickTime is a file format that your Mac uses to save video and audio (just as Photoshop saves pictures in its own file format, and Microsoft Word saves text in its own file format). QuickTime files are standard on the Mac, and any Mac software program — including Final Cut Express — that uses video or audio is designed to play and save QuickTime files.

However, all QuickTime files are not alike. For starters, the video/audio media within a QuickTime file can be compressed or left uncompressed. (*Compression* is a process where the digital data that describes media is paired down to its essential parts. This process has benefits and tradeoffs, which I discuss in a moment). QuickTime media can be compressed using a one of many different compression technologies.

Compression is particularly common in QuickTime video files. The reason is that uncompressed digital video is so incredibly rich in data that computers and cameras have to be very powerful — and therefore expensive — to capture, play, and store it all. When video is compressed, a lot of its data is tossed out, which makes it easier for ordinary computers (like your Mac) and consumer video cameras to manage. The tradeoff is that compressed video may not look quite as crisp and clear as raw video because less data is used to describe it.

Clever programmers have designed lots of compression technologies called *codecs* that are custom tailored to particular jobs. For instance, one codec called MPEG-2 is used exclusively to compress video that goes on commercial DVD movie disks, and another codec called Sorenson 3 is used to compress QuickTime video that will be downloaded via the Internet.

The compression technology that matters most to you is called DV. DV video is compressed five times (meaning it uses one-fifth the data that raw video needs), and this compression sacrifices some image quality in your video — that is, DV's images are never quite as crisp as uncompressed video, and its colors aren't quite as true. Still, DV video looks great to most people, especially when it's seen on regular TVs, and it's become a big standard. For instance, many video cameras these days are designed to record and play their images and sound in DV (look for the miniDV logo on these devices), and this DV footage looks good enough to be used in home videos, documentaries, some news programming, reality TV shows, industrial and wedding videos, and independent films. (Of course, some professional markets demand uncompressed video's perfection, which is why DV is not used for major broadcast programming and slick TV commercials.)

Final Cut Express works natively with QuickTime files that use DV compression. This means that although Express can actually import video and audio that isn't compressed with DV, Express converts anything media you import so that it uses DV compression. (This conversion is done through a process called *rendering*, which I talk about later.) The result is that this non-DV media ends up using DV compression anyway.

A fully functional Final Cut Express system needs only a few things:

> ✔ **A half-decent Mac:** For your purposes, a half-decent Mac meets the following minimum requirements:

- A 300 MHz G3 or G4 processor

- 256MB (megabytes) of RAM

- A hard drive with 40MB of free space for the Final Cut Express application

Your Mac needs to run the OS X operating system (version 10.2 or better — nope, OS 9 won't work). Your system also needs a built-in FireWire port, which lets you connect different devices to your Mac.

✔ **A DV video camera or playback deck:** You need a camera or deck to play existing video footage into Final Cut Express, so it can be captured to the hard drive. However, any old video camera or deck won't work; you need a device that works with video/audio in the digital video (DV) format. (See the sidebar, "QuickTime, compression codecs, and DV," if you're curious about the ins and outs of DV video.) You'll know these devices because they tend to have a little miniDV logo on them (but I just say "DV" for short). Most consumer video cameras these days work in DV, and some models of VCRs do, too.

So these requirements are all you actually need to get started with Final Cut Express, but within these two requirements, you have plenty of different options to consider. For instance, would your ideal Mac be a laptop or desktop model, and how should it *really* be configured so that you can get your work done comfortably? (The Express system requirements are bare minimums. You may want a faster CPU, more RAM, and a bigger, faster hard drive than Express officially requires.) Also, although all you *need* is a Mac and a DV camera (or playback deck) for editing, you may appreciate extra hardware and software components, such as a DVD burner to record your finished movies to DVDs, or a television monitor so that you can watch your movie-in-progress on a real TV instead of a small window on your Mac.

Selecting and Configuring a Mac

Final Cut Express demands more hardware firepower than a word processing program or Internet browser demands, but you don't need a top-of-the-line Mac to run it. In fact, Express runs comfortably on just about any Mac made since 1999 or 2000 (except for some of the older iMacs and iBooks). This section looks at some Mac models you may want to consider, as well as what you need in terms of RAM, hard drives, monitors, and more:

✔ **PowerMacs:** The stylish, upright Apple towers known as PowerMacs are the crown jewels of the Mac line. They sport the fastest CPUs (dual CPUs, in fact), the largest hard drives, the most RAM, the capability to drive two video monitors at once. PowerMacs also offer expansion card slots that let you add an uncompressed video capture card or high-speed SCSI controller, but these extras aren't necessary for editing DV video and might be wasted on Final Cut Express. If your top priority is building a high-performance editing workstation with lots of room to grow, then PowerMacs are the way to go. That being said, you can easily get a lot out of Express without going for these top-of-the-line Macs.

✓ **PowerBooks:** The Apple PowerBooks have become so good that they can handle tons of editing work without breaking a sweat. PowerBooks aren't as feature-packed as desktop Macs, but don't underestimate the benefits of tucking your editing system in a small shoulder bag and taking it wherever you go. You can also work around PowerBook limitations: You can boost memory, attach a second screen, and add more storage via small, external FireWire hard drives. The only thing you can't upgrade is its CPU, but PowerBooks these days feature G4 processors, which are usually fast enough.

✓ **iBooks:** Although not as fast or feature-packed as PowerBooks, you can still get quite a lot done with an iBook. Limitations include its smallish screen (12 or 14 inches, which might cause occasional squinting), as well as slower CPUs (G3s as of this writing), and no option for attaching a second screen. For the money, however, an iBook can still deliver quite a lot of editing bang for the buck.

✓ **iMacs/eMacs:** You can also build a fine Express editing system around either the iMac or budget eMac. These systems also have fast G4 processors, and while they can't accept expansion cards or work with two monitors at once, you can easily live without such frills.

CPU speed

The brain of your Mac is called its *central processing unit* (CPU), and a CPU's speed is typically measured in megahertz (MHz). The faster your Mac's CPU is, the faster Final Cut Express runs. How fast should your Mac's CPU be to run Final Cut Express comfortably? The answer totally depends on the kind of editing work you're doing.

If you're largely doing "cuts-only" editing, in which most of your work is simply cutting up media clips and arranging them on the Timeline with a cross fade or other transition here or there, even a G3 CPU running at 400 MHz can do the job. (However, I don't recommend something as slow as the Apple 300 MHz requirement.) Things may certainly feel peppier on a faster machine — say, a 700 or 800 MHz G3 — but the difference won't make or break your productivity.

On the other hand, when you do a variety of effects work in Final Cut Express (tons of transitions, color correction, motion graphics, and/or compositing lots of images together), the CPU can make a big difference. All those effects have to be *rendered* (calculated) before you can play them in real time, and how fast they're rendered depends almost entirely on the brute strength of the CPU. To give you an idea of the difference a fast CPU can make, suppose that you want to render a movie in Express. A G3 would take almost twice as long as a G4 CPU and close to three times when compared to a PowerMac with two G4s inside. If you're going to be rendering a lot, I recommend splurging for the fastest Mac you can afford.

A CPU MHz rating isn't the only major factor that determines its speed. G4 CPUs have special units called Altivec engines built in, which turbo-charge graphics and video work even further. So if you want to cut down your rendering times, go for a Mac with a G4 (even if it has the same MHz as a G3).

Memory (RAM)

I recommend you have at least 384MB of RAM in your Mac to run Final Cut Express. Technically, you can get away with using only 256MB of RAM, but if you try do so, the Mac OS X operating system uses your hard drive to temporarily store data that would normally go into RAM (this is called *virtual memory*). Unfortunately, your Mac tends to pause while it temporarily stores data, which can get downright annoying.

When you run Final Cut Express with 384MB of RAM, you still get pauses from time to time but far less frequently that you do with less RAM. You also have enough room to keep a few other applications open at the same time (programs for e-mail, Web browsing, and sound and graphics work) so that you can switch from one program to another quickly and easily.

If you want to run Final Cut Express with other memory-hungry applications open at the same time (typically photo or effects programs such as Adobe Photoshop and After Effects), you'll probably want to stock your Mac with 512MB or even a gigabyte (GB) of RAM.

Disk storage for DV video

DV video eats up a ton of hard drive space. You need about 13GB for every hour of DV video stored. Unless you're doing short home videos, commercial or quick music videos, you probably need to add more drive space than an internal hard drive offers. Fortunately, one of the nice things about working with DV video is that you can use affordable hard drives to store it — as opposed to the pros who work with uncompressed video need very fast and very expensive drives. Your options come in two basic flavors:

✔ **An internal Ultra-ATA drive:** This drive can replace your main system drive (if you're using an iMac or Mac laptop) or be added to it (in the case of PowerMacs, which can accommodate one to three extra drives in addition to your main system drive).

✔ **An external FireWire drive:** This drive plugs into a Mac FireWire port. Most Macs made since 2000 have them.(If yours doesn't, you can usually buy an add-on card that adds this port.) I like external FireWire drives for a number of reasons:

• You can easily move them around — to bring footage to another Mac or PC somewhere off-site, for example.

• They're hot-pluggable, meaning you can plug one into your Mac and use it without restarting the Mac.

• You can connect dozens of FireWire drives together (called *daisy-chaining*) so that you can easily add more storage when you need it.

• If you're running Final Cut Express on a laptop, you can buy small FireWire drives that draw power from your Mac battery, so they don't need AC power — the ultimate in mobility.

Not all Ultra-ATA or FireWire drives make the cut for video editing. Make sure your drive runs at least at 5400 RPM (Revolutions Per Minute); 7200 RPM is ideal, but if you're buying an internal drive for a laptop, 5400 RPM is currently the best you can get. And if you're choosing a FireWire external drive, make sure that it uses the Oxford 911 bridge chip set. Otherwise, the drive may not be fast enough to capture video in real time without missing frames here and there (a big no-no) or to play all the frames in a clip smoothly. Drive manufacturers don't often advertise whether their products use the Oxford chip set, so you may have to scrutinize the drive datasheet or call the manufacturer.

In practical terms, a hard drive never has as much free space as advertised. For starters, after the drive is formatted, it loses around 7 to 8 percent of its size. Secondly, leaving 5 to 10 percent of your drive free is good because filling it completely with data not only slows it down (which can lead to skipping frames during capture or playback) but also increases the risk of crashes. In other words, if you have a 100GB drive, it's good for only about 85GB, so factor that into your decision about how much hard drive space your projects need.

When you're in the thick of editing, you can often give your hard drive quite a workout by saving and deleting media files. This data is written on a spinning magnetic disk inside your hard drive, and over time, the disk's surface starts to resemble a patchwork of areas containing data and empty areas. At this point, your drive is said to be *fragmented*. The result of this fragmentation is that when your hard drive reads or writes data, it has to work harder to find data or to find room to store data. This searching slows drive performance significantly and can lead to missing frames when recording or reading data. To counter this tendency, you can *defragment* your drive by using software such as Norton Utilities, which is available from retail stores or online at www.symantec.com.

The official documentation for Final Cut Express recommends not capturing your audio and particularly video to the hard drive where you installed the operating system and software applications. Doing so can fragment your hard drive more quickly and lead to other minor headaches; you may want to factor this in while you decide how much hard drive space you need. On the other hand, I've created plenty of DV video projects using my main system drive and had no problems whatsoever, so take Apple's advice with a grain of salt.

Monitors and LCDs

When running Final Cut Express, the most important element regarding a monitor (or LCD screen) is not its physical size but its pixel resolution. This isn't to say a physically bigger monitor won't be easier on your eyes (it will), but the monitor resolution determines how much information you can see on-screen at the same time (the more pixels, the better). For instance, the resolution determines how many media clips you can see on the Timeline or in the Browser without scrolling.

The lowest screen resolution that works with Final Cut Express is 1024 x 768 pixels, which is what you get with most 15-inch monitors (like those found on many iMacs) and the LCD screens on some PowerBooks and iBook models. Although this resolution isn't exactly spacious, it's actually quite workable, especially if you learn to use the Express keyboard commands to quickly call up overlapping windows or zoom in and out of the Timeline.

Any screen resolution higher than 1024 x 768 is gravy. If you can have your druthers, I recommend a 19-inch monitor running at 1280 x 1024 resolution, or one of the Apple Cinema Display LCD screens, which runs widescreen as high as 1920 x 1200 (and will duly impress family, friends, neighbors, and so on). Some editors, though, prefer to use two monitors at the same time (one monitor usually displays the Final Cut Express Timeline, Viewer, and Canvas windows, while the other monitor plays host to the Browser and secondary windows, such as the Tool Bench, Favorites, or Effects). To use two monitors, you need to install two video cards in your Macintosh or use a video card that offers outputs for two simultaneous displays (some G4 Macs ship with these 2-for-1 cards installed). A PowerBook also lets you hook up a second monitor (in addition to its LCD screen), and run it at a resolution as high as 1600 x 1200 pixels.

Not all monitors and LCD screens are created equally! Different models from different manufacturers vary in sharpness and brightness, which can make a difference when you're working in Final Cut Express. Apple's Cinema Displays have good reputations, but they can be a bit more expensive than other models, so if you're considering a non-Apple brand, you might want to use an online search engine like Google to find reviews and feedback on the model you're considering.

A monitor can often work at a variety of resolutions, some of which may be better suited for Final Cut Express than others. You can change your screen resolution in OS X by choosing Apple⇨System Preferences, clicking the Displays icon (in the Hardware section), and then choosing from any of the resolutions that are 1024 x 768 or higher. A word of caution: Some LCD screens offer lots of different resolutions, but look sharpest at the default resolution, which is typically the highest resolution offered.

FireWire port

Make sure that your Mac has at least one FireWire port. FireWire is the interface used to hook your Mac to a DV camera or deck so that you can capture video and audio from DV tape, or record your finished movies back to tape. You can also use a FireWire port to hook up fast and affordable hard drives for storing DV video, so it's very important!

All new Macs made today feature one or two FireWire ports (you can easily get by on one), and many models have featured FireWire since 1999 or 2000. If your Mac doesn't have FireWire, you can probably buy a third-party card that adds the capability (old iBooks and iMacs may be the exceptions, where add-on cards may not be available). However, if your Mac is old enough to not have FireWire, it may also not have the hardware muscle to play DV video anyway.

Apple is now including a next-generation FireWire port, called FireWire 2, in some of its machines. This new FireWire port can transfer data between your Mac and other devices (like new FireWire 2 hard drives) up to five times faster than the original FireWire standard, but it's not at all essential for editing DV video in Final Cut Express. FireWire 2 will be helpful for creating drives fast enough to handle uncompressed video (good news for high-end pro work), but the original FireWire is fast enough for hard drives that capture and play DV video, and DV camera makers are also likely to stick with regular FireWire interfaces because it suits their needs as well.

DV video cameras and playback decks

Just for the record: You don't *have* to connect a DV camera or deck to your Mac to run Final Cut Express. However, you'll need to make the connection if you want to capture video/audio from DV tapes to your Mac and later record back to tape. If you don't need to connect your camera (for instance, if someone else has given you an external FireWire drive with media files already on it), you can load Express without any DV equipment attached.

The easiest way to capture video into Final Cut Express (and to record it back to tape) is to simply use any DV video camera as a playback/recording deck, because these cameras have all that functionality built in. The second option is to buy a dedicated DV deck, which works just like a VHS VCR, except it uses the same DV tapes that DV cameras do. (If you're taking this route, check out the Sony offerings.)

Why go for a dedicated deck if your camera can fill that role anyway? Well, your camera isn't built to the same industrial-strength standards as a dedicated deck is, so if you're going to do hundreds of hours of capturing and recording, you might wear out the camera (buying an extended warranty for your camera can address this concern). Also, if you work with other people, you never know whether someone will be using your camera out in the field when you need it to pinch-hit as a deck. On the other hand, DV decks can cost as much as a camera, and most people find that using their DV camera for playback is just fine.

Either way, getting a DV camera or deck working with your Mac is quick and painless. All you need is a single FireWire cable (typically a 6-pin to 4-pin connector, which costs about $15 at computer or electronics stores) to hook the camera or deck to the FireWire port. Final Cut Express senses that the camera or deck is connected and knows how to control it without further ado.

Final Cut Express may not work perfectly with every model and brand of DV equipment. For instance, a particular camera may not always respond precisely when Express tries to control its rewind and fast forward functions. Although these kind of annoyances are rare, you can sidestep them entirely by making sure your DV camera or deck is fully supported by Final Cut Express. Apple keeps a list of such supported equipment online at www.apple.com/ finalcutexpress/qualification.html.

Other optional hardware

Although your Final Cut Express system doesn't have to have the following goodies, you may want to add them, depending on your needs and tastes:

- ✓ **Television monitor:** Although not absolutely necessary, adding a television to your Final Cut Express system is a good idea. That way, you can see your media clips and edited movies on TV as you work. (If your project is intended for TV, seeing your movie exactly as your audience will see it can be an especially big help.) Watching your footage on a TV screen is also helpful for spotting subtle problems in your images, which are harder to see if you're watching video in a small window on your Mac. Any TV with either RCA (also known as Composite) or S-Video input jacks will do. To find out how to set your TV up with Express, see the "Connecting and preparing all your hardware" section, later in this chapter.

- ✓ **DVD burner and authoring software:** One of the coolest aspects of digital media is that you can record your movies to DVDs and then play them in just about any consumer DVD player sold these days, just like a Hollywood flick. If this floats your boat (and how could it not?), you'll need a DVD-R drive. If you have a newish Mac, you may already have one built in (Apple calls its DVD-R drive a SuperDrive and includes it with many newer machines), along with the free, award-winning iDVD software to encode your movies for DVD and to create the fancy menus and such.

  If your Mac doesn't come equipped with a DVD-R drive, you can get an add-on drive from companies such as LaCie or FireWire Direct, but you must buy your own DVD authoring software because iDVD currently works only with SuperDrive-equipped Macs.

  Buying add-on DVD authoring software, such as DVD Studio Pro from Apple, can get costly — as much as $1,000. So if putting your movies on DVD is something you're interested in, consider getting a SuperDrive-equipped Mac right from the start, which includes iDVD as a bonus.

- ✓ **Zip disk or CD-R(W):** To be safe, back up your Final Cut Express project files somewhere other than your hard drive (not your media files, just the project files that describe what to do with those files). You can burn projects to a CD if you've got a burner, but putting them on a Zip disk is also an easy option.

- ✓ **Final Cut keyboard:** Post-Op sells a keyboard with Final Cut keyboard shortcuts printed directly on the keys (obviously in small print). Some editors like working with these keyboards because they make it easier to invoke Final Cut's many keyboard shortcuts. And although the keyboard is designed specifically for Final Cut Pro, most of the same keyboard shortcuts apply to Final Cut Express.

✓ **Turbocharged mouse:** You can buy a multibutton mouse (some with a built-in jog shuttle, track ball, or fly wheel), and program those extra buttons to perform Final Cut Express operations with a simple click. Using these handy devices can save a lot of time when you're editing.

✓ **Speakers or headphones:** The built-in speakers on your Mac aren't good enough to play all the nuances in your audio (or highlight any problems that should be corrected). To upgrade the audio, you have a few options. If you're hooking up a TV to your Mac, choose one with stereo speakers. Otherwise, connect a pair of speakers to your Mac or invest in a good pair of headphones.

Getting Started

After you've installed the Final Cut Express software on your hard drive, you need to take a few steps to configure Express to work with your hardware. *Note:* The steps in the following section work whether you're using a DV camera or DV playback deck, but I focus on DV cameras from now on.

Connecting and preparing all your hardware

Before loading Final Cut Express, connect and prep all your hardware using these steps:

1. **Connect your DV camera to the FireWire port on your Mac using a FireWire cable (most likely a 6-pin to 4-pin variety).**

   The Mac may have more than one FireWire port, but either will do.

2. **Turn your camera on, and make sure it's in Play mode.**

   Your camera can either record or play back video. You want it in playback mode, so you need to look for a switch or dial on the camera that says VCR, VTR, or Play, and make sure it's enabled.

3. **Connect and turn on your FireWire hard drive, if you have one.**

   If you want to use an external FireWire hard drive with Final Cut Express, turn it on before launching Express as well, and make sure it's hooked into your Mac FireWire port too. (Remember, you can connect FireWire devices to each other, in case you have only one FireWire port.)

You may also want to add a television to your setup, so that you can watch video in Final Cut Express on a TV screen instead of a smaller window on your Mac. How exactly you do this depends on your DV camera and your TV, so I can't give you step-by-step instructions. However, here's some general guidance:

1. **Identify the Video/Audio Out connector.**

   Most DV cameras have an Video/Audio Out connector on them, which sends the video/audio signal in your camera to an outside device (like a TV) that's attached. Depending on the brand and model of the camera, this connector will consist of a single connector or three connectors (one for video and two for stereo audio, like your stereo system offers).

2. **Identify the Video/Audio In connector.**

   Most TVs have Video/Audio In connectors — usually on the rear of the TV — that can receive a video/audio signal from an outside device (like a VCR or a video camera) that's attached. On TVs, there are usually 3 connectors for each kind of device you can attach (one connector for video and two for stereo audio).

3. **Use cables to connect the Video/Audio Out on your camera to the Video/Audio In on your TV or to your VHS VCR.**

   The type of cables that you use depends on the kind of connectors your camera and TV have. The most common cables are called RCA (also known as *composite*). Many DV cameras include the necessary cables to connect a TV and your DV camera, or you can buy them at an electronics store. Just connect the cables, and you're ready to go.

   You don't have to hook your DV camera directly to a TV. Instead, if you already have a VHS VCR (which is probably already hooked to your TV), you can hook your camera to the VCR, so the video/audio signal goes through the VCR to the TV. Another benefit of this setup is that you can record your Final Cut Express movies to your VHS VCR. (See Chapter 15.) If you opt for this setup, look on your VCR for the Video/Audio In and Out connectors, and connect the VCR to your camera.

After you have a TV hooked up to your DV camera, you have to switch the TV to one of its video channels (which show signals coming from its Video In jacks) before you can see the video coming from Final Cut Express. How to do this depends on your television setup (and whether you've connected the TV to a VCR, cable box, or some other device as well), but I can offer you this guidance: Look on your TV or remote control for a button that says TV/Video and press it. (Try pressing it repeatedly or press your Channel Up and Down buttons after pressing Video.) If you see a video clip displayed in the Express Viewer or Canvas windows, you're in business. If not, check out your TV manual to see how to switch to its video input channels. Also, make sure that you have your DV camera and TV connected properly.

When displaying video through a TV, Express loses the ability to give you real-time previews of its rendered effects. Ordinarily, Macs with fast G4 CPUs can give you previews of certain transitions and other effects elements that would normally require you to render them before playing them in your movie. (See Chapter 17 for more information.) This is a nice time-saver if your movie calls for you to render lots of material, but you lose this handy option when viewing video on a TV. If you find yourself missing real-time previews of rendered effects (assuming your Mac can handle them to begin with), then you can temporarily turn off Express's TV output by choosing View⇨Video⇨Real-Time. To return back to TV viewing, choose View⇨Video⇨FireWire.

Launching Final Cut Express

With your hardware set up and raring to go, use the Mac Finder to find the Final Cut Express application on your hard drive (it should be in the Applications folder), and double-click the Express application icon. Express begins to load all sorts of files and modules, but if you're running it for the first time, it prompts you for a few important settings.

The quickest way to load Final Cut Express is to add its icon to your Mac Dock (as shown in Figure 2-1). Then you can launch it by simply clicking its icon in the Dock. In the Finder, just drag the Final Cut Express application icon to the Dock to add it there. (Don't worry; you're not actually moving or affecting the original application file on your hard drive.) If you ever want to remove Express from the Dock, you can also click that same icon and drag it outside the Dock again.

Figure 2-1:
The Final Cut Express icon added to the OS X Dock.

Choosing an initial setup

When Final Cut Express loads for the first time, it opens a Choose Setup dialog box, shown in Figure 2-2, which prompts for two important settings: Easy Setup and Primary Scratch Disk. The following sections explain what each means to you (and remember that these setting aren't carved in stone — you can easily change them later on):

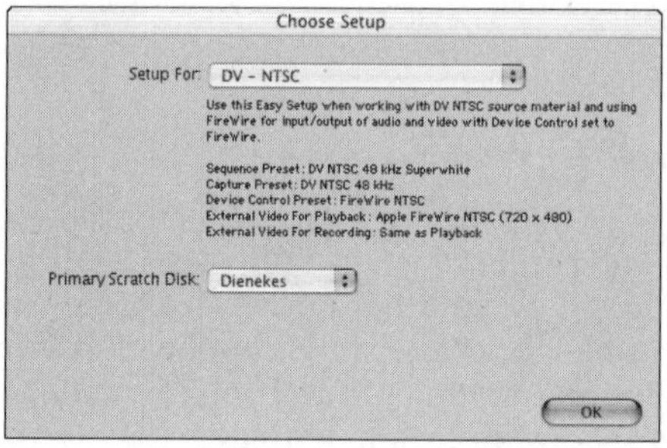

Figure 2-2: Choose Setup dialog box.

Easy Setup

An Easy Setup is a collection of settings that Final Cut Express applies to your movies, based on the kind of DV media you want to work with and the kind of DV hardware you've got.

When you click the Setup For button in the Choose Setup dialog box, you see a pop-up menu of all the setups Final Cut Express offers, based on some variations of the DV format. Select the one that suits your needs, using these guides:

- DV cameras record DV audio at different quality levels, depending on their make and their current settings. For instance, you can choose between audio at 32KHz or the higher quality 48KHz variety. Choose whichever option matches the audio quality of your DV source footage.

- If your source footage was shot in a 16:9 aspect ratio (widescreen), but you want your project to stretch it to fill a standard TV screen's 4:3 aspect ratio, then you can choose the Anamorphic option here.

- North American and European video equipment (TVs, VCRs, cameras, video tapes, and so on) use different signal standards. North Americans use a standard called NTSC, and the Europeans use PAL. These two standards aren't compatible, so you can't hook an American NTSC camera up to a PAL television or play a PAL DV tape in an NTSC camera. You need to tell Final Cut Express what standard your DV footage was recorded with.

If you don't know which of Express' many setups to choose, the two can't-go-wrong defaults are DV-NTSC (if you're working with NTSC gear), or DV-PAL.

After you pick an initial setup for Final Cut Express, you'll probably never need to tweak those settings again, provided your hardware setup and video/audio requirements don't change. But if they do, you can easily change the settings again by choosing Final Cut Express⇨Easy Setup, and selecting a new option from the Setup For pop-up menu. Remember, changing the Easy Setup doesn't affect settings for movies (that is, Timeline sequences) you've already created — only new ones.

Primary Scratch Disk

The scratch disk is the hard drive to which Final Cut Express saves all your captured video and audio (and other files, such as rendered media). If your Mac has only one hard drive (including the internal system drive), it's automatically your scratch disk. But if you have multiple drives, you can specify which one serves as your scratch disk by selecting it from the Primary Scratch Disk drop-down list.

You can change your scratch disk at any time by choosing Final Cut Express⇨ Preferences and then clicking the Scratch Disks tab. (See Chapter 3 for more information about the scratch disk.)

When you're finished making your choices, click OK. Final Cut Express opens a new project for you, and you're ready to get down to business.

If you initially set up Final Cut Expess with a DV camera that was turned on when attached to your Mac, Express will check for the camera every time you launch the software. If it can't find the camera when you launch it (maybe it's no longer attached, or you forgot to turn it on), Express opens a dialog box warning you that it can't find your device. Just make sure that it's properly connected and click the dialog boxes Check Again button. Or, if you don't mind the fact that your camera is no longer attached, click the Continue button instead.

Working with Projects and Sequences

After you've established your initial setup, Final Cut Express automatically creates a new, untitled project, which in turn includes a new, untitled Timeline sequence, as shown in Figure 2-3. In other words, you're ready to roll! Before moving forward, however, you need to know a few things about projects and how to manage them.

A project is a Final Cut Express document file — like a Word or PhotoShop document file you'd create in those applications — that you can create, save, close, and open again, like any other document on your hard drive. A typical Express project contains two elements, which are unique to it:

- ✔ Any media files (video, audio, and still pictures) you capture or import into it

- ✔ One or more Timeline *sequences,* which are collections of the project's media clips that you've edited together in the Final Cut Express Timeline window

Generally, you create a new project for each movie or other unique, stand-alone program you're working on. For instance, if you're a big-time Hollywood editor, you would have a project for each of the films on your plate. And within those projects, you'd create multiple Timeline sequences to break each movie's edited clips into smaller, more manageable pieces. For instance, you might create a Timeline sequence for each major scene or act in the film.

You can have multiple projects open at the same time. Each open project is represented in the Browser by a tab, which you'll see at the top of the Browser window. The tab lists the name of the project or Untitled Project, if you have not yet saved the project. (Refer to Figure 2-3.)

Saving and autosaving projects

To save an untitled project (like the one Final Cut Express automatically whipped up for you after you installed the program), follow these steps:

1. **Choose File⇨Save Project As.**

   After you've used Save As to save your project with a name, you can now save the project (as you work on it) by choosing File⇨Save or press the familiar ⌘+S. This saves the project using the name you've already given it. If you ever want to save the project using a different name, then just choose File⇨Save As again.

2. **In the Save dialog box (shown in Figure 2-4), type the new project name in the Save As text box.**

3. **Use the horizontal scroll bar or click the Where drop-down list for major folders to navigate to a folder on your hard drive.**

4. **Click the Save button.**

   After you save a project, its new name appears in its tab at the top of the Browser window.

Figure 2-4:
The Save
dialog box.

When you save a project, you automatically save all the sequences that are a part of that project. You can't save individual sequences, just projects.

Final Cut Express also includes a nice autosave feature that automatically makes a backup copy of your project at intervals you establish. Imagine that Express suddenly crashes after you've done a fair amount of work on your project without doing a manual ⌘+S save. (It's been known to happen.) When you relaunch Express, it opens the last project you manually saved but doesn't show all the latest work you may have done since the last manual save. But Express *also* asks if you want to open a newer autosaved version (provided you have the feature turned on, and an autosave time interval passed while you were working before the crash). If you open this autosaved version and want to keep it, just choose File⇨Save Project, and Express replaces your original project with the newer version, which now assumes the original project name so that it's a seamless transition.

You can tweak the Autosave settings (or turn it off) by choosing Final Cut Express⇨Preferences. Look for the Autosave Vault setting in the General Preferences tab (as shown in Figure 2-5), and make whatever adjustments you want.

Figure 2-5:
The
Autosave
Vault in the
General
Preferences
tab.

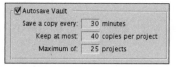

☑ Autosave Vault

Save a copy every: 30   minutes

Keep at most: 40   copies per project

Maximum of: 25   projects

Final Cut Express keeps your autosave backups in a folder called Autosave Vault, which you can probably find in the Final Cut Express Documents folder, in your Home directory Documents folder. Within the Autosave Vault folder are subfolders for each of your projects, and within these are your actual backup files, in case you want to load one (or delete old ones taking up space). These backups use the same name as your original project but append -auto at the end of the filename. By default, Express keeps up to 40 successive backups per project. You can tweak the default via Preferences.

Managing projects

If you have any experience using other applications in Mac OS X, managing projects in Final Cut Express is pretty standard stuff:

- **Create a new project:** To create a new project from scratch, choose — you guessed it! — File⇨New Project. Final Cut Express opens an untitled project tab in the Browser window and makes it your active project. I recommend saving the project right away.

- **Open a project:** To open a project, you have a several of options:

  - At the bottom of its File menu, Express lists files that you've opened most recently. If your project is listed there, just select its name from the File menu to open it.

  - If your project isn't listed on the File menu, then you have to open it by choosing File⇨Open. In the Choose a File dialog box (see Figure 2-6), browse your hard drive (use the horizontal scroll bar), and double-click the project name when you see it. Final Cut

Express opens the project as a new tab in the Browser and makes it active.

- You can also open a project from the Mac's Desktop by double-clicking its icon.

Figure 2-6:
The Choose
a File dialog
box.

✔ **Close a project:** To close a project you're no longer working on, make it active in the Browser window (click its tab at the top of the window) and choose File⇨Close Project.

You can have multiple projects open at the same time. To work with an open project, just click its tab at the top of the Browser to make it active. You'll see all of the project's clips, bins, and sequences listed in the Browser's window, as shown in Figure 2-7.

Figure 2-7:
The
Browser
shows three
open
projects:
Click a
project tab
to make it
active.

When you quit Final Cut Express with open projects (that is, without closing them first), Express automatically opens those same projects the next time you load it. This feature is handy when you're working on the same project, day in and day out, but can be downright annoying when you're finished with a project and find that it keeps opening each time you launch Express. To put an end to this vicious cycle, just close a project you're finished with before quitting Express. After you close it, it won't come back until you open it again.

Part II
Importing and Organizing Your Media

In this part . . .

Part II explains how to capture, import, and organize all the media you use in your Final Cut Express projects (video, dialogue, music, sound effects, still pictures, and so on). I cover how to capture media from DV videotape and how to bring media into Express from other sources, such as digital video or audio files already on your hard drive, songs from a music CD, graphics from Photoshop, and so on.

Finally, I describe how to name, annotate, and organize all these different media clips in the Express Browser window so that you can easily find them when you need them.

Chapter 3

Capturing Media from Tape

· ·

In This Chapter

▶ Setting up a camera or deck

▶ Understanding timecodes

▶ Capturing clips in the Capture window

▶ Saving captured clips

▶ Recapturing an entire project

· ·

*F*inal Cut Express can bring in media from a number of sources (music CDs, still pictures from a camera, and QuickTime movies already on the hard drive), but you'll probably get most of a project's content by capturing video from MiniDV tapes (from now on, just *DV*) by using a DV video camera or DV playback deck attached to a Mac.

Capturing video requires you to think about a few issues: how exactly to capture the video (Final Cut Express gives you two different options), where on the hard drive to store video while it's captured, and how to properly name and describe video clips so that you easily manage them later on (very important when you add more and more media to projects!).

Final Cut Express generally works well with all DV cameras and decks, but you may run into occasional glitches with a couple of models. I suggest that you go to www.apple.com/finalcutexpress/qualification.html and look up the list of DV devices qualified by Apple to work with Express. If you want to be absolutely sure that your Mac and DV camera or deck work harmoniously, use a device listed on that site. However, if you don't use a device listed there, it's probably not the end of the world — it should still function well in most cases.

Connecting a DV Camera or Deck

Before you can capture video from a DV camera or deck, you need to connect it to the Mac by using a FireWire cable. *FireWire,* also sometimes known as IEEE-1394, is an Apple-invented technology that lets you very quickly move a whole lot of data (which DV video and audio require) through a thin, little cable. Most DV cameras and decks have a built-in FireWire port. A common FireWire cable has a 4-pin connector on one end (for the camera/deck) and a 6-pin connector on the other end (for the computer). To get all gear ready for capture, follow these steps:

1. **Use a FireWire cable to connect a DV camera to the Mac (or deck, but I'll assume a camera from now on).**

   Mac laptops typically have only one FireWire port. If you're using an external FireWire hard drive with a Mac that is already using the single FireWire port, how do you connect the camera to the Mac? Well, most FireWire hard drives have two FireWire ports on them, so just connect the camera to the open FireWire port on the hard drive. The camera then works with the Mac through the hard drive.

2. **Turn the camera on, if it's not already.**

3. **Insert a DV tape.**

4. **Make sure that you have switched the camera to the VTR setting (on some models, it's called VCR, or Playback).**

   This setting lets the camera play DV tape, like a VCR plays a tape, instead of recording images seen through the camera.

5. **Choose File➪Capture in Final Cut Express (or press ⌘+8).**

   This command brings up the Express Capture window, which I'll explain in a moment. In the bottom left of the window, check the VTR status area to make sure that you have good communication with the device:

   - When you see the message VTR OK in the status area, all is well, and you're ready to proceed.

   - When you see the message No Communication in the status area, the camera is either turned off or not connected to your Mac via a FireWire cable. Or, perhaps you have faulty equipment.

Decoding Timecodes

A *timecode* is a series of numbers that describe time; and as an editor, there's no escaping timecodes. For instance, timecodes can be used to record where in time a shot begins or ends, how long a shot lasts, and so on.

Timecodes are made up of four sets of double-digits separated by colors and semicolons (like 00:12:23;07). From left to right, the numbers indicate hours, minutes, seconds, and finally frames. Frames are always last (after the semi-colon), and there are 30 frames in a second, so frames act as a measurement of time, too. If you were speaking in timecode, you could say, "The shot that I want to capture on my DV tape starts at 00:05:10;04," which means that the shot starts at 5 minutes, 10 seconds, and 4 frames into your tape.

You see timecode values all over Final Cut Express. For instance, the Viewer window uses a timecode to note the duration of a shot. In the Timeline, you can see timecode values displayed across the Timeline's ruler, and the Canvas window reports the entire length of your movie as a timecode. Additionally, the Final Cut Express Capture window displays the timecode that it reads off your DV tapes (each frame of video recorded to DV tape has a timecode stamp), and when you set In and Out points to mark video for capturing, Express records these marks as timecode values, too.

Capturing in the Capture Window

Capturing clips means that you take digital video data on DV tape and bring it into a Mac as digital QuickTime files. The center of the video-capturing universe is the Final Cut Express Capture window, shown in Figure 3-1, which you can access by choosing File➪Capture. The Capture window lets you perform these three basic steps in the capturing process:

1. **Navigate through a DV tape until you find the piece of video that you want to capture.**

2. **Describe this video by giving it In and Out points, naming it, and writing any other useful, descriptive comments about it (such as the name of the DV tape that you're capturing it from).**

3. **Capture the video by saving it on the hard drive as a QuickTime digital file and also adding it to the Browser window of a project as a media clip, which you can now edit on the Timeline.**

The following sections outline these three steps.

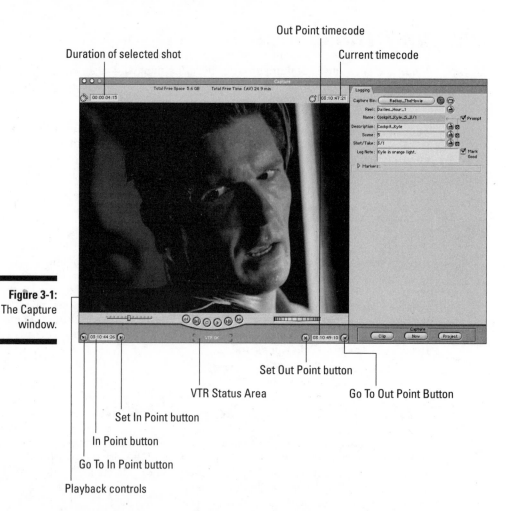

Out Point timecode

Duration of selected shot

Current timecode

Figure 3-1:
The Capture
window.

Set Out Point button

VTR Status Area

Go To Out Point Button

Set In Point button

In Point button

Go To In Point button

Playback controls

Navigating through a DV tape

Use the Capture window's playback controls (shown in Figure 3-2) to move
through tape and find a piece of video that you want to capture. While you do
this, you'll see the video playing in the Preview pane. You have several controls available so that you can either move quickly through the tape or proceed frame by frame (for high-precision work):

   ✔ **Play, Stop, Fast Forward, and Rewind buttons:** Clicking the Play button
     begins your DV tape immediately in the Preview pane of the Capture
     window, and clicking Stop . . . well, you can imagine what that does. To
     move to another part of the DV tape quickly, use the Fast Forward and

Rewind buttons. Unfortunately, you can't preview the video while the tape speeds by, but you can watch the Capture window's Current Timecode box to see where you currently are on the tape.

✔ **J, K, and L keys:** Although using shortcut keys is a matter of preference, I find that the best way to quickly and precisely navigate through a tape is by pressing J, K, and L on the keyboard:

- Pressing J plays the tape in reverse.

- Pressing K pauses playback.

- Pressing L plays the tape forward.

Even better, pressing the L or J key repeatedly increases the speed of the forward or the backward motion while showing you the video in the Preview pane. Try it: Press either key once, and then again, and then again, and watch your video fly by super fast. The fact that this approach lets you see the video moving by is preferable to using the window's Fast Forward and Rewind buttons, which move through the tape quickly but don't show your video in the process.

✔ **Arrow keys:** Occasionally, you may want to move through a tape frame by frame. Press ← on the keyboard to move back one frame and → to move forward one frame.

✔ **Jog and Shuttle (see Figure 3-2):** Honestly, not many people prefer using these controls instead of keyboard commands (J, K, L, and the arrow keys). However, you can drag the Shuttle control to the left and right to move back and forward through a tape at different speeds. (The further from center that you drag the control, the faster you go.) You can move the Jog wheel to the left or right to slowly roll back or forward as little as a frame at a time.

✔ **Current Timecode field:** The Current Timecode field, in the top and center of the Log and Capture window, always shows the timecode of the frame that appears in the Capture window. By entering a timecode in the Current Timecode field, you tell Final Cut Express to go to that time-code location. This field comes in handy when other people (such as your producer or a client) screen source tapes in advance and make notes about shots that they like on the tapes.

Figure 3-2:
These controls determine the playback of DV tape.

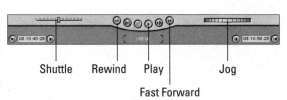

Shuttle   Rewind   Play   Jog

Fast Forward

Describing and capturing video —
the long way

When you find a clip of video that you want to capture, you need to give Final Cut Express some details about it before capturing it. For instance, you need to give the clip a name, and you also need to tell Express at what point in time on the tape to start capturing the video to the hard drive and at what point to stop (by setting what Express calls *In* and *Out points*):

1. **Move to the frame on a DV tape where you want to begin capturing video and then press I to mark an In point.**

   The timecode for that beginning first frame appears in the Capture window's In Point Timecode field (refer to Figure 3-2).

2. **Move to the last frame that you want to capture on the DV tape and then press O to mark an Out point.**

   The timecode for this last frame appears in the Out Point Timecode field. Just so you know: Final Cut Express doesn't care whether you mark the Out point before you mark the In point.

3. **Type the reel name in the Capture window's Reel field, shown in Figure 3-3.**

   Reel names are nothing more than the tape names that you may have created for DV videotapes. For example, Birthday#1 and Birthday#2 are names that you can enter if you used these names on the tapes that you shot for someone's birthday. Although entering this information isn't mandatory, noting the tape that your video was captured from makes going back to that source tape easier in case you ever need to recapture media from it. (It's much easier to find a tape when you've given it a name in Express and physically labeled the tape with that same name.)

   Make sure that you change the reel name each time that you put in a new tape. Express reminds you each time that you put a new tape in your camera, but make sure to heed its advice!

Figure 3-3:
Describe the captured clips in these fields in the Capture window.

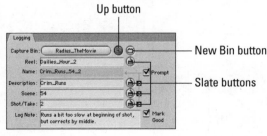

4. **Fill in the fields that describe important stuff about a clip (refer to Figure 3-3).**

   Final Cut Express gives you lots of information to record about a clip — for instance, a description of the clip, scene, shot/take data, and general notes (such as `John blinks a lot` or `slightly shaky camera`). Recording this information may be overkill for your purposes, but if you're going to be working on projects that use dozens or hundreds of clips, having this info embedded into clips can help you better organize them and search for them in a hurry. (See Chapter 5 for info on finding clips.)

   You can click the Slate button next to each field to increase the current value (by one) shown in that field. For instance, when a 2 is in the Scene field, clicking the field's Slate button turns that value into a 3, saving you time from keying in a number yourself. Also, when you click the Slate button in the Scene field, Express is smart enough to increase not only the current scene number by one but also reset the current Shot/Take number to 1.

   If you really like a particular shot, select the Mark Good check box. After you've captured all your clips, Express can quickly search out the most promising shots that you marked in this way. (See Chapter 5 for more information.)

5. **Type a name for the clip and click OK.**

   By default, Final Cut Express generates a name for the clip based on information that you provide into the Capture window's Description, Scene, and Shot/Take fields (provided that you've selected the check box to the right of each of these fields — see Figure 3-3 again). For instance, when you type `Sunrise` in the Description field and `Scene54` in the Scene field, Express automatically names the captured clip `Sunrise_Scene54` (again, provided that the Description and Scene fields have checks next to them). If you don't want the clip's name to use one or all these fields, just select the field's check box to toggle the field off. However, even when you have a field's check box turned off, Express records any info that you enter in the field with the clip. You can search to find the clip by its scene or description, but the information won't be added to the clip's name.

   I strongly suggest that you develop a naming system to keep clips organized. See the sidebar, "Tips for capturing clips."

   When you don't want the clip's name to include *any* of the Capture window's fields, toggle each field's check box off but toggle the Prompt check box so that it's enabled. When you capture the clip, Final Cut Express opens a new dialog box and lets you type a name and any additional comments for the clip.

   When you don't select the Prompt check box or any other fields, Final Cut Express names the clip something like `Untitled 0001`, and you don't want that! Make sure that you come up with a good name.

6. **Click the Clip button at the bottom of the Capture window to capture the clip.**

   Final Cut Express cues the camera to the In point that you set and captures the clip from the DV tape until it reaches the Out point that you set. (You can abort the capture any time by pressing Esc.) The clip then appears in the Browser window under the name that you gave it. Express also stores the clip as a QuickTime file on the hard drive, using that same name. (See the section "Locating captured clips" for information on controlling exactly where Express saves those QuickTime files.)

By default, Express aborts a capture if it encounters a break in your DV tape's timecode. A break means that the tape's timecode starts over at 00:00:00;00. A break usually occurs because you turned your camera off and then on again while recording footage. These breaks can have some bad side effects if you ever plan to recapture the clip that you're capturing now, so see the section "Avoiding timecode confusion" later in this chapter to fully understand the consequences. On the other hand, if you don't care about these breaks, choose Final Cut Express➪Preferences, deselect the Abort Capture on Timecode Break option, and then recapture your clip.

Changing your logging bin

When you capture a clip, Final Cut Express adds it to the Browser window. However, you might want your captured clips to go directly into a bin in the Browser. Putting clips in a bin keeps you from having a bunch of captured clips cluttering up the Browser.

You can create a new bin in the Browser directly from the Capture window. Just click the New Bin button (refer to Figure 3-3), and Express creates a new bin in the Browser (see Figure 3-4). This new bin is designated as the Logging Bin so that any new clips that you capture go there automatically. The Browser displays a Logging Bin icon to the left of this new bin, but you may want to rename the bin to be more descriptive. (See Chapter 5 for more on working with bins.) To toggle off this designation (so that captured clips go directly into the main Browser and not a bin), click the Up button in the Capture window.

You can turn any existing Browser bin into your logging bin. In the Browser window, hold the Control key, click the bin that you meant to use as the logging bin, and then choose Set Capture Bin from the pop-up menu.

A small slate icon indicates the
current Logging Bin in your Browser

Figure 3-4:
A logging
bin.

Capturing the video — the short way

Capturing a video clip by using the steps that I describe in the previous section can sometimes get tedious because you have to navigate through the DV
tape, set In and Out points for each clip, and then wait while the camera
again returns to those points to capture each clip to the hard drive. Although
this process is fine when you're capturing a couple of clips at a time, it can be
inefficient when you have lots of capturing to do. Instead, you can use the
Final Cut Express Capture Now feature, which captures whatever happens to
be playing on the camera at the moment and spares you from setting In and
Out points or even naming the clip:

1. **Begin playing the tape in the Capture window.**

   You can press L to start playing the tape forward or just click the
   window's Play button.

2. **Click the Now button in the Capture window when you want to start
   capturing the video that's playing.**

   Click the Now button a few seconds before you want the capture to begin
   in case the Mac has to "wake up" the hard drive. Either way, Final Cut
   Express starts capturing the video that's playing through the camera.

3. **Press Esc on the keyboard to stop the capture.**

   Final Cut Express automatically names the captured clip something
   generic like Untitled001, adds the clip to the Browser window, and
   saves it as a QuickTime file on the hard drive. If you want to know where
   the QuickTime file has been saved on your drive, select the clip in the
   Browser and then choose Edit⇨Item Properties. In the Item Properties
   dialog box, you can see the media file's location listed in the Source File
   field.

Tips for capturing clips

You may find the following advice helpful when you capture clips:

✔ **Capture only what you need:** To save hard drive space, capture only the footage that you know that you want. Each 4.5 minutes of DV video takes about 1 GB of disk space, so don't set your In and Out points too wide (thereby capturing excess footage) or try to capture each shot in the source video as a separate clip.

✔ **Use Start/Stop Detection:** Conversely, if you don't mind capturing excess footage, using the Final Cut Express Start/Stop Detection feature lets you capture long segments of video in one fell swoop and then automatically break any unique scenes within that video into separate pieces. See "Letting Final Cut Express Find Scenes for You" in this chapter for more information.

✔ **Develop a good naming scheme:** The name of the clip is the first item that appears in the Browser and is one that you will refer to most often. Take some time to develop a naming scheme that makes sense. For example, you can develop a shorthand for naming clips, using names and also two-letter short descriptions, such as Erica-CU for *Erica's close up,* Bob-MS for *Bob's medium shot,* and House-LS for a *long shot of the house.* When naming clips, also consider the fact that the Final Cut Express Browser organizes the clips alphabetically by name (although you can change this — see Chapter 5). By naming shots of similar items with the same beginning word, such as Bob exits-MS and Bob walks away-LS, you make sure that Express groups all the clips of Bob together.

✔ **Make sure that you have correct reel numbers for all clips:** When capturing shots, be sure to type the DV tape's reel name in the Capture window's field. (You also should label each DV tape with that same reel name, using the little labels that come with each tape.) Final Cut Express records this information with each clip that you capture, and if you ever want to recapture any of the clips, you can easily figure out which DV tape you need. Also, remember to *change* the reel name every time that you put a new DV tape into the camera.

This Capture Now process is very quick and painless, but the only drawback is that you get a bunch of clips with not-very-useful names such as Untitled 0001. Of course, you can quickly change the clip's name in the Browser window after it's captured. (See Chapter 5 for more about renaming clips in the Browser.) However, the QuickTime media file saved to the hard drive will keep its original, generic name, and that can lead to some confusion if you want to look at the media files from the Mac desktop.

If this naming issue doesn't bother you, then you're all set. However, Final Cut Express offers a middle ground that lets you name a clip quickly, before doing a capture now, so that it winds up in the Browser and on the hard drive with a more useful name:

1. **Before playing the tape, name the clip to be captured by typing some descriptive information in the Capture window fields.**

See Step 5 in the section "Describing and capturing video — the long way" for a description of how these fields work. Make sure that Express automatically incorporates your entries into the Capture window's Name field. You can also enter the clip's reel name here, but be aware that Express uses any information that you enter into the window's other fields (Scene, Shot/Take, Description, and so on) only for naming the clip. When captured, the clip doesn't retain any of this information; it's simply used to build the clip's name.

2. **Do a Capture Now, as you normally would (see the previous set of steps).**

   Final Cut Express captures the clip, using the name generated in the Capture window's Name field.

Locating captured clips

When you capture clips from DV tape, Final Cut Express saves them to whatever hard drive you set as the Scratch Disk. (You did this the first time you launched Express, after installing it.) Additonally, Express puts the files in specific folders on that hard drive. To determine where exactly those folders are (and change that location, if you want), choose Final Cut Express➪Preferences and then click the Scratch Disks tab, as shown in Figure 3-5.

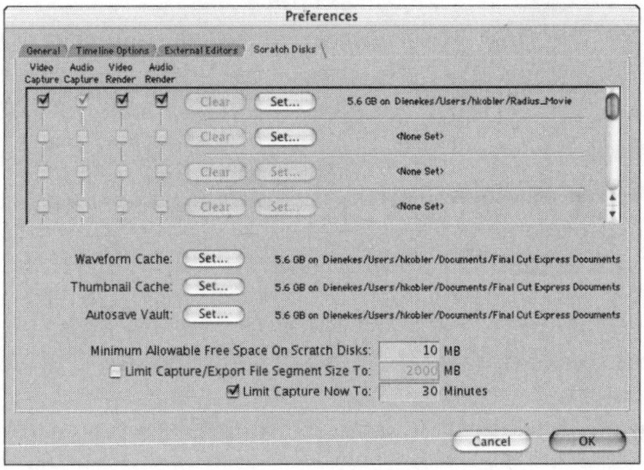

Figure 3-5: The Scratch Disks tab, found in the Preferences dialog box.

To the right of the Scratch Disks tabs, you should see a pathname that tells you the folder in which Final Cut Express saved the video. In that folder, Express creates yet another folder called Capture Scratch, as shown in Figure 3-6, and within that folder, it creates *yet another* folder using the same project name that you used in capturing the video. (For instance, if you name the project Radius_TheMovie, the folder's name is Radius_TheMovie as well.) And it's in that folder (finally!) where you can find the captured QuickTime files.

Dropping frames during capture?

When you capture clips, Final Cut Express may interrupt the capture process to tell you that it's *dropping frames* while capturing, which means that the hard disk is not recording all the frames of video flowing from your camera in real time. Captured clips missing some of their frames play with slight stutters or pops, so Express thankfully warns you that this is happening ahead of time. If you're dropping frames during capture, consider these culprits:

✔ **The hard drive isn't fast enough.** Lots of factors determine how fast a hard drive can write data, but a major one is its revolutions per minute (rpm) speed — that is, how fast the drive's physical magnetic disk spins around. A drive with a 4,200 rpm speed (particularly ones in older Macs) can suffer from dropped frames, but drives with 5,400 and especially 7,200 rpm ratings should be safe.

✔ **The hard drive is fragmented.** Hard drives write data onto the surface of a spinning magnetic disk. Ideally, when writing a video file, that spinning disk has enough empty space to record the file from start to finish in the same physical place. As you use a hard drive more and more (writing files to it, deleting files from it), the disk's surface becomes a patchwork of filled and empty areas of different sizes. And when the hard drive can't write a video file from start to finish in one spot, the drive writes parts of it in different places on the disk's surface (wherever the disk has empty space), and that means the hard drive's *heads* (which do the writing and reading of data) have to move around the disk, back and forth, to write the file. All this moving around takes extra time and sometimes slows the drive down so that it can't record the video frames fast enough — in other words, dropped frames. The solution is to defragment the disk with a third-party utility such as Norton Utilities, which can cleverly rearrange all the data on the drive so that it can keep each file's data together, and the free space on the drive is physically in the same place on the drive's disk surface. The result is a faster drive!

✔ **The hard drive is too full.** If a drive has only about 10 percent free space, it can lose enough speed to start dropping frames. The solution: Delete some files that you don't need anymore. (You may want to back them up to CD-ROM or some other media beforehand.)

You can change the folder or even the hard drive where the files are captured:

1. **Click the top-most Set button in the Scratch Disks tab (refer to Figure 3-5).**

   The Choose a Folder dialog box appears, and you can navigate to any folder on the hard drive(s).

2. **Find the folder you want to capture to and click it once to select it.**

3. **Click the Choose button.**

   Final Cut Express updates the Scratch Disks tab to show this new folder as the capture destination.

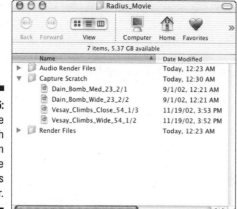

Figure 3-6:
The Capture
Scratch
folder, seen
from the
Mac's
Finder.

You can actually set up multiple scratch disk folders by clicking the other Set buttons of the Scratch Disks tab. But Final Cut Express captures only to the disk/folder that has a check mark in the Video Capture check box to the left of the tab. I like to set up multiple scratch disks and switch between them, depending on the project that I'm working on.

Letting Final Cut Express Find Scenes for You

Final Cut Express has a feature that can save you loads of time and free you from the burden of capturing many clips — one after the other — from the same DV tape. The feature is DV Start/Stop Detection, and it detects each instance on a DV tape where you or your cameraperson stopped and then started recording the action again. Express treats each Start/Stop instance as a separate unique scene and quickly turns each into a separate clip in the Browser window for easy organization. By using this feature, you can save yourself from manually capturing one clip after another on the DV tape.

To take advantage of the DV Start/Stop Detection feature, follow these steps:

1. **Capture the entire length of the tape following the steps presented earlier.**

   For example, if you have a half-hour tape, capture it all in one go. (Just make sure that you have enough disk space for it; each 4.5 minutes of DV video takes up 1GB of disk space.) You can capture this media using a variety of techniques, but doing a Capture Now is probably quickest.

2. **After the clip appears in the Browser, select it and choose Mark⇨DV Start/Stop Detection.**

   Final Cut Express scans the clip and marks all locations where you pressed the Record/Pause button on the camera during the shooting. Small markers appear wherever you paused the camera, as shown in Figure 3-7.

Select the markers and create
subclips for scenes

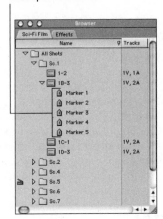

Figure 3-7:
The markers
indicate the
points when
you paused
the camera.

You can even go further and create subclips from these markers. *Subclips* are pieces of a long clip that has been divided into smaller clips. To create subclips, follow these steps:

1. **In the Browser, select all the markers within your clip.**

   You can hold down the ⌘ key while clicking each marker to select them individually, or you can use your mouse to highlight all the markers and select them as a group.

2. **Choose Modify⇨Make Subclip.**

   All the material between the markers appears as subclips in the Browser (no longer under the original clip that they came from). The subclip icons look just like the clip icons in the Browser but have jagged edges (as if they were ripped from a longer clip).

At this point, you may want to rename some of the subclips to better reflect what they contain. (See Chapter 5 for more information.)

Recapturing a Project's Clips

Another way to capture clips in Final Cut Express is to recapture an entire project of clips that you've already captured, using the Capture Project feature.

You may wonder why you'd want to capture clips you already captured, and that's a good question. The answer is that you may have deleted a project's original captured clips (or lost them in a rare hard drive crash) and want to revive your project by recapturing its clips yet again.

Using the Capture Project feature

The beauty of the Capture Project feature is that it lets you clear media that you're not using from your hard drive (freeing up precious space) but gives you the option of bringing the media back if you need it later. Just load up your earlier movie's project file, and Final Cut Express will tell you that your media clips are all offline, which means that Express cannot find them. (See Chapter 5 for more about offline media.) However, your project still remembers all the clips of media that you originally captured from your DV tapes and where on each DV tape to find each clip. By using the Capture Project feature, Express prompts you for all the different DV tapes that you used to capture your original clip and searches out those clips and recaptures them to your hard drive.

Follow these steps to do a Capture Project:

1. **Make sure that your project is active in the Browser window.**

   Make sure that the Browser is open and active (choose Window⇨ Browser if you can't see the Browser), and then click a project tab at the top of the Browser window to make an open project your *active* project. You then see the active project's media listed in the Browser window. You can have multiple projects open, but only one is active at a time.

2. **Choose File⇨Capture Project.**

   Alternately, you can open the Express Capture window and then click the Project button in the lower-right corner.

3. **Define how you want to recapture your project in Capture Project window (as shown in Figure 3-8).**

   The Capture Project window lets you determine three key things about how Final Cut Express recaptures your project:

   - **Offline Items or All Items:** From the Capture pop-up menu, you can decide to recapture all the clips used in your project or just the ones currently offline (that is, the clips no longer available on your hard drive). You can choose Offline if you deleted some clips from a project (these are offline) but not all of them. On the other hand, you choose All Items if you no longer have any of your original media.

You also choose All Items even though some the clips are still on your hard drive and online because Final Cut Express puts the new, recaptured clips in the same folder. This is helpful when you have a bunch of online clips in different folders all over your hard drive(s), and you want Express to consolidate and organize them.

- **Handles:** You can recapture your clips with handles, which are extra frames of audio or video added to the beginning and end of a captured clip. Why would you want to capture longer versions of your original clips? Well, you may want to capture a little more footage for each clip if you plan to make subtle editing changes to your movies later on. Having a second or two added to each clip gives you a few more options when editing. To recapture your original clips with handles, select the Handles check box and type the length (in timecode) of handles that you want captured at the beginning and end of each clip. (For example, you type 2 seconds and 15 frames of handles as 00:00:02;15.) Remember, though, that adding handles means that you're capturing more video per clip — and requires more hard drive space.

- **Capture Preset:** Click this button, and choose the option that best describes the format that your tape's video and audio is in (NTSC DV video with audio at 32 kHz or PAL DV video with audio at 48 kHz and so on.) See Chapter 2 for more about what these options mean, but you probably want to match this option with whatever preset is selected in Final Cut Express Easy Setup menu (choose Final Cut Express⇨Easy Setup).

4. **Click the Capture button.**

Final Cut Express then begins recapturing your project media clips from their DV source tapes. Express prompts you to insert each DV tape that you originally captured clips from, using the reel name that you gave each tape the first time that you captured them. That's why it's very important to properly label your DV tapes and carefully give each tape a unique name in the Reel field when you capture your clips the first time (as I describe earlier in this chapter). Otherwise, if you don't have labels on your DV tapes or you were too lazy to change the Reel names in Express, Capture Project begins recapturing all your clips and asks you to insert Reel 001 into your camera (or some other reel name), and you have no idea what tape that name actually refers to.

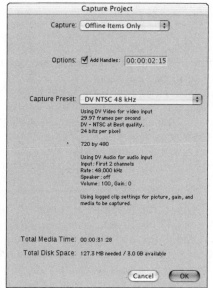

Capture Project

Capture: Offline Items Only

Options: ☑ Add Handles: 00:00:02:15

Capture Preset: DV NTSC 48 kHz

Using DV Video for video input
29.97 frames per second
DV - NTSC at Best quality.
24 bits per pixel

720 by 480

Using DV Audio for audio input
Input: First 2 channels
Rate: 48.000 kHz
Speaker: off
Volume: 100, Gain: 0

Using logged clip settings for picture, gain, and media to be captured.

Total Media Time: 00:00:31:28

Total Disk Space: 127.3 MB needed / 3.0 GB available

Cancel   OK

Figure 3-8:
The Capture
Project
window.

Final Cut Express captures all project clips to whatever hard drive and folder that you set as your Scratch disk. To learn exactly where Express saves those files, choose Final Cut Express⇨Preferences and then click the Scratch Disks tab (refer to Figure 3-5). To the right of the Scratch Disks tabs, you then probably see a path name identifying the folder that Express captured your video to. In that folder, Express creates yet another folder called Capture Scratch (refer to Figure 3-6), and within that folder, Express creates *yet another* folder, using the same name as the project you're currently working with.

When Final Cut Express finally finishes recapturing your media, you see that it's all online again in the Browser window and in the project Timeline sequences.

Not all offline media has to be recaptured. Your media may still be on your hard drive but just moved or renamed somehow, making Final Cut Express declare that it's offline and not giving your project access to it. If you know that your media is there but Express thinks that it's offline, don't try to use Capture Project to get the media back online. Instead, see Chapter 5 for more about relinking media that's gone offline for one reason or another.

Avoiding timecode confusion

Doing a Capture Project can become a real mess if the DV tapes that you're recapturing media that have timecode breaks in them. A *timecode break* is when timecode restarts at any point on your tape, going back to 00:00:00;00. Timecode breaks usually happen when you're recording video with your DV camera (and thereby laying down timecode on the DV tape as well), you turn the camera off, you turn it on again sometime later, and then you start recording more video — thereby resetting the timecode with this new round of footage that you're recording. (*Note:* Pausing or stopping your recording doesn't reset timecode, so pausing when you can is better than turning your camera off.)

How do timecode breaks affect your attempts to recapture an entire project? When you recapture your clips, Final Cut Express looks at each tape that you originally captured media from and notes all the clips that it should recapture by their timecode value (capture a clip starting at two minutes on the tape, then another clip at five minutes, and so on). However, if your tape has timecode breaks, it may have several instances of video with the same timecode (for example, two minutes), so how does Express know which instance to capture? It doesn't! Instead, Express just finds the nearest two-minute mark on the tape and starts capturing there. Unfortunately, Express may be capturing video from the wrong segment of your tape, thereby giving you the wrong clip of video.

How do you avoid this timecode confusion? The best way is to use special technique to prepare a DV tape *before* you actually record any footage to it. When you get a new DV tape, rewind it to the beginning, start your camera recording (leave the lens cap on), and let it record for a full hour until it reaches the tape's end. This process lays down uninterrupted timecode on the tape. Now rewind the tape and shoot your footage with the camera like you normally would; the footage will use the uninterrupted timecode already on the tape, meaning that you'll have no timecode breaks, no matter what.

If your tape has timecode breaks, you have to take some extra steps when you name and capture your video clips the first time around (not when you're recapturing a project — at that point, it's too late). Basically, you want to give each clip that you capture a unique reel name, depending on which timecode segment the clip is in on your DV tape. For example, if my fourth DV tape has four timecode breaks, I name the unique timecode segments on the tape Reel 4A, Reel 4B, Reel 4C, and Reel 4D. I also write down, on the tape itself, the fact that it has four timecode breaks and when in time each one occurs.

When I capture a clip, I save the appropriate reel name with that clip (Reel 4C, not just Reel 4). This way, when I run the Capture Project command and

Final Cut Express captures a clip at, say, two minutes on Reel 4C, I can cue up the tape to that third timecode segment, near the two-minute mark. Express then captures the clip from the right timecode segment.

If all this sounds like a lot of work, you're right, it sure is! However, it's really your only option if your DV source tapes have timecode breaks, and you still want to reserve the right to recapture your project sometime down the road.

 If you want to see or edit clip reel information (as you recorded it when you captured the clip), select the clip in the Browser window, choose Edit⇨Item Properties and click the Logging Info tab. If you want to change the Reel field (for example, to account for timecode breaks on the tape), you're in the right spot to make your changes.

Chapter 4

Importing Media Already on Your Mac

Most likely, plenty of the media you use in Final Cut Express won't have to be captured from DV videotape. You probably already have the media in a digital form on your hard drive. These media may consist of a sound effects file in the AIFF format, an MP3 song from your favorite album, still pictures from a digital camera, or a video clip already digitized into the QuickTime format. And if the media are already on your Mac, you can bring it into Express — that is, import it — with little trouble. That's what this chapter is all about: I tackle all the ways you can import media into your projects, and I also look at some high-powered tools that help convert media from one digital format to another so that it works best with Express.

Importing media into Final Cut Express is completely safe. No matter how you edit your media files going forward, Express doesn't modify or delete the original media files on your hard drive.

Your Media Are Welcome Here

What kinds of media can you use with Final Cut Express? The good news is plenty, though I point out a couple of notable exceptions to avoid any unpleasant surprises.

For video, you can import any video files in the QuickTime file format. Because you're using a Mac, any digital video files you have on hand are probably in QuickTime anyway: That file format is the preferred "homegrown" format for multimedia on the Mac.

On the flip side, Final Cut Express doesn't work with video in other file formats, such as RealVideo or Microsoft Windows Media Format — both are popular on PC machines. If you have a video file in these formats (maybe you downloaded it from the Internet), you can find a small utility program to export the individual frames as Targa images and then reimport those images into Express.

For importing still pictures, Final Cut Express isn't very discerning (thankfully). You can import pictures in just about every file format known to Macs and PCs. In Table 4-1, you can see a list of some of the popular file formats that you can use.

Table 4-1	Popular File Formats for Still Pictures
File Format	*Description*
JPEG	A common format for photos taken by digital cameras and used on the Internet that permits varying degrees of image compression. (The more compression, the smaller the picture's file size, but image quality can suffer.)
TIFF	A photo favorite.
TGA	Known as Targa, a biggie on the PC.
SGI	Images created on professional workstations made by SGI.
PNTG	The MacPaint file format.
PICT	A Macintosh format for graphics.
PNG	A compressed file format that doesn't lose image quality (though its compression can't be as extreme as JPEG). This format is found mostly on the PC.
QTIF	Pictures saved as QuickTime Image Files.
BMP	A popular Windows format.
PSD	The native Photoshop file format.

For sound and music, Final Cut Express welcomes all major formats: AIFF, WAV, and any other audio format that the QuickTime architecture supports. (QuickTime carries not just video but also audio.) These formats are popular on both the Mac and PC, so you can work with just about any audio you dig up.

The only major sound format that Final Cut Express doesn't work with (work well with, at least) is MP3. A favorite in the music world, MP3 compresses music into small files so that they can be easily stored and traded. Unfortunately, an MP3 file imported into Express plays with weird distortion that your audience isn't likely to appreciate (unless you want to call it modern art, in which case you'll be hailed as a deep, brooding genius — maybe not so bad). Anyway, all is not lost. You can solve the MP3 problem with some easy steps, which I talk about later in this chapter, in the section "Converting MP3 (and other kinds of audio) with iTunes."

You can see the compression technology a QuickTime file uses by opening it in the QuickTime Player. From the Mac desktop, double-click the QuickTime file, which launches the QuickTime Player and brings up the movie file. Then choose Window⇨Show Movie Info. The compression information is visible in the Format field of the Movie Info window.

Rendering Media

Although Final Cut Express can import any video or audio that's in the QuickTime format, you may have to render those clips before playing them on the Timeline. _Rendering_ isn't the end of the world — it's just a process where Express has to calculate how a media clip should look or sound before you can play it in your movie. (Admittedly, rendering is a hassle if you have many media files to render.)

Final Cut Express is very clear when you need to render your media files: When you play them on the Timeline, you hear beeps for audio that needs to be rendered, and the Canvas window shows a message that says Unrendered for any video clips. (At the top of the Timeline, above all the tracks, Express also draws a thin red horizontal line over any clips needing rendering.)

But what determines why you must render some media and not other media? For audio clips, it's straightforward: You must render any compressed audio (for instance, an AIFF file that's been compressed with the IMA or MACE compressor). As for video clips, when the video doesn't use DV compression, you must render it. (Remember, Apple designed Final Cut Express to use DV video, and when non-DV video is rendered, it's converted into DV so Final Cut Express can work with it.)

When Final Cut renders a media clip, it writes its calculations out as an entirely new clip to your hard drive. It does this behind-the-scenes; you don't have to worry about where this rendered clip is on your hard drive, and don't have to reimport it. Express doesn't change your original clip at all, but essentially makes a copy of it, but in the format that Express can work with natively.

Be aware that just because a video file is in the QuickTime format doesn't mean it uses DV compression. For instance, a title artist may give you a QuickTime title sequence animation that uses no compression at all or uses the popular Animation compression. Still pictures never use DV compression; they are in formats like JPEG and TIFF, so you need to render them too. If your Mac is powerful enough to give real-time previews of rendered effects, you may be able to play your still pictures on the Timeline without immediate rendering. (See Chapter 17 for more about real-time rendered effects.)

Importing Your Media into Final Cut Express

Okay, so you have digital media on your hard drive, and you're ready to import them into the Final Cut Express Browser window (you've got some editing to do, after all). You have a few options. You can import a single file, which is good for bringing in a random file or two after you're already in the thick of editing, or you can bring in an entire folder of files, which is the best way to get things rolling when you're working with a lot of media. You can also import those files and folders either by using a plain old vanilla dialog box in Express, or by dragging files and folders from your Mac desktop directly into the Express Browser if that's easier for you.

Whatever your tactic, your end goal is the same: getting those media files into the Final Cut Express Browser window (see Figure 4-1), which acts as the central repository for all the media in your project. When you bring a media file into the Browser, the file becomes a *clip,* and it's from the Browser that you can watch or listen to your clip, make a variety of adjustments to it, and ultimately move it to the Timeline for editing. You know that a file has been imported successfully because a little clip icon appears in the Browser window, with your media filename next to it. (Check out Chapter 5 for a full rundown on the Browser.)

If you create or open a Final Cut Express project (see Chapter 2) and you don't see the Browser, you can turn it on by choosing Window⇨Browser from the menu bar, or toggle it on and off by pressing ⌘+4 as a shortcut.

Sometimes you may want to import media that's on a CD-ROM, a DVD-RAM or DVD-ROM (which is like a super-charged CD), a puny old little Zip disk, or even another computer connected through a network. If this is the case, first copy that media to your own hard drive (internal or external will do) and then *import* from the hard drive. This method guarantees that Final Cut Express always has the media available, and can access them quickly. (See Chapter 17 for mote tips on keeping your media organized.)

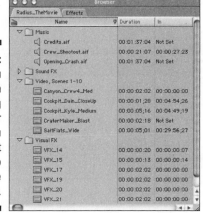

Figure 4-1:
Before you
can begin
working
with your
clips, you
must import
them into
the
Browser.

Importing one file or more at a time

To import a single file or collection of files, try this:

1. **Select the Browser window to make it active.**

   When you have another window selected, Final Cut Express may not let you import files. If the Browser isn't active, you can also select it by pressing ⌘+4 on your keyboard.

2. **To import your files directly to an existing bin in the Browser window, double-click that bin so that it opens in a new window.**

   Remember, a bin is the Final Cut Express version of a folder. If a Bin window isn't open and active, Express imports your files into the top level of the Browser.

3. **Choose File⇨Import⇨Files from the menu bar or use the ⌘+I shortcut.**

   The Choose a File dialog box, shown in Figure 4-2, appears.

4. **Use the Choose a File dialog box to navigate through your hard drive folders until you see the media file you want.**

   The dialog box is divided into columns: When you click a drive or folder name in the left column, the column to its right shows the drive or folder contents. Just keep clicking folders until you see the file you're looking for. If you accidentally choose the wrong folder, move the scroll bar back a bit until you see the previous levels of folders.

   You can speed up your file search by telling Final Cut Express to show you only movies, sound clips, or still pictures. Just select your preference from the Show drop-down list at the bottom of the dialog box.

Figure 4-2:
Navigate
through the
Choose a
File dialog
box to find
the media
you want to
import.

5. **Select the media file(s) you want and then click the Choose button to add the media to the Browser window.**

   To select a continuous range of files for importing, click the first and the last files of the range while holding down Shift (called *Shift-clicking*). Or you can select multiple files, regardless of their order in the file list, by holding down ⌘ while clicking them.

   Either way, Final Cut Express adds your media files as new clips in the Browser window (refer to Figure 4-1), where you can now play with them to your heart's content. (If you can't see the Browser, choose Window⇨Browser from the menu bar, or press ⌘+4).

Just because the filename in the Choose a File dialog box is grayed out does not mean that it can't be imported. The key to selecting a valid file for importing is the icon for the file. If the file's icon is *not* grayed out, it will import.

If you often import files from the same folder, you can make that folder a Favorite by highlighting its name in the Choose a File dialog box, and then clicking the Add to Favorites button. From now on, you can access that folder quickly by opening the From drop-down list and selecting your folder name from Favorite Places. No more navigating all the way through your hard drive.

Importing a folder full of files (or other folders)

If you want to import several media files into Final Cut Express at once, go to your Mac desktop, drag all your files into a single folder, and follow these simple steps:

1. **Make sure the Browser window is active.**

2. **Choose File⇨Import⇨Folder.**

   The Choose a Folder dialog box appears, as shown in Figure 4-3.

3. **Select the folder you want to import and click the Choose button.**

   Final Cut Express now adds your folder to the Browser, making it a bin. When the folder you imported contains other folders inside it, you see that those folders have become bins within the master bin.

   Navigating this dialog box is just like navigating the Choose a File dialog box. Refer to the previous section ("Importing one file or more at a time") if you aren't sure how to navigate this dialog box.

Figure 4-3:
Importing
the Scene 54
folder moves
all the files
and folders
inside it to
the Browser.

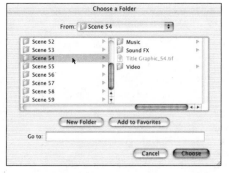

Importing whole folders instead of individual files not only saves you time but also has a nice side effect: It encourages you to keep your media files organized in folders that make sense. For instance, maybe you keep all your video clips in a Video folder and your music in its own folder as well. The point is that you work a lot faster when you corral your media into folders, instead of leaving random files strewn all over the place.

Importing files by dragging them from the Finder

A quick way to import media files and folders is by dragging their icons directly from your Mac Finder to the Final Cut Express Browser window. But why do this when you can just use the Import File or Import Folder option within Express? Because you may instinctively know how to find a file quicker by navigating to it via the Finder, rather than by using the Express dialog boxes. Follow these steps to import files via the Finder:

1. **From Final Cut Express, click the Finder icon in the OS X Dock (see Figure 4-4).**

   The Finder becomes active, but if you don't have any open windows in the Finder (which pop up automatically), you may not notice the change because you'll continue to see the Final Cut Express windows visible in the background.

2. **In the Finder, find the files or folders you want to import into Final Cut Express.**

   If you don't currently have a Finder window open, choose File⇨New Finder Window. Then use the window to navigate to your files or folders.

Figure 4-4:
The Finder icon and the Final Cut Express icon on the Dock.

3. **Click and drag the files from the Finder window to the Express Browser window.**

   You may have to move the Finder window so that it doesn't cover up the Browser. When you drag your files to the Browser, they become clips. When you drag a folder, it becomes a bin with the files/clips inside.

Importing music tracks directly from a CD

Final Cut Express can also import music tracks from all your audio CDs. The best way to import CD tracks is to first copy the CD tracks to your hard drive and then import the tracks into Express as you would any media file. Follow these easy steps:

1. **Place a CD in the CD-ROM drive.**

2. **From the Mac Finder, double-click the CD icon so you can see its contents (as shown in Figure 4-5).**

   You can go to the Finder by clicking its icon in the OS X Dock (refer to Figure 4-4).

Figure 4-5:
A window in the Finder shows the tracks of an audio CD.

3. **Copy the CD track(s) you want to import to your hard drive.**

   The Finder lists the CD tracks as files. Just click and drag the files you want to your hard drive (or preferably a folder inside your hard drive, but you can also copy the files to your desktop if that's easier). While in the Finder, you may want to give your copied tracks more descriptive names now, but you can also do this within Final Cut Express.

4. **Go back to Final Cut Express, and import the track(s) as you normally would.**

   You can jump back to Final Cut Express by clicking its icon in the Dock. When you import a track file, you'll see it listed in the Browser window as an audio clip.

Importing Photoshop files (layers and all)

You already know that you can import all sorts of still picture formats into Final Cut Express, but if you've created graphics in Photoshop that use its layers feature (for instance, a fancy title made up of overlapping images and effects), I have some good news: Express can actually preserve your layers so that you can animate and otherwise manipulate them individually. I explain how it all works in this section.

When you import a Photoshop PSD file, Express imports the file not as a single image clip, but as an entire Timeline sequence. (A *sequence* is the Express way of organizing a group of clips; see Chapter 6 for a full explanation.) In the sequence, Express places each Photoshop layer on its own video track (track V1, track V2, and so on). Express also preserves the order of your Photoshop file layers by assigning the background layer to the sequence's first video track (V1) and ordering every other layer as you did in your Photoshop file. For instance, your fifth layer, including the background, would be on the V5 track.

Final Cut Express also interprets many of the settings you gave your layers in Photoshop — for instance, opacity settings, modes, and visibility. (See Chapters 12 and 14 for more on effects and compositing, respectively). On the other hand, Express tosses out any layer masks you create, and if you're using some weird compositing modes that Express can't understand, it ignores those layers.

In general, though, you can successfully import some pretty sophisticated Photoshop masterpieces into Final Cut Express and, with a little tweaking, get them ready to take the stage in your movie.

When you import a Photoshop file with layers, Final Cut Express doesn't make a copy of that image; it just references the original Photoshop file on your hard disk. If you go back to Photoshop and change the artwork, you see the changes reflected in your Express sequence. That's pretty cool, but if your changes include adding or deleting layers in your Photoshop file, you're likely to confuse the heck out of Express. If you ever want to add or delete layers in a Photoshop file that you've already imported into Express, I recommend importing the file again rather than working with the earlier version.

A few words about still pictures

When you work with video in Final Cut Express, it sizes each video frame at a resolution of 720 horizontal pixels x 480 vertical pixels (this is true of all standard, NTSC-based DV video). But when you import a still image into Express, the image probably won't match that standard video resolution. A still picture could be 640 x 480 pixels, 1280 x 960 pixels, 2560 x 1920 pixels — all depending on how it was taken, scanned, or otherwise edited before winding up in Express. The result? When you import that image into your movie, it'll either be too small or too large to fit the video frame. A black border appears around an image that's too small; if the image is too large, you don't see the whole image, which makes it look cropped.

Sometimes that's a good thing. For instance, if you bring in an oversized high-resolution picture (say a high-res scan of an old map), you can use the Final Cut Express animation features to slowly pan or scale it through your 720x480 video frame. (You see this effect used a lot in documentaries, like those historical masterpieces done by Ken Burns.) On the other hand, sometimes you simply want your still pictures to fill the screen — nothing more, nothing less.

Fortunately, Final Cut Express gives you full flexibility to handle your still pictures any which way. You can bring them in with the intention of showing just parts of them, or you can resize them to fit the frame of your movie. I cover the "how-to" behind this in Chapter 13.

Converting MP3 (and Other Kinds of Audio) with iTunes

One of the most popular file formats for audio these days is MP3, which compresses audio into very small file sizes while keeping very high quality (that's why MP3 files are so popular on the Internet — they don't take long to download but still sound pretty good). At some point, you may want to use an MP3 file in your movie. For example, a composer may e-mail you the latest version of a movie musical score as an MP3 file so you can quickly try it out. However, it turns out that the MP3 file and Final Cut Express didn't work well together, thanks largely to the MP3 extreme compression. For starters, when you imported that MP3 file into Express, you had to render the file before playing it, and that took a couple minutes. Even after rendering, the MP3 file sounded warbled. Your best bet is to convert the MP3 file to a friendlier file format, such as AIFF, before importing it.

You also have problems when you import audio clips in the MP4 format, which is a successor to MP3. You can use the same steps to convert either format to AIFF.

Fortunately, converting an MP3 file to a Final Cut Express-friendly format is pretty easy, but you need to rely on another program already on your Mac, called iTunes, to do it. Just follow these steps:

1. **Launch iTunes from your Mac Finder.**

   If you're not sure where to find iTunes, check the OS X Dock for the iTunes icon, and click it (the icon shows musical notes on a CD disk). If you can't find an iTunes Dock icon, open your Applications folder, and look there. Still no iTunes? Then you can download the software for free at `www.apple.com/itunes`.

2. **If your MP3 file is not in your iTunes library, then add it.**

   To add a song to your iTunes library, choose File⇨Add to Library. Use the Add To Libary dialog box to select the MP3 on your hard drive, and click Choose. iTunes adds the MP3 file to its library — look for its name in iTunes main window (see Figure 4-6). If you don't see your file listed, select Library under the iTune Source list to make sure that iTunes is showing you all the files in its library and not some other information, such as Internet radio stations.

3. **Choose iTunes⇨Preferences to open the iTune Preferences dialog box.**

   The Preferences dialog box displays (see Figure 4-7).

4. **From the Import Using pop-up menu, choose AIFF Encoder.**

Figure 4-6:
An MP3 file
selected in
the iTunes
library.

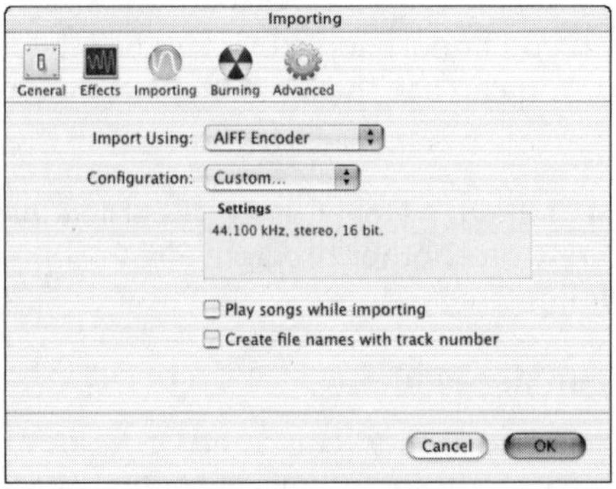

Figure 4-7:
The iTunes
Preferences
dialog box.

5. **From the Configuration pop-up menu, choose Custom.**

   A settings dialog box for the iTune AIFF Encoder appears (see Figure 4-8).

6. **In the AIFF Encoder list, select a sample rate of 44.1 kHz from the Sample Rate drop-down list, select Stereo channels and a 16-bit sample size, and click OK.**

   You're telling iTunes to use its highest quality settings when it converts MP3 audio files to an AIFF version.

7. **Click OK in the iTunes Preferences dialog box to close it.**

8. **From the iTunes main library, select the MP3 file you want to convert.**

9. **Choose Advanced⇨Convert Selection to AIFF to convert the MP3 file to a AIFF file format.**

   iTunes begins converting the MP3 file. Depending on the iTunes settings, iTunes may start playing the MP3 file while converting it. You can watch the progress of the conversion (it can take a few seconds or longer), by selecting Converting Songs under the Source list of the iTunes main window.

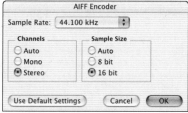

Figure 4-8:
Setting your
AIFF
settings.

10. **Use the Mac Finder to find the new AIFF file.**

iTunes saves the new AIFF file to its default folder. If you haven't changed this folder, the file is in the Home folder. Open that folder, the Music subfolder, the iTunes subfolder, and then the iTunes Music sub-folder. (Yup, that's a lot of folders!)

Within the iTunes Music subfolder, iTunes may have created yet another folder, using the name of the artist who created your original MP3 file (such as U2, The Rolling Stones, or my personal favorite, Lawrence Welk) for the converted file. If not, look for a folder named Untitled Artist.

Your converted AIFF file used the same name as its MP3 parent but with the .aif extension. You can import the AIFF file into Final Cut Express the same way you import any other clip.

You can verify where iTunes saves your files by choosing iTunes⇨Preferences, and clicking the Advanced button in the Preferences dialog box. You'll see the file iTunes used in the box named iTunes Music Folder Location. Click the Change button to create a different path.

When you convert an MP3 file to the AIFF format, the AIFF version doesn't improve on the MP3 sound quality even if you kept your AIFF sound settings as high as possible. Why not? Well, the MP3 source is already compressed, and the AIFF file iTunes spawns can't magically recover data lost during the MP3 original compression. You may say, "Fine by me. The MP3 file sounded great anyway!" But here's the catch: While the sound of an MP3 file holds up on your Mac built-in speakers or an average television or headphone set, when you compare the sound to that of the same uncompressed file (especially on a good sound system), the MP3 rendition isn't as good. I say this only to warn you about converting MP3 sound to an AIFF format and then using it in your finished Final Cut Express movies. MP3-based sound is great placeholder mate-rial, but when you're finally ready to wrap up your movie, you may want to use sound that you have never compressed to get the best results.

Chapter 5

Organizing Your Media Clips

As you edit your movies — especially long ones — keeping all of the media clips and Timeline sequences for your project well organized is very important. A good method of organization allows you to find them fast, and because a project may use hundreds of clips, working with them can be a nightmare if you don't have a good system for keeping track of them. Fortunately, Final Cut Express gives you plenty of tools to run a tight ship.

Working in the Browser

When you capture or import media clips or when you create new Timeline sequences, Final Cut Express places all of these elements into its Browser window, which is shown in Figure 5-1. The Browser is like the central repository for all the stuff your project uses, just as your hard drive is the central repository for all the data your Mac uses. In fact, the Browser works much like your hard drive. A hard drive is full of many different files, stored in many different folders, just as the Browser will be filled with many different media clips and sequences of clips, stored in many different *bins*, which act just like folders within the Browser.

Chances are, you'll be able to see the Browser on your screen at all times, but if it ever gets covered up by another window, you can call it forward by choosing Window⇨Browser, or just press ⌘+4.

Bin icons

Figure 5-1:

Figure 5-1:
The
Browser
window can
show its
contents in
both Large
icon view
and List
view.

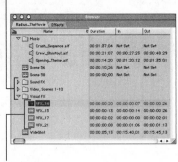 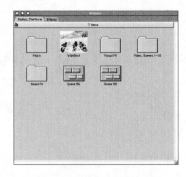

Clip icons

Besides letting you organize clips and sequences (preferably into bins), the Browser can also show you a great deal of information about your media clips arranged in columns that you can scroll through horizontally. You can also list the contents of the Browser by all sorts of criteria; for instance, you can see clips in alphabetical order, from longest to shortest, by their data rate, and so on.

The Browser shows all the media and sequences available in your current project, but you can have multiple projects open at a time, in which case, each open project gets its own tab in the Browser (the tab displays the project name). You can click a tab to see its project media and sequences within the Browser, or you can drag each tab outside the Browser to open the project in a new Browser window. To close a project, Control+click its tab (hold down Control as you click) and choose Close Tab from the pop-up menu.

By the way, Final Cut Express can display items in the Browser window as a list of text or as icons of different sizes (refer to Figure 5-1). The Browser, by default, opens in an icon view, but I recommend switching to List view for best results. Choose View⇨Browser Items⇨as List.

Figuring out the Browser icons

Each type of item in the Browser has its own icon. Table 5-1 shows the icons in the Browser window and what they stand for. The chapters in the table indicate where you can turn find more information.

Table 5-1	Icons of the Browser Window	
Icon	*Item*	*To Find Out More, See...*
	Bin	Chapter 1
	Open bin	
	Locked bin	
	Marker	Chapter 3
	Video/Audio Clip	Chapters 8 and 11
	Subclip	Chapter 3
	Audio Clip	Chapter 11
	Offline Clip	Chapter 3
	Sequence	Chapter 2
	Graphic/Still	Chapter 4
	Video Filter	Chapter 12
	Video Transition	Chapter 9
	Audio Filter	Chapter 11
	Audio Transition	Chapter 9
	Generator	Chapter 10

Using bins

Keeping your media clips and sequence files organized into bins is always a
priority as you work. Take the time to set up bins in advance, for files such
as video clips, music, sound effects, or you can organize bins according to
scenes in your movie. The following list describes some functions you can
perform with bins.

✔ **Making New Bins:** To make a new bin in your Browser, choose File⇨ New⇨Bin (⌘+B). You see a new bin appear in your Browser with its name highlighted for renaming. Click in the name field of the bin and give it a new name.

✔ **Adding Items to Bins:** Adding items to bins is like adding files to your folders in the Mac OS. Simply drag any item into your bin to add that item to that bin. You can also drag a bin into another bin.

✔ **Opening Bins:** Each bin has a small triangle next to it. (Apple calls it the *disclosure triangle*. Whoopee-doo — how impressive!) To open your bin, you can click the triangle so that it points down and reveals the contents of your bin. You can also double-click a bin to open it in its own Browser-like window.

Using Browser Columns

The Browser columns let you see lots of facts about your media clips and Timeline sequences, such as duration, scene and shot information, frame size, audio format, and plenty more. While this information may not be useful to you on a daily basis, it can come in handy more often than you'd think.

Understanding the column headings

The Browser boasts 33 different column headings that you can display or hide. You may not need many of them in your project, but most editors prefer to see a lot of information about their media in the Browser.

Some of the column headings you will probably use the most are as follows:

✔ **Name:** The name column is the first column of your Browser, and nothing you do will change that. (It's a stubborn column and likes to be first.) The name of your clip is the name you entered in the Log and Capture window. You can also rename the clip in the Browser by double-clicking the name of the clip. Be aware, though, that the actual media file (which also uses the name of the clip) maintains the old name.

✔ **Reel:** This column shows the reel name as you entered it in the Log and Capture window.

✔ **Capture:** You can see the current capture status of your clip in this column. The indicators that appear in this column are Not Yet, OK (which means the clip has been captured), Aborted, and Queued. Another indicator that appears in this column is Error, indicating that your clip dropped frames during the capture process.

✔ **Data Rate:** This column indicates the data rate of your captured clip. For DV clips, it always hover around 3.6 Mbps (megabytes per second).

✔ **Size:** This column shows the size of your clip in megabytes (MB) as it exists on the drive. Using this column, you can identify unnecessary clips that take up large amounts of hard-drive space. *Note:* The Browser normally hides the Size column. To reveal the column, see the section "Working with column headings" later in this chapter

✔ **Source:** Final Cut Express stores each clip you capture as a media file on a drive. This column enables you to see the path of the media file. In short, if you want to find out exactly where you stored a file on your drive, look in this column. *Note:* The Browser normally hides this column too, because it can be very wide. To reveal the column, see the section "Working with column headings" later in this chapter.

✔ **In:** This column indicates the timecode of an In point. This point may not necessarily be the very start of your clip. If you move the In point, the timecode changes here to reflect that move.

✔ **Out:** This column shows the timecode of an Out point. Again, this point is not necessarily the very end of your clip, as you might have set an Out point before the actual clip ends.

Sorting clips by column

The Sort feature is one of the more helpful features in the Browser window. To sort by name, click the top part of the name column. You see a small green arrow pointing downwards (indicating a sort), and your clips sort themselves in alphabetical order. Similarly, you can click the Duration column, and Final Cut Express sorts your clips by how long they are.

To reverse sort, click the column heading again so that the small green arrow points upwards. This indicator means that Final Cut Express has reverse-sorted your column. In a reverse-sorted name column, for example, clips with names starting with a Z are at the top, and the ones with names starting with an A are at the bottom.

Working with column headings

With so many different column headings, you need to manage them and organize them in some logical fashion. You can add or delete columns, rearrange their order in the Browser, and change their widths to match your needs. The following list gives a few simple things you can do to keep the columns looking just the way you like them.

✔ **Add columns:** To add a new column heading that is not visible, Control+click any column heading and choose a heading from the pop-up menu that appears.

✔ **Hide columns:** To hide any column, Control+click the column heading you want to hide and choose Hide Column.

✔ **Rearrange columns:** To rearrange the order of the columns, you can click and drag any column heading to move it to the left or right.

✔ **Change column width:** Many times, you may find the width of the columns to be too narrow. For example, your clip names may get hidden behind other columns. You can click between two column headers and drag left or right to change the width of the columns.

✔ **Save column layout:** After you've created a column layout, you can save it for later use. Saving is especially helpful if several people are using the same Final Cut Express workstation, and each has his or her own tastes. To save a layout, Control+click any column heading and choose Save Column Layout from the pop-up menu that appears. Name and save your layout.

✔ **Restore column layout:** To restore a column layout, Control+click any column heading and choose Restore Column Layout from the pop-up menu that appears. Select the column layout you named and saved.

Modifying settings in a column

All the columns in the Browser show you information about the clips or the sequences in the Browser. You can change many of these column settings by using one of the following on-screen elements:

✔ **Browser item names:** You can rename any bin, clip, subclip, sequence, or marker in the Browser by selecting the clip, clicking it again (two single clicks, not a fast double-click), and typing a new name.

✔ **Check marks:** Some fields in the columns show check marks. By changing the check marks, you can change the clip's settings. For example, in the Good column, you can change the Good status by clicking the check mark that appears in the field. (The Good setting is a carryover from the Capture window and indicates that a clip you felt was good for use during the capture phase.)

✔ **Fields in the Browser:** You can modify fields in the Browser (such as Reel, Log Notes, Scene, and Take) by single clicking them twice (not a double-click, but two single clicks) and entering the new information, such as a new reel name. Depending on the fields, you may need to single-click or double-click.

   ✔ **Pop-up menus:** You can change a clip's settings in other Browser fields by Control+clicking the field and selecting a new setting for the clip from the pop-up menu that appears. For instance, you can change a clip's composite mode, its alpha channel settings, or its Reel Name. A common example is when you've used multiple reels for a project and later realize that, for one of the clips, you've forgotten to change the name of the reel during the Capture phase. Control+clicking the Reel field in the Browser opens a pop-up menu with the names of all the reels you've been using. You can then choose a reel from this pop-up menu to reflect the correct reel name.

Viewing Clips as Icons or in Lists

In the Browser, you can see the clips in a few different views, as shown in Figure 5-2. To select the method of viewing, choose View⇨Browser Items and choose from one of the four views in the submenu:

   ✔ **List:** The List view is the most efficient and shows the most information. The only drawback is that you don't see an icon for the image of your clip (so only its name can tip you off to its contents). You can, however, Control+click any column heading and choose Show Thumbnail to bring up small thumbnails for each clip. (*Thumbnails* are small postage-sized views of the video contained in your clip.)

   ✔ **Small Icons:** The Small Icon view displays small icons for clips and items in the Browser. In practice, this view isn't helpful because the icons are too small to be seen clearly.

   ✔ **Medium Icons:** Medium Icon view displays a slightly larger view of the icons. The thumbnails are fairly large and easy to view.

   ✔ **Large Icons:** The Large Icon view shows the largest icons of any of the views. This view is helpful for looking for a shot if you can recall the first video frame, which is the frame shown in each clip icon.

The Large Icon view (choose View⇨Browser Items⇨As Large Icons) has a few features that I find very useful when editing a project. The first feature is that the Large Icon view shows a thumbnail frame of each video clip, called a *poster* frame. By default, the poster frame is the very first frame in a clip, but you can change the poster frame to be any other frame. While scrubbing the clip with the Scrub Video tool, find the desired frame and then press the Control key while releasing your mouse button. Now your clip will use that new frame as its poster frame.

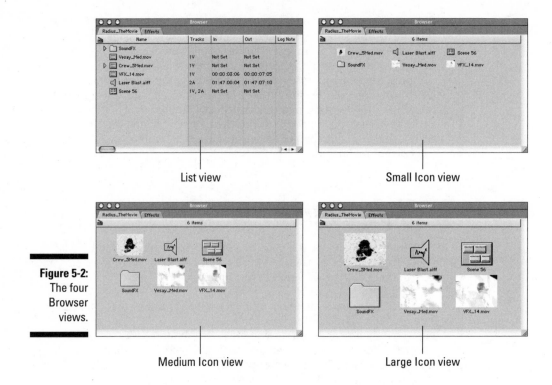

List view

Small Icon view

Figure 5-2:
The four
Browser
views.

Medium Icon view

Large Icon view

In the following steps, I show you how to quickly scan through a video clip's frames without having to open the clip in the Viewer window:

1. **Make sure that your Browser is selected and choose View⇨Browser Items ⇨As Large Icons.**

   Your Browser window switches to the Large Icon view.

2. **Clean up your Browser by choosing View⇨Arrange.**

   This step is necessary because, whenever you switch to the Large Icon view, you may find that your clips become disorganized like a messy drawer full of socks.

3. **Select the Scrub Video tool from the Tool palette.**

   If the Tool palette isn't visible, choose Window ⇨Tools to bring it up. The Scrub Video tool looks like a hand with two small arrows and is part of the fly-out menu of the Zoom tool, which looks like a magnifying glass (see Figure 5-3).

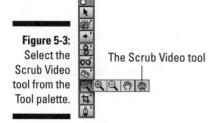

Figure 5-3:
Select the
Scrub Video
tool from the
Tool palette.

The Scrub Video tool

4. Click and drag any video clip with the Scrub Video tool.

With the Scrub Video tool, you can quickly scroll through your video clips to find the shot you may be searching for. This method is often a whole lot faster than loading each clip into the Viewer and searching through it. Drag to the left to go back and to the right to go forward in your clip.

If, during scrubbing, you need to move a clip around in the Browser window, turn off scrubbing by pressing ⌘ to get your pointer back. Then click and drag the clip to its new location.

Adding Transitions and Effects to the Favorites Bin

The Browser window features an Effects tab. Click this tab, and you can find all the effects that Final Cut Express offers, such as Dissolves and Wipes. (By the way, you can also see the same effects on the Effects menu. For more on transitions and effects, see Chapters 9 and 13.) The Effects tab has a Favorites bin where you can store transitions and effects that you may have modified for your use and want to reuse again. You can rename these effects and transitions as well. For example, you may find that you're using a Dissolve of ten frames in your Timeline again and again. You can drag this Dissolve from the Timeline into the Favorites bin in the Browser's Effects tab and reuse it as many times as you like:

1. Select the Transition or effect you want to add to the Favorites bin.

To select a transition or an effect, click the Effects tab in the Browser. (If one is not visible, choose Window⇨Effects to bring it up.) Then open the category folders and select a transition you like.

  2. Choose Modify⇨Make Favorite Effect.

    Final Cut Express copies the transition to the Favorites bin. You can rename this transition by double-clicking its name in the Browser and typing a new name.

    From now on, you can drag this transition or effect from the Favorites bin (instead of having to burrow like a rabbit through all those folders full of effects and transitions) and add it to your clips.

These effects in the Favorites bin are also available to you when you choose Effects⇨Favorites.

Editors use the Favorites bin to store modified effects and transitions. For example, you can double-click any transition in the Browser to open it in the Viewer window and change its duration. Then you can drag the transition into the Favorites bin and rename it as you like. This way, you can have various modified effects and transitions available to you in your Favorites bin.

Locating Clips

On a large project of any scope, the Browser can quickly become a rabbit hole, strewn with media clips stored and cluttered bins within bins. If you ever find your Browser in this state of disarray, finding a particular media clip or sequence in all this mess can become very time consuming.

Thankfully, the designers of Final Cut Express have included an awesome search function to help find the proverbial needle in a haystack.

Searching by clip name or comments

The most basic search is to look for a clip or sequence by name. (Of course, you have to remember the name of the item you're looking for.) You can also search by comments you may have added to the missing clip. For more on the different types of criteria, flip ahead to "Searching by other criteria."

To do a basic name search in Final Cut Express, follow these steps:

  1. Choose Edit⇨Find or use the shortcut ⌘+F.

  2. In the Find dialog box that appears (shown in Figure 5-4), select the name of your project in the Search pop-up menu.

Figure 5-4:
The Find
dialog box.

3. **In the For pop-up menu, choose All Media.**

4. **In the two pop-up menus at the bottom, choose Name in the left one and choose Contains in the right one.**

5. **Type the name for the clip you want to search for in the lower-right field of the Find dialog box and then click Find Next.**

   You can type part of or the whole name in the Name field. The Find dialog box closes and the first clip in the Browser matching the name is highlighted.

6. **Choose Edit⇨Find Next or use the shortcut ⌘+G to find the next clip based on the name you entered.**

You can also click Find All so that the search function finds all the clips with the text in their names. Find All brings up a Find Results window containing all the clips Final Cut Express found. Each time you use ⌘+G, Express highlights the next clip that has the same name you were searching for.

Searching by other criteria

The Find dialog box is a versatile search tool. You can search by an almost endless array of criteria, such as Name, Type, Length, and any one of the four Comment fields you may have supplied for a clip. You can also create more than one criterion for a search by clicking More and adding to the list of your criteria. A creative mixing and matching of the options available in the Find dialog box can narrow down just about any item you may go searching for.

If your results produce more than one clip, Final Cut Express presents the results in the Find Results window. In this window, you can select an item and click the Show in Browser button to locate the selected item in the Browser.

Defining the scope of your search

The top part of the Find dialog box enables you to define the scope of the search you are about to begin.

✔ **Search:** Choose an option from the pop-up menu to determine which open projects or folders you want to search. The options are All Open Projects, Effects, or Current Open Project.

✔ **For:** With this setting, you can indicate which type of media you want to restrict the search to: All Media, Unused Media, or Used Media. This setting is important because you may not want to search through media you have not used in the sequences.

✔ **Results:** This option tells Final Cut Express what to do with the results after the search feature presents them. The options are

- **Replace Find Results:** Choosing this option replaces the results of a previous search.

- **Add to Find Results:** Choosing this option adds the results of the current search to any previous search you may have done.

Defining the criteria of your search

You can add or eliminate search criteria by using the More and Less options. The More and Less option buttons are located in the lower-left section of the Find dialog box.

✔ **More:** Clicking More gives you additional criteria that you can use for your search. For example, you may want to search for a name and also a log note.

✔ **Less:** This button reduces the next level of criteria. This button is available only when you have enabled some of the More options.

✔ **Omit:** Select this check box in the lower-left corner if you want to omit certain criteria rather than add it. For example, you may want to omit any clip with the name *car* from your criteria of search.

✔ **Any Column:** In this drop-down list, which is next to the Omit check box, you can specify any column you may want to search. Using this setting, you can search any and all columns in the Browser.

✔ **Contains:** This drop-down list, which is to the left of the Column drop-down list, allows you to narrow your search.

The Contains options are Starts With, Contains, Equals, Ends With, Less Than, or Greater Than. At first glance, these options may seem confusing, but after you experiment with them, you realize they are quite powerful.

For example, you may have some clips that end in the word *cars,* while others begin with the word *cars.* To search only for the clips that end in *cars,* select Ends With.

✔ **Text field:** Type the text you want to search for in the text field in the lower-right corner.

✔ **Find Next and Find All:** These buttons are in the top-right corner of the Find window, and you use them to start your search. The Find Next button highlights the next item in the Browser that matches your search criteria. From here, you can then press ⌘+G to locate the next item that matches the search. The Find All button tells Final Cut Express to locate all the items that meet your search criteria and gather them in the Find Results window, shown in Figure 5-5.

Figure 5-5:
The Find
Results
window.

Dealing with Offline Media

The Browser is also an early warning system when your project's media suddenly goes *offline* — when Final Cut Express can no longer find the media your movie depends on.

Remember, any clip that you import or capture into the Browser is simply just a pointer to a real, live digital media file somewhere on your hard drive (like a QuickTime movie, a TIFF image from Photoshop, or an AIFF music file). Usually, Final Cut Express knows exactly where to find all of your project's media files — Final Cut Express knows each file's name, which hard drive it's on, and in which folder it resides in. However, things can go awry if you alter your digital media files in such a way that Final Cut Express can't find them. For example, if you import a piece of media into the Browser (where it's represented as a clip), but go to your Mac's Finder, and rename, move, or delete the media file you just imported, then you'll be in trouble: Final Cut Express won't be able to play your clip, because it can't find its associated media file anymore. Tragically, your clip has gone from being *online* (a happy and productive member of your fine film) to *offline* (lost and presumed dead).

Express constantly checks your hard drive to make sure that the media for your project is online. If Express finds that any media is missing in action, you are alerted via the dialog box you see in Figure 5-6. Also, your Browser puts a slash through each offline clip's icon, as shown in Figure 5-7, and Final Cut Express displays the message `Media Offline` when you play the clip in the Viewer or from the Timeline.

Figure 5-6:
Final Cut Express tells you the name of every media file it can't find, and also notes where on your hard drive it expected to find the media.

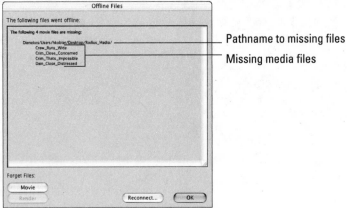

Pathname to missing files

Missing media files

Figure 5-7:
The Browser shows that a clip is offline by putting a slash through its icon

When Final Cut Express reports that a clip is offline, you have a couple of options for bringing it back, as the next sections discuss.

Recapturing deleted clips

If you deleted media clips from your hard drive (you may have done this on purpose, to clear some space), then you have only one option. You have to use the Capture Project command, which can recapture media from the original DV tapes it came from.

The Capture Project command cannot always save the day, however. If your offline media didn't come from DV tape — if you imported a TIFF image from Photoshop, for example — then you're out of luck. You'll have to recover your offline file some other way (possibly by redoing it), or just give it up for lost. Secondly, even if your offline media comes from DV tape, Final Cut Express won't be able to find it easily unless you noted some key information about the clip, such as the name of the tape and the clip's timecode location on that tape, when you originally captured it from tape. If you recorded this info when you captured your now-offline clip, Final Cut Express remembers it, and you can use its Capture Project feature to look up the clip on DV tape again. (See Chapter 3 for more information.) If you didn't record this key information when you originally captured a clip from tape, then you have to determine the DV tape your clip's media came from, and recapture the clip manually. This isn't the end of the world, especially for an occasional clip here or there, but if you're trying to recover a large number of clips, it can be pretty tedious.

Reconnecting an offline clip

If a clip has gone offline, but you know its media file is still on your hard drive, then you reconnect the clip with its media in one of two ways:

- ✔ When Final Cut Express displays a dialog box warning you that clips in your project have gone offline (refer to Figure 5-6), you can click the Reconnect button in the dialog box.

- ✔ You can select any offline clips in the Browser (these are the clips that show slashes through their icons), and then choose File➪Reconnect Media.

Either way, Final Cut Express responds with the Reconnect Options dialog box, which asks what kind of clips you want to reconnect, as shown in Figure 5-8. Make sure to check Offline (it should be checked already), and click OK.

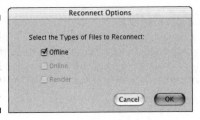

Figure 5-8:
Check the
media types
you want to
reconnect.

In response to your input in the Reconnect Options dialog box, Final Cut Express opens the Reconnect dialog box, shown in Figure 5-9. The Reconnect dialog box lets you navigate through your hard drive's folders and files, and show Final Cut Express where, on your drive, to find each piece of offline media.

In the File Name field of the Reconnect dialog box, Final Cut Express prompts you for the media file it's looking for. Use the dialog box's file selector to browse to the file on your hard drive, select it, and click the Choose button to reconnect it and bring it online again.

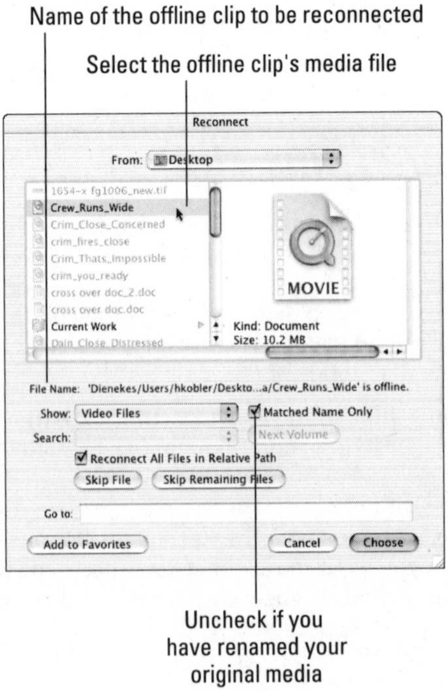

Name of the offline clip to be reconnected

Select the offline clip's media file

Figure 5-9:
The
Reconnect
dialog box.

Uncheck if you
have renamed your
original media

If there are multiple offline files, Final Cut Express prompts you to find each file, one after another. To skip finding a file (maybe this file in particular is not on your drive anymore), just click the Skip File button.

After you reconnect a file in a particular folder on your hard drive, Final Cut Express can automatically reconnect any other offline files that happen to be in that folder as well, saving you from handling each file manually. To take advantage of this, just make sure that you've checked the Reconnect All Files in Relative Path option in the Reconnect dialog box.

If your clips have gone offline because you renamed their media files on your hard drive, make sure to uncheck the Match Name Only option in the Reconnect dialog box. This allows you to associate an offline clip with *any* media file on your drive, not just a file that matches the clip's original name. Just make sure you're reconnecting a clip to the right media file — otherwise, when you use that clip in the future, it won't play the media you expected!

Part III
Editing Your Media

The 5th Wave — By Rich Tennant

"I found these two in the multimedia lab morphing faculty members into farm animals."

In this part . . .

I kick off Part III with the basics of editing video and audio: how to move clips to the Final Cut Express Timeline window and then how to resize them, cut them up, or move them in time. You round out your new skills by mastering the finer points of the Timeline, and you also tackle the advanced editing features — many of which let you perform editing tasks in a single step rather than two or three steps.

Chapter 6

Editing Basics

*E*diting is a unique form of magic. You begin the process with hordes of raw, rambling video, audio, and still pictures that, taken on their own, mean nothing. But through editing, you weave all those disparate parts into a new whole — something with its own identity, something with the power to entertain, inform, provoke, gall — take your pick.

The process of editing may seem complex and mysterious to the uninitiated (again, like magic), but that's just an illusion. In fact, after you begin to explore editing tools and methods, you'll realize that they're all very straight-forward, even — dare I say — *simple*.

Final Cut Express is stuffed with keyboard shortcuts, and the more shortcuts you use, the faster you can edit. Of course, keyboard shortcuts may not be as intuitive as other methods, but I think you'll benefit in the long run if you start getting used to them! For a quick reference to the most frequently used short-cut commands, check out the Cheat Sheet inside the front cover of this book.

Understanding the Editing Process

At the center of all your editing work is the Final Cut Express Timeline window, where you visually arrange all your video clips, audio clips, and still pictures in time. But the other major windows play a big part in editing, too:

✔ **The Browser:** As shown in Figure 6-1, the Browser is where you store and organize all the media clips you've imported into your project before you move them to the Timeline.

✔ **The Viewer:** The Viewer window is where you watch (or listen to) clips before you move them from the Browser to the Timeline (double-clicking a clip in the Browser opens it in the Viewer).

✔ **The Canvas:** The Canvas window plays whatever clips you've arranged in the Timeline window. In other words, it's the window you use to pre-view your movie-in-progress.

✔ **The Tool palette:** Although it's not technically a window, the Tool palette contains the editing tools for cutting, moving, and resizing clips, among other things.

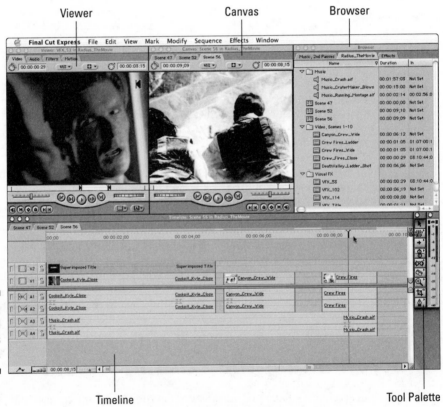

Viewer   Canvas   Browser

Figure 6-1:
The Final
Cut Express
interface.

Timeline   Tool Palette

As you edit, you constantly move back and forth between the Final Cut Express windows. The overall process goes something like this:

1. **Find a clip using the Browser.**

2. **Preview the clip in the Viewer to see how you like it.**

3. **Add the clip to the Timeline, making it part of your movie.**

4. **Watch your movie, in the Canvas, to see how your new clip fits in with all the other clips.**

5. **If you want to tweak how your clip works with the rest of the movie, use the appropriate tool from the Tool palette to resize, split, or rearrange the clip on the Timeline.**

6. **Check out your movie *again* in the Canvas window to see how your edits look.**

7. **Move on to the next shot or scene, and do it all over again.**

If this process sounds a bit daunting, don't worry. Editing in Final Cut Express is like learning to drive a car with a stick shift: You wonder how you can possibly steer the wheel, hit the gas or brake, *and* shift gears at the same time (not to mention tune the radio, chat on the phone, and decipher those directions you scrawled on a napkin). But sure enough, before you know it, it's all second nature. So it goes with Final Cut Express.

You work more quickly when you are comfortable using these keyboard shortcuts to switch between the Final Cut Express windows: ⌘+1 activates the Viewer window; ⌘+2, the Canvas; ⌘+3, the Timeline; and ⌘+4 the Browser. Go ahead and try them out. Just watch out: If a window is already active when you select it with these keystrokes, it will disappear. To bring it back, just use the same keystroke again.

A nice thing about editing in Final Cut Express is that it never offers just one way to do something. For instance, if you want to trim frames from a clip, you can do it by using the Viewer window, clicking and dragging the clips' edges on the Timeline, or doing a cut and then a lift edit or ripple delete. I explain what all these terms mean in due time, of course, but the point is that you have lots of flexibility to develop your own style of working.

Getting to know the Timeline

The Final Cut Express Timeline, which you can see in Figure 6-2, lets you arrange all your video and audio clips so that they tell the story you want to tell. To understand how the Timeline works, think of it as a page of sheet music, but instead of placing musical notes of different lengths of time (quarter notes, half notes, whole notes), one after another, you're placing video and audio clips of different lengths of time, one after another. And when you want to see how your clips play together, you can watch your movie-in-progress in the Canvas window.

Final Cut Express is a nondestructive editor

If you're new to editing, you may be seized with the fear that you accidentally change or even destroy your precious video or audio media — for good. And to this I say, "Get a grip. It just ain't gonna happen!" Final Cut Express is a nondestructive editor, which means that some important safeguards are built in:

✔ When you move media clips to the Timeline and then cut off some frames, you can retrieve those lost frames with a simple click and drag of your mouse.

✔ When you delete clips you've imported into the Browser, Final Cut Express *does not* erase them from your hard drive. To retrieve them, you just have to reimport them.

✔ You can always undo up to your last 32 actions. So even if you cut, trimmed, moved, or deleted a clip 30 minutes ago, you can probably get it back.

In other words, you're invincible! Nothing can hurt your project (at least what you do within Final Cut Express), so fear not. Dive in, experiment, and feel free to brew up endless combinations of clips with the knowledge that a big fat safety net is just below you.

The following sections point out the key features of the Timeline.

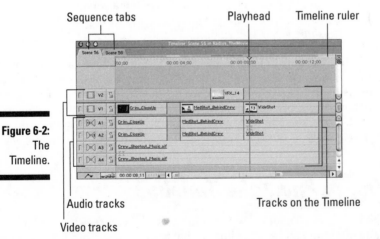

Figure 6-2:
The
Timeline.

Timeline ruler

The Timeline ruler stretches across the top of the Timeline and looks like a conventional ruler (see Figure 6-2), except that it marks increments in time (4 seconds, 8 seconds, and so on), not distance. When you place a media clip on the Timeline, the clip plays at the point in time where you've placed it on the Timeline ruler. For instance, if the clip starts at the 4-second mark on the ruler, the clip plays 4 seconds into your movie.

The ruler markers show hours, minutes, seconds, and finally frames of video; these values are known as the *timecode*. A timecode measurement that reads 00:02:40;04 means you're in the first hour, second minute, fortieth second, and fourth frame of your story.

The playhead

The playhead (refer to Figure 6-2) is like a record needle on an old LP record player: The music plays wherever the needle is, and your movie plays wherever the playhead is on your Timeline. In the Timeline ruler area, click the spot where you want the playhead to start playing. The playhead automatically jumps to that point in time, and you see whatever video frame happens to be under the playhead in the Canvas video. To begin viewing your movie from that point, click the Play button in the Canvas window.

Timeline tracks

The Timeline is divided into horizontal rows called *tracks*. You use tracks to play two or more clips at the same time by placing the clips on different tracks, stacked on top of each other (refer to Figure 6-2 again). For instance, if you want your movie to feature dialogue and background music playing together, just put the dialogue clip on one track and the music directly below it on a different track.

Timeline tracks come in two flavors — video and audio — so you put your video clips on video tracks and your audio clips on audio tracks. You can have up to 99 tracks of each, but for most purposes, you need only a handful of them. Video tracks are numbered V1, V2, and so on, while audio tracks are A1, A2, and so on.

Final Cut Express gives you lots of control over tracks, which comes in handy if your movies need a fair number of them. For instance, you can lock tracks in case you don't want the clips on them to be affected by other editing you're doing, and you can turn tracks off, so they don't play (for instance, if you just want to hear the dialogue track, not the music tracks). See Chapter 7 for more details.

Sequence tabs

If you recall, a sequence is a collection of clips you've organized on the Timeline (you typically use sequences to break a movie down into smaller, more manageable parts — for instance, you might create each of your movie scenes in its own sequence). You can open your project sequences by double-clicking them in the Browser window, and every open sequence is represented by a tab in the upper-left corner of the Timeline window. You can work with each sequence by clicking its tab. (See Chapters 5 and 7 for more about how to create and manage sequences.)

Playing back video: The Viewer and Canvas windows

Before you get into the thick of editing, let's talk a moment about the one thing you do in Final Cut Express more than anything else, which is play back video using either the Viewer or Canvas windows.

The Viewer window plays a single media clip so that you can check it out, see what you like about it, and possibly make edits to it, which I get to later in this chapter. You open a clip in the Viewer by double-clicking the clip either from the Browser window or from the Timeline, if you've already moved the clip there.

Although the Viewer lets you play a single clip, the Canvas window plays the sequence of clips you've assembled in the Timeline window — in other words, you use the Canvas, shown in Figure 6-3, to watch your movie-in-progress so that you can judge how all your edited clips work together.

Zoom

Timecode duration

Current timecode

Figure 6-3:
The Canvas
window.

Scrubber bar

Playhead

Jog Control   Play Button   Shuttle Control

The Viewer and Canvas windows do two very different things, but they work very much alike in that they both offer essentially the same playback options: You can play video forward and in reverse at normal speeds, you can zoom through it with a super fast-forward and rewind, move slowly, or jump to any point with a single mouse click. Take a look at some of the controls that work in both the Viewer and the Canvas:

- ✔ **Play button:** Click it to play and click it again to pause.

- ✔ **Scrubber bar and playhead:** The scrubber bar runs horizontally across the Viewer and Canvas windows, right under your video. The length of the scrubber bar represents the length of your clip (Viewer) or movie (Canvas), and you can position the scrubber playhead anywhere on the bar by clicking your mouse button there. The window shows whatever frame of video is at the playhead position. By the way, notice that the Canvas and Timeline playheads mirror each other: When you position the playhead in the Canvas scrubber, the playhead in the Timeline jumps to the same position.

- ✔ **Jog control:** Click and drag the jog to the left or right to slowly roll the Viewer or Canvas playhead forward or back, as little as a frame at a time (you can also move the playhead frame by frame with the arrow keys).

- ✔ **Shuttle control:** Click and drag the shuttle left or right to rewind or fast-forward. The further you drag the shuttle head from its middle point, the faster your playback is.

As intuitive as these play controls are, they do have a downside. As you play your clips over and over again, scrutinizing each little frame or edit, you may start to tire of constantly moving and clicking the Viewer or Canvas. Take a break. Put your fingers on the keyboard and try out these three keys:

- ✔ **J:** Play backward (in reverse, like a rewind)

- ✔ **K:** Stop

- ✔ **L:** Play forward

Keeping your fingers on these keys gives you lightning-quick control over video playback. Plus, you can use the same keys to quickly go into fast-forward or fast-rewind modes, rather than use the Shuttle control. For instance, to fast-forward, just press L twice. Press L a third or fourth time for an even faster fast-forward.

Alternatively, you can use the space bar to play and stop video in the Canvas or Viewer, instead of pressing L and K .You can also use your right and left arrows keys to move forward or backwards a frame a time, or the up down arrow keys to move a clip at a time.

If the Viewer or Canvas windows don't play your video smoothly, click the Zoom icon at the top of either window (see Figure 6-3), and choose Fit to Window from the Zoom pop-up menu. Doing so scales your video to match the size of your window and allows it to play without any jerkiness.

Looking at timecode data in the Viewer and Canvas

Both the Viewer and Canvas windows give you handy timecode information about the clip or Timeline sequence you're working:

- **Timecode Duration:** The Timecode Duration field (see Figure 6-3) tells you how long your clip or your entire Timeline sequence is. The Viewer window reports the length of the clip, and the Canvas reports the length of the sequence, measured at the last frame of the last clip of your Timeline sequence. If you've selected a segment of a clip or sequence by using In and Out points — more on those in a moment — then this field shows the length of whatever media falls within those points.

- **Current Timecode:** The Current Timecode field tells you the timecode of whatever frame the Viewer or Canvas playhead happens to be on. See for yourself — click inside the scrubber bar of either window to move the playhead from place to place, and watch the Current Timecode value change.

Again, timecode measures hours, minutes, seconds, and frames, so the timecode value 00:04:40;26 means zero hours, 4 minutes, 40 seconds, and 26 frames.

Moving Clips to the Timeline

When you're editing, you spend a lot of time moving media clips from the Final Cut Express Browser window to the Timeline (more specifically, to a video or audio track on the Timeline) as you weave them into your story. Express gives you a few options for accomplishing this; I start with the easiest, most intuitive approach and end with the quickest, most flexible.

Inserting and overwriting

When you add a clip to a track on the Timeline, you're making what's called an *edit*. And the two edits you're most likely to make in Final Cut Express are *Insert edits* and *Overwrite edits*. The difference between these two edits is simple:

✔ **Insert:** With an Insert edit, Final Cut Express creates new room on the Timeline track for your clip, so it doesn't copy over other clips that are already there (in other words, this edit works and plays well with others).

✔ **Overwrite:** When you do an Overwrite edit, Final Cut Express adds your clip to the Timeline. If the new clip is long enough to run into other clips already on that track, however, the new clip erases the existing ones (a decidedly selfish kind of edit).

Figure 6-4 shows the original arrangement of Clips A, B, and C and then what happens when Clip D is added after Clip A with both an insert and Overwrite edit.

Figure 6-4:
The effects of an Insert edit and an Overwrite edit.

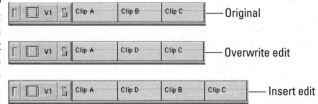

Which type of edit should you use? The answer depends on what you're trying to do. If you want to add a clip to a bunch of other clips, use an Insert edit. If you don't like how a certain clip is working on the Timeline and want to see how a new one does in its place, an Overwrite edit probably is better. The important thing is that you don't think too much about any of this. You'll develop a natural feel for it all soon enough. In any case, the easiest, most intuitive way to do either edit is this:

1. **Position the Timeline playhead wherever in time you want to add your new clip.**

   Final Cut Express places your clip wherever the playhead is on the Timeline. Click in the Timeline ruler to position the playhead at that point in time. (To fine-tune the playhead position, you can move it frame by frame with your left and right arrow keys.) The Canvas window shows the current frame the playhead is on (if a frame is there, as opposed to empty space).

   Although you can position the playhead anywhere, you usually position the playhead at the edge of existing clips (at the first or last frame of a clip). If this is the case, make sure that the Final Cut Express Snapping feature is turned on (check the View menu). This feature makes positioning the playhead at the edge of a clip easy work. (See the section, "Speeding Up Editing with Snapping," later in this chapter.)

You can also press your up and down arrow keys to move the Timeline playhead from the beginning of one clip to another. This works whether Snapping is on or off.

 2. **Drag your clip from the Browser window to the Canvas window.**

    Yes, drag it to the Canvas, not the Timeline. As you drag, a number of "buttons" pop up over the Canvas window. These buttons are actually called *sections,* and as a group, they make up the Edit Overlay. This overlay gives you several choices for the kind of edit you want to make, as shown in Figure 6-5. Don't release the mouse button yet!

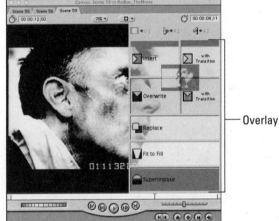

Overlay

Figure 6-5:
The pop-up
edit window
of the
Canvas
window.

 3. **Move the mouse pointer over either Insert or Overwrite, and then let go of the mouse button.**

    Final Cut Express either inserts or overwrites your clip to the Timeline. If your clip includes both video and audio in it, the video portion appears on the Timeline video track, while its audio goes on one or two audio tracks (one track for mono audio and two tracks audio captured in stereo — see Chapter 11 for more on audio).

    How simple was that?

When you move some clips to the Timeline, you have to render them so that they play properly. (*Rendering* is when Final Cut Express figures out ahead of time how to play a clip.) You know you need to render a clip because Express draws a thin red horizontal line above it in the Timeline window. Also, for an unrendered video clip, the Canvas window displays the message "Unrendered" when you try to play the clip; for an audio clip needing rendering, the Canvas will play a repeating beep instead of the real audio you expect. To render the clip, select it on the Timeline, and then choose Sequence⇨Render Selection (or just press ⌘+R).

Choosing the right track on the Timeline

If your Timeline has a lot of tracks, you need a way to tell Final Cut Express which track gets which clips. For instance, if you have multiple audio tracks for stereo dialogue, sound effects, and music, you don't want to insert a clip of music on a track you're using for dialogue clips. To make sure a clip goes to the right track, you make the desired track your *target* track, which tells Express to edit any clips to that track (until you make another track your target track).

You can make any video track a target track, but you can only have one target video track at a time. You can have two audio target tracks — one each for the left and right channels of stereo audio.

Look at the left side of the Timeline, where the tracks begin. As shown in Figure 6-6, to the left of each track name is a little icon called a Target Track control — a filmstrip for video tracks and left/right speakers for audio tracks. (Audio tracks have a 1 in the left speaker if they're designated stereo left audio and a 2 if they're designated for right audio — see Chapter 11 for more about stereo audio.)

You can click these icons to toggle their settings on and off. Note that an icon turns yellow when it's on, and only one track can be turned on at a time. When a track icon is turned on, it's your target track — that is, it's the track where all your clips go when you do an edit. (Just for the record, you don't have to designate a track each time you make an edit — just when you want to change the currently designated track to a new one.)

Figure 6-6:
Click a track icon to turn it on or off.

Using a shortcut to insert and overwrite

When you are comfortable doing Insert and Overwrite edits by dragging clips to the Canvas (and designating your target tracks on the Timeline), you may want to try out this more direct approach.

Click a clip icon or name in the Browser window and drag it to any point in time on the Timeline (regardless of the playhead position) and any track on the Timeline (regardless of your target tracks). As you drag your clip to its track (video or audio), notice that the upper third of the track has a horizontal line running through it (see Figure 6-7, it's easy to miss). This line is the dividing line between inserts and overwrites:

- ✔ **Insert:** When you drag your clip *above* the line, Final Cut Express inserts your clip on the Timeline. Your mouse pointer becomes an arrow pointing to the right, signaling an insert.

- ✔ **Overwrite:** When you drag your clip *below* the line, Final Cut Express overwrites your clip on the Timeline. Your mouse pointer becomes an arrow pointing down when you're in Overwrite mode.

Figure 6-7:
Moving
clips to
tracks on
the Timeline.

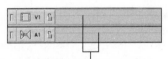

Drag a clip above these lines for an insert;
drag below for an overwrite

Setting in and out points

When you're moving clips to the Timeline, you can move either the entire clip or just a part of it. At first, you may feel more comfortable dragging entire clips to the Timeline and then trimming them down after they're there. But in many cases, it's better to look at the clip ahead of time, identify only the part you're interested in by setting In and Out points, and *then* move the abbreviated clip to the Timeline. This method keeps the Timeline less cluttered. To set In and Out points, follow these steps:

1. **Find the clip in the Browser and double-click it to open it in the Viewer.**

2. **Within the clip, find the first frame you want to move to the Timeline.**

   To find the frame, click in the Viewer scrubber bar (see Figure 6-8) to move the playhead until it is on the frame you want. The frame in the Viewer window corresponds to the frame that the playhead is on.

3. **To set an In point, click the Mark In button in the Viewer or simply press I.**

   You'll see an In point symbol — which looks like a triangle pointing to the right, as you can see in Figure 6-8 — appear at the Viewer playhead and also in the top-left corner of the frame you've marked (this symbol makes it easy to find marked frames).

Figure 6-8:
The Viewer
with In and
Out points.

Scrubber Bar   In and Out Points

Out point button

In point button

4. **Mark an Out point at the last frame you want to move to the Timeline.**

   Follow the same procedure as in Steps 2 and 3, but click Mark Out in the
   Viewer window (or just press O).

Congratulations: You've now marked a range of frames within a larger clip.
When you move this clip to the Timeline (using any of the steps I just cov-
ered), Final Cut Express moves *only* the frames that fall within your In and
Out points.

If you set an In point on a clip, but no Out point, Final Cut Express assumes
the Out point is the last frame of the clip. And if you set an Out point, but no
In point, Express assumes the in point is the first frame of the clip.

To move an In or Out point, just click and drag the in/out arrow in the Viewer
scrubber bar to a new location. You can clear In and Out points by choosing
the option from the Mark menu, or by pressing Option+X.

Recycling a clip by changing its In and Out points

In the thick of editing, you may want to use the same clip over again, but set different In and Out points. For example, you have a clip whose early frames are great at the beginning of your movie, but its later frames work nicely towards the end of the story. When you want to use different parts of the same clip, you open it in the Viewer, set In and Out points for the first part of the clip, and move those frames to the Timeline. Then go back to the Browser, open the same clip in the Viewer window again, set different In and Out points, and move the clip *again* to the Timeline. Voilà: You now have two entirely different clips on the Timeline, each one taken from the same master clip.

You can also copy and paste a new copy of a clip into the Browser, rename it, and set different In and Out points for the new copy. To copy a clip, select it in the Browser, choose Edit⇨Copy, and then choose Edit⇨Paste.

Selecting Clips on the Timeline

After you get your clips to the Timeline, you usually have to select them before you can edit them in various ways (for instance, move or delete them). Doing so isn't rocket science: You select a clip on the Timeline by using the Selection tool, the arrow-shaped tool on the Tool palette.

To select a single clip on the Timeline, just make sure that you're using the Selection tool and click the clip.

If you select a clip or clips but then decide not to do anything with it, deselect it. To deselect a clip, try clicking in the Timeline window, but outside of a track (provided you don't have a All Tracks selection tool active), or press ⌘+D with your free hand (for Deselect All) to save you from mousing overload.

Sometimes, you may want to select a number of clips at once, or a range of frames within one or a group of clips. Table 6-1 runs down some of the handy tools that Final Cut Express offers for selecting multiple clips.

Table 6-1	Tools for Selecting Clips on the Timeline	
	Tool	*What It Does*
▲	**Selection tool**	To select multiple, continuous clips, click the first clip and then hold down Shift while clicking the last clip. Final Cut Express selects all clips in between. To select multiple clips with a selection marquee, you can click your mouse over an empty spot on your Timeline tracks (as long as no clip is there), and drag your mouse to select multiple clips. To select multiple but noncontinuous clips (those that aren't one after another), hold down the ⌘ key while clicking each clip.
	Group Selection tool	Select a range of whole clips by dragging a selection marquee across any clips you want. You can also hold down Shift to select multiple groups of clips with this tool. When your clips are linked (the way audio clips are usually linked to their corresponding video), this tool selects those linked clips too. But honestly, you can also make group selections with the standard Selection tool, so you may want to skip using this tool in favor of the more versatile Selection tool.
→	**Track Forward tool**	This handy tool selects whatever clip you click *and* every clip on that track that follows it (that is, to the right of the clip you click). This tool is a godsend when you trim or delete one clip amid a long continuous sequence and create an unwanted empty gap among the clips. The solution is to select all the clips *after* that gap and then move them over to close the gap in one fell swoop.
⇥	**All Tracks Forward tool**	This tool works just like the Track Forward tool, but when you click a clip, you select both it and *every* clip that follows it — on not one but all tracks. This option is great when you want to select not only clips on your video track, for instance, but also your audio tracks at the same time (moving or deleting them all together).

After you select clips with any of the tools listed in Table 6-1, you can quickly move the entire group by clicking one of the highlighted clips and then dragging.

Moving a Clip That's Already on the Timeline

After you have a clip on the Timeline, you can click and drag it to a different time or to another track. (For instance, you can move an audio clip from Track A1 to A2, no problem.) But Final Cut Express offers something new: When you drag a clip elsewhere on the Timeline, you can *overwrite* it to its new location or you can do what's called a *Swap Edit.*

Overwrites are straightforward. When you move your clip, it fills as much space on the Timeline as it needs, erases any clips already there, and leaves an empty gap on the Timeline where it was, as shown in Figure 6-9. To do an Overwrite edit, you click and drag your selection to the point on the Timeline where you want it. As you'll see from practice, overwrites usually aren't the most helpful of edits, partly because you usually don't want to leave an empty gap on your Timeline.

Figure 6-9:
An Over-write edit, as Clip C moves into Clip B's position.

The Overwrite edit leaves a gap

When you do a Swap Edit, like the one shown in Figure 6-10, Final Cut Express inserts the selection (meaning it creates new space on the Timeline so that it doesn't overwrite any existing clips) *and* closes the gap left behind. For instance, say you've arranged Clips A, B, C, and D on the Timeline one after another, but decide that Clip C should actually come *before* Clip B. Simply drag Clip C in front of Clip B, as shown in Figure 6-10, and you have a seamless sequence of clips: A, C, B, D, and no empty space where Clip C was.

Follow these steps to do a Swap Edit:

1. **Click the clip to select it.**

2. **Drag the to its new spot.**

3. **But before releasing the mouse button, press and hold your keyboard's Option key.**

   With Option pressed, your mouse pointer becomes an curved arrow pointing downwards, indicating you're about to make a swap edit.

   If you want to swap a clip, but press your Option key before dragging the clip, you won't make a swap edit. Instead, you'll insert a copy of the clip into the new spot you drag it to. (Your mouse cursor becomes a big arrow pointing right, indicating an insert and copy.)

4. **Release your mouse button.**

Figure 6-10:
A Swap Edit,
as Clip C
moves into
Clip B's
position.

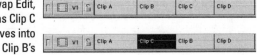

You can overwrite or swap a clip or clips directly *into* another clip, not just to its border. For instance, you can drag Clip B to the 5th frame of Clip A, not just to the beginning or end of Clip A.

You can move (overwrite or swap) not only single clips by clicking and dragging but also large groups of clips (or just a range of frames within a clip). To select those clips, use one of the many selection tools in the Tool palette. Refer to Table 6-1 for a rundown of these tools.

You can also move clips by using the time-honored, no frills Cut, Copy, and Paste commands. Select a clip or clips, and choose either Cut or Copy from the Final Cut Express Edit menu (or press ⌘+X or ⌘+C respectively). Position the Timeline playhead where you want to paste the clips, and then choose Edit ➪ Paste to overwrite the clips at that point, or Paste Insert to insert them. Express pastes the clips to whatever track you've designated as your target track.

Linking and unlinking clips

If a clip on the Timeline includes both video and audio, Final Cut Express normally keeps those related elements linked: When you try to select, move, resize, cut, or delete a linked clip on the Timeline video track, Express does the same to its related clips on the audio tracks as well (and vice versa). At times, however, you may want to unlink related clips or link unrelated clips together.

To unlink video from audio (and vice versa), select the linked clip on the Timeline, and choose Modify⇨Link to toggle linking off. Be warned: If you unlink video and audio and then move one without the other, they become out-of-synch; for instance, an actor's dialogue will no longer match his lip movement. Final Cut Express makes it easy to spot such cases by

displaying a red tag on each Timeline clip that's out of synch, along with a time value telling you how much the clip is off.

To link video and audio clips back together (whether they were originally linked or are totally unrelated), just select the clips on the Timeline, and choose Modify⇨Link to toggle linking back on. A little underline appears beneath the clip names to indicate that they're now linked.

Although you rarely need to, you can also unlink the two channels that make up a stereo audio clip. First, make sure the audio clip is no longer linked to a video clip. Then, select the stereo audio clip and choose Modify⇨Stereo Pair. See Chapter 11 for more about stereo clips.

Speeding Up Editing with Snapping

Snapping makes aligning media clips on the Timeline easy because it makes clips magnetically stick to each other or to other elements on the Timeline (such as the Timeline playhead, In and Out points set on the Timeline, or markers you've placed). Go ahead and try out this feature: When you move a couple of clips to the Timeline, drag one towards the other — when the clips get close, they automatically snap together.

You can turn Snapping on or off in Final Cut Express, but you'll want it on for most editing work. It's on by default, but you can verify that by making sure that Snapping is checked on the View menu. On rare occasions when you want to make precise edits and Snapping interferes, just turn off Snapping by choosing View⇨Snapping (or just press N for quicker results).

Resizing Clips Already on the Timeline

After you place your clips on the Timeline, you devote most of your editing energy to resizing those clips — that is, trimming frames from one clip or adding frames to another. You can do these edits one of two ways:

✔ Drag the edges of a clip in or out on the Timeline.

✔ Open the clip in the Viewer window and set new In and Out points for it, which automatically resizes the clip on the Timeline.

Which tack should you take? When you open a clip in the Viewer, you can play through the entire clip, back and forth, until you've found the right frame to extend or trim it to. It's the easiest way to gauge the clip you're working with, but you can't beat the speed of resizing clips directly on the Timeline. In the end, give both methods a try, and you'll develop a natural feel for when each is best.

Resizing clips directly on the Timeline

If you want to resize clips as quickly as possible, do it directly on the Timeline:

1. **Choose the Selection tool from the Tool palette.**

   The Selection tool may already be selected, but you can also press A just in case.

2. **Move your mouse pointer to the edge of a clip on the Timeline.**

   When the mouse pointer is over either left or right edge, the pointer becomes a resize symbol, as shown in Figure 6-11.

Figure 6-11:
A drag of a clip on the Timeline.

3. **Drag the edges of a clip in or out to resize it to a new frame.**

   Dragging inwards (towards the center of the clip) trims the clip, and dragging outwards extends it (if the clip has unseen frames that you didn't edit onto the Timeline by using In and Out points). Keep an eye on the Canvas window: As you drag, it shows which frame is at the clip end. Also, on the Timeline, a pop-up number shows you how many frames you're trimming or extending the clip to.

When you're trimming a clip on the Timeline, you can use the Final Cut Express Snapping feature to easily drag the clip edge to whatever new frame you're trimming to. Just follow these steps:

1. **Make sure Snapping is turned on.**

   On the View menu, Snapping is checked if it's on.

2. **Position the Timeline playhead at the frame you want to trim your clip to.**

   You may want to play the clip a couple of times to look for the best place to trim it to. To position the playhead precisely on that frame, move it frame by frame with your keyboard arrow keys.

3. **Drag either the start or end edge of the clip towards the playhead.**

   Final Cut Express quickly snaps that edge to that point (and therefore the frame you're trimming to).

When you resize a clip by dragging its edges, you may find that you can't move the clip edge to the exact frame you want — even if you drag the mouse an insy-tinsy bit, the edge can jump several frames at a time. To fix this, zoom in on the Timeline for more precision. You can zoom by pressing ⌘++ (the ⌘ key and the plus key, I'm partial to using the keyboard) or by using the Zoom In tool on the Tool palette, shown in Figure 6-12. With the Zoom tool selected, click the Timeline anywhere. To zoom in even further, keep pressing ⌘++ or keep clicking the Timeline with the Zoom tool. To zoom out, press ⌘+− (⌘ and the minus key) or use the Zoom Out in the Tool palette.

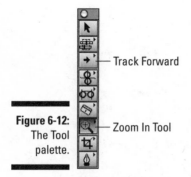

— Track Forward

Figure 6-12:
The Tool
palette.

— Zoom In Tool

Resizing clips in the Viewer window

The Viewer window method isn't as quick as resizing clips directly on the Timeline, but it's the way to go when you want to do a precise edit:

1. **Make sure the Selection tool in the Tool palette is active.**

2. **On the Timeline, double-click the clip you want to resize.**

   Final Cut Express opens the clip in the Viewer window (check out Figure 6-13). You can see the entire clip, even if you originally moved only part of it to the Timeline. But if you've already trimmed the clip (maybe you set In and Out points when you first moved it to the Timeline), you see the current In and Out points on the Viewer scrubber bar.

Figure 6-13:
Set In and Out points in the Viewer window to resize a clip precisely.

3. **Mark any new In and/or Out points to trim or extend the clip.**

   To adjust the first frame, you set an In point at the frame where you want the clip to start. To adjust the last frame, you set an Out point at the frame where you want the clip to end.

   As you mark a new In or Out point, Final Cut Express automatically adjusts the size of your clip on the Timeline (making it longer or shorter — with a few exceptions, which I cover in a moment).

Understanding the limitations of resizing clips

Just when you think you've mastered the fine art of resizing clips, I've got a bit of bad news: The steps I just outlined have some annoying limitations. The two biggest culprits are the following:

✔ **Closely packed clips:** Final Cut Express won't let you extend a clip if another clip is next to the edge you're extending. In other words, if you have Clips A, B, and C arranged side by side and want to extend either edge of Clip B, you can't do it. Clips A and C effectively block it, refusing to move over on the Timeline to make room for the extended frames of Clip B.

✔ **Gaps on the Timeline:** If you trim a clip that's next to other clips, your trim creates a gap in the Timeline. In other words, if you have Clips A, B, C, and D next to each other and decide to trim frames off the end of Clip B, then Clips C and D don't automatically move over to fill the space left by trimming Clip B. Your Timeline looks like this: Clip A, trimmed Clip B, empty space, and then Clips C and D.

But now for the good news! You can use some of the other Final Cut Express tools to solve these two headaches. One handy option is the Track Forward or All Tracks Forward tool (check out Figure 6-12 again), which enable you to quickly select a group of clips on one or all tracks, and move them either forward or back on the Timeline in one fell swoop. By doing this, you can quickly create room for a clip you want to extend, or close gaps left by a clip you just trimmed.

The most quick and efficient way to deal with resizing clips is to use the advanced editing tools from the Tool palette — tools like Roll Edit, Ripple Edit, Slip Item, and Slide Item — which let you extend and trim clips in all sorts of ways, while Final Cut Express seamlessly adjusts all the other clips in the Timeline, sparing you from worrying about them.

By now, you're probably wondering: "Why didn't Helmut mention these tools in the first place?" Well, they can be a bit overwhelming to new editors and are harder to appreciate if you haven't worked without them first. Try resizing your clips by using the steps that I explain here, but when you think you're ready, head on over to Chapter 8, where I tackle the advanced Final Cut Express tools in all their glory.

Cutting a Clip into Two

After you've dragged a clip to the Timeline, you sometimes find the need to cut it into smaller pieces. For instance, you might want to cut a clip in two for various reasons:

✔ To use its early frames at the beginning of your sequence and its later frames in another place

✔ To trim off an extra frame you don't need

✔ To insert a third clip between the two, freshly cut parts

Final Cut Express lets you cut clips in two different ways: You can cut a single clip on *one* track of the Timeline, or your cut can carry through *all* tracks on the Timeline, simultaneously splitting any clips carried on those tracks, as shown in Figure 6-14.

The Razor Blade All tool even cuts through tracks that you've turned off, but it *doesn't* cut tracks you've locked. I cover these track topics in Chapter 7.

Figure 6-14: Clicking the Razor Blade tool in a track cuts only the clip in that track; the Razor Blade All tool cuts through all the tracks.

The type of cut you choose depends on what's going on in your movie. For instance, say you're working on a sequence that uses three tracks on the Timeline: one video track, one audio track for dialogue, and another audio track for background music. Suppose your video track features a stock analyst talking about stocks and bonds, but while the analyst is blabbering on and on, you decide to quickly cut to new video of the New York Stock Exchange — all the while, the analyst's dialogue and your background music continue to play over this new shot, uninterrupted. To insert the clip of the Stock Exchange, you have to make a cut in the video clip featuring your analyst, but should you cut through just the clip on the video track, or through the clips on the dialogue and music tracks as well? In this case, you want to cut only the analyst clip on the video track and leave the clips on the audio tracks untouched, because you don't want the change in the video to interrupt the audio.

Alternately, suppose that in the middle of your stock analyst interview, you decide that Mr. Analyst is getting a little dry, so you want to cut away to an entirely different scene, perhaps an establishing shot of some glistening corporate campus, with a new voice over in your dialogue track and new background music, too. To cut from the stock analyst segment to this new scene, you want to cut the stock analyst clips on *all* your tracks because you want them all to end at the same point, which is also the point where you begin your new scene.

To cut clips on one or multiple tracks, follow these steps:

1. **Move the Timeline playhead to the frame where you want to make a cut.**

   Click in the Timeline ruler to move the playhead to that point, or use your keyboard arrow keys to move frame by frame for extra precision. Keep an eye on the Canvas window — it shows whatever frame the playhead is on.

2. **Use the Razor Blade tool or the Razor Blade All tool.**

   If you want to cut a clip on only one Timeline track, press B for blade or choose the Razor Blade tool from the Tool palette, as shown in Figure 6-15.

   If you want to cut clips on *all* the Timeline tracks, use the Razor Blade All tool. You can just press B twice on your keyboard, or you can select the tool from the Tool palette. (It's hidden beneath the Razor Blade. Just click and hold down your mouse button with the pointer over the Razor Blade icon, and the Razor Blade All tool pops out as well.)

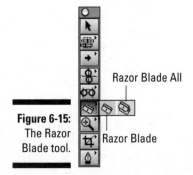

Razor Blade All

Razor Blade

Figure 6-15:
The Razor
Blade tool.

3. **Click the clip you want to cut.**

   Line up the blade with the Timeline playhead so that you cut the frame you selected in Step 1. When you have the Snapping feature turned on, Final Cut Express automatically snaps the blade to the playhead, so you can line up the two very quickly. (Turn Snapping on and off from the View menu, or press N.)

What happens if your Timeline sports many tracks, and you want to make a cut through *some* of those tracks, but not all of them? It's easy: Use the Razor Blade All tool, but before cutting, lock any tracks you don't want your cut to affect. To lock a track, click the little lock icon to the left of each track. By locking a track, you protect any clips on it from being cut, moved, or otherwise changed.

When you cut a clip in two, each new clip remembers all the video/audio media that the razor cut off from the larger, original clip. You can recover this media by dragging outwards the edges of each of the cut clips.

You may be tempted to use the Razor Blade to cut a clip in two so that you can insert a third clip in between (for instance, to show actor A, cut to actor B, and then cut back to your original shot of actor A). However, you can use an even easier alternative that doesn't involve the Razor Blade at all. See the "Moving a Clip That's Already on the Timeline" section, earlier in this chapter, for the technique to use when you want to insert one clip into another (effectively splitting the first clip).

Deleting Clips from the Timeline

When you have no more use for a clip on the Timeline, you delete it so that it doesn't play in your movie or clutter up the Timeline. (**Remember:** Even when you delete a clip from the Timeline, it stays put in the Browser window, so you can use it again.) Final Cut Express offers two ways to delete a clip: the first way is called a *lift edit,* and the second is a *ripple delete.*

Doing a simple lift edit or a ripple delete

A lift edit is your no-frills, garden-variety delete. You select a clip and then delete it, leaving an empty gap in your Timeline, which plays as black void in your movie. This deleting may be fine by you, but if other clips follow the deleted clip on the Timeline, you probably want to move all those clips to the left so that they fill in the empty gap. And that's where the ripple delete comes in: It deletes your clip and automatically "ripples" all the following clips to the left so that the Timeline has no empty gap, as shown in Figure 6-16.

However, sometimes a Ripple Delete can change how clips in different tracks synch up together, leading to problems. For instance, say you're editing a music video and just spent endless hours timing your video cuts to beats in the music track. But suppose you decide you don't like a video shot in the middle of your sequence, and you use a Ripple Delete on it. All the video clips to the right of your deleted clip now shift over (to close the gap on the Timeline) and, unfortunately, fall out of synch with your music because you didn't delete anything from the music track. To dodge this headache, skip using a Ripple Delete altogether. Instead do a lift edit and find a new video clip to fill in the gap left by the deleted one.

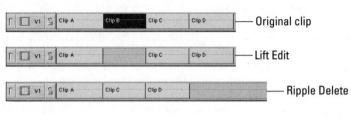

Original clip

Lift Edit

Ripple Delete

You'll probably use the ripple delete most in your work, but the following steps outline how to do either a lift edit or a ripple delete:

1. **Select the clip or clips you want to delete on the Timeline.**

   You can select a single clip by clicking it with the Selection tool, or select a group of continuous clips by clicking each one while holding down Shift.

   You can also use other Final Cut Express tools to select groups of clips, entire Timeline tracks, or just parts of tracks. See the "Selecting Clips on the Timeline" section, earlier in this chapter. for more about selecting clips.

   In many cases, you may have placed a video clip on your Timeline that comes linked with its own audio clips. When video and audio clips are linked, deleting the video clip also cuts the linked audio clips (or vice versa). If you don't want to do this, you can always unlink the video and audio clips by selecting the clips and then choosing Modify⇨Link so that the Link command is unchecked.

2. **Press Delete to do a lift edit or press Shift+Delete to do a ripple delete.**

Cutting and pasting clips on the Timeline

You can cut clips from one place in the Timeline and paste them somewhere else, which is a pretty handy trick. Just follow these steps:

1. **On the Timeline, select the clip or clips you want to cut.**

   See the "Selecting Clips on the Timeline" section for more about selecting clips and all the wonderful selection tools on the Tool palette.

2. **Cut the clip using either a lift edit (press ⌘+X) or a ripple delete (press Shift+X).**

Alternatively, you can also do a lift edit by choosing Edit⇨Cut. (See the preceding section if you don't know what a lift edit or a ripple delete is.)

3. **Position the Timeline playhead where you want to paste your clip(s).**

4. **To paste the selection you cut, choose Edit⇨Paste (press ⌘+V) or Paste Insert (press Shift+V).**

When you paste a selection, it's overwritten on the Timeline, while Paste Insert inserts it. See the earlier section, "Inserting and overwriting," for more information.

Deleting parts of clips on multiple tracks

You can delete just a portion of a clip (or a range of clips) by setting In and Out points on the Timeline. (You'll delete any video and audio that fall within those points.) As you become comfortable with Final Cut Express, you'll probably favor this tactic — it's so direct:

1. **Move the Timeline playhead to the first frame of the range you want to delete.**

    The Canvas window shows whatever frame is currently under the playhead.

    Make sure you haven't accidentally selected another clip in the Timeline before setting your In and Out points — otherwise, Final Cut Express deletes the selected clip, not what you designate now. You can quickly deselect any clips on the Timeline by pressing ⌘+D.

2. **Mark your In point by pressing I for in or by clicking the Mark In button in the Canvas window (see Figure 6-17).**

    An In point (a triangle pointing to the right) appears in the Timeline and in the Canvas window scrubber (both display In and Out points that you've set in your movie).

3. **Move the Timeline playhead to the last frame of the range you want to delete and mark an Out point.**

    You can click Mark Out in the Canvas window (see Figure 6-17), choose it from the Mark menu, or just press O for Out. Train yourself to use the keyboard shortcut if you can.

4. **Do a lift edit or ripple delete by pressing Delete or Shift+Delete, respectively.**

    Final Cut Express now cuts out all the frames that fall within your in and out points on all tracks of the Timeline.

In and Out Points   Canvas

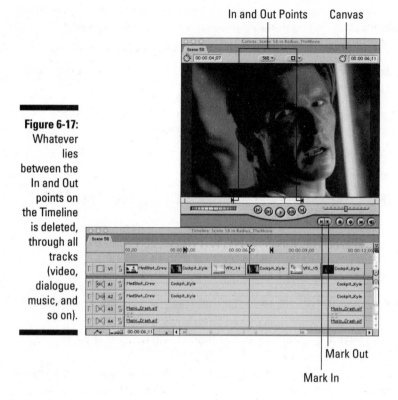

Figure 6-17:
Whatever
lies
between the
In and Out
points on
the Timeline
is deleted,
through all
tracks
(video,
dialogue,
music, and
so on).

Mark Out

Mark In

When you delete media by using In and Out points, Final Cut Express makes
your cuts through *all* the tracks on your Timeline (video and audio). This
might be fine by you, but if not (for instance, if you want to cut out frames
from a video track, but leave dialogue and music tracks untouched), you can
protect those tracks by locking them. Click the Lock icon to the left of each
track you want to preserve before making a cut.

Chapter 7

Getting to Know the Timeline

*I*f you've read Chapter 6, you've already bit off and chewed quite a bit: namely, all the skills that you need to edit an entire video from start to finish. In this chapter, you nibble on smaller fare — the kind of things that can help you work more smoothly with the Final Cut Express Timeline, which is where most of your blood, sweat, and tears spill while you edit.

Investigating Timeline Tracks

One of the most important things that you can do with the Timeline is to take control of your tracks. (You remember Timeline tracks, don't you? For a refresher, see Chapter 6 or check out Figure 7-1.) For instance, sometimes you want to turn off certain tracks so that Final Cut Express won't play any of the clips on them — turning off your music tracks to better hear dialogue, perhaps. Or you may want to lock a track so that any clips on it can't be accidentally resized or moved. Or you want to ensure that when you move new clips from the Browser to the Timeline, they go to exactly the tracks that you want. The Timeline enables you to do all this and more.

Figure 7-1: Using tracks helps you organize different kinds of clips on the Timeline.

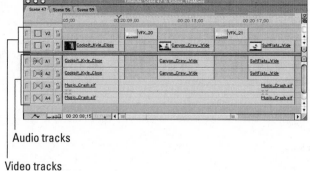

Audio tracks

Video tracks

Locking tracks so they can't be changed

When you lock a track on the Timeline, you prevent any clips on that track from being resized, moved, deleted, or changed in any other way. Why would you want to freeze a track like this in the course of your editing? For any number of reasons, all of which involve your wanting to make changes to clips that are on *some* of the tracks in your movie but not on *all* of them. For example, suppose that your movie sports a number of tracks (a video track and audio tracks for dialogue, sound effects, and music) and you want to cut out the video, dialogue, and sound effects of a scene but leave the music tracks completely untouched (the bottom screen of Figure 7-2).

In this case, you need to lock the music tracks first and then make your cut to the rest of the Timeline tracks. (See Chapter 6 for options on the best way to make the cuts.) The end result is that Final Cut Express cuts through the clips on all your tracks *except* the music tracks because they're locked!

To lock a track, just click the Lock Track control for that particular track. (The Lock Track control is a little padlock icon to the left of each track, as shown in Figure 7-3.) Final Cut Express draws diagonal lines through the entire length of the track to let you know that that track is now off limits.

To unlock a track, just click the Lock Track icon again, and your locked track becomes fully editable.

One other reason to lock your tracks is when you know that you're finished tinkering with them. If you've labored over a group of clips and honed them to picture-perfect perfection, just lock the tracks that carry those clips so that you don't accidentally change them while working on other parts of your video.

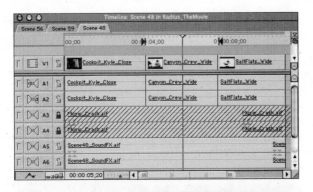

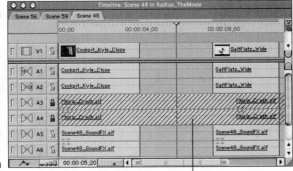

Figure 7-2:
Before and
after
cutting:
All tracks
except the
protected
ones are
cut.

The protected tracks are uncut

Figure 7-3:
The Lock
Track
control
icons, both
locked and
unlocked.

Click to lock

These tracks are locked

Hiding and soloing tracks

If your movie uses a lot of tracks, you may sometimes want to play only some of the tracks but not others. For instance, maybe you want to watch your movie while carefully listening to its dialogue track but without hearing all the tracks that carry your sound effects and music. In this case, you may want to hide those distracting tracks. On the other hand, if you have a single track that you want to see or hear all by itself, you can easily tell Final Cut Express to play this track only and ignore all the others; this technique is called *soloing* a track.

To hide a track so that its clips don't play in your sequence, just click the Track Visibility control (the little rectangular icon at the far-left side of that track), shown in Figure 7-4. When you're ready to bring the track back to normal, just click that icon again.

Figure 7-4:
The Track
Visibility
control,
showing
some tracks
turned on
and some
not.

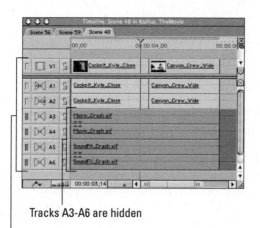

Tracks A3-A6 are hidden

Track Visibility control

To solo a single track so that it's the only one that Final Cut Express plays, just hold the Option key down while clicking the Track Visibility control for that track.

In one instance, hiding tracks on the Timeline has an unwanted effect: When you render some of your video or audio clips before Final Cut Express can play them, you lose those renders when you hide the track that they're on. Don't panic too much. Losing the renders doesn't hurt your original clips; it just means that you'll have to re-render them. If you don't want to wait for re-rendering, you can also get your renders back by undoing the action of hiding your track (choose Edit⇨Undo).

Designating your target tracks

Final Cut Express lets you designate one of your video tracks and two of your audio tracks (for left and right stereo channels) as so-called *target tracks*. A target track is the track that will be affected by whatever editing work that you're doing, regardless of how many other tracks are on your Timeline.

Setting a target track is like selecting text in a word processor. Whatever text you select gets the style, font, and color changes that you make without affecting any text that's not selected. The same thing goes for target tracks.

In these instances, Final Cut Express works with the target tracks that you select:

- ✔ When you move video and audio clips from the Viewer or Browser to the Timeline (other than by dragging them), they go to whatever tracks that you've targeted.

- ✔ When you copy and paste clips on the Timeline, the pasted clips appear on whatever tracks that you've targeted.

- ✔ When you use the Match Frame feature (good for syncing video to audio — see Chapter 8), Final Cut Express matches to the clip that the playhead is on. But if your playhead is on multiple clips, Express chooses the one on your target track.

- ✔ When you want to mark clips or add keyframes to them, Final Cut Express works with clips on your target tracks.

Targeting a video track

To turn any video track into your target video track, just click the Target Track control for the track, as shown in Figure 7-5. Clicking the control again turns off targeting for that track. (The control turns yellow for on and gray for off.)

Targeting two audio tracks

You can target two audio tracks because most of the audio that you work with uses two tracks to carry its left and right stereo channels (refer to Figure 7-5).

To make an audio track your left channel target track, click the Left speaker icon on the Target Track control for the audio track. A little numeral 1 appears in the icon, showing that it's now your channel 1 (that is, the target track). To target a track as your right channel target track, just click the Right speaker icon on the Target Track control of a track; a little numeral 2 appears in the icon. You can click these icons again to turn off targeting for the tracks as well.

Turning off your target tracks

Editing with your video and audio tracks targeted is usually best, but sometimes you may want to turn off that targeting when you don't want to affect those tracks with an edit that you're about to make. For instance, suppose that you want to add a clip of video to the Timeline, but that clip also has two channels of audio built in (typical of DV video). To move the video without the audio, just turn off your targeted audio tracks, and Final Cut Express moves only the video to the Timeline. On the other hand, to move only the audio to the Timeline, make sure that no video tracks are targeted when you do the move.

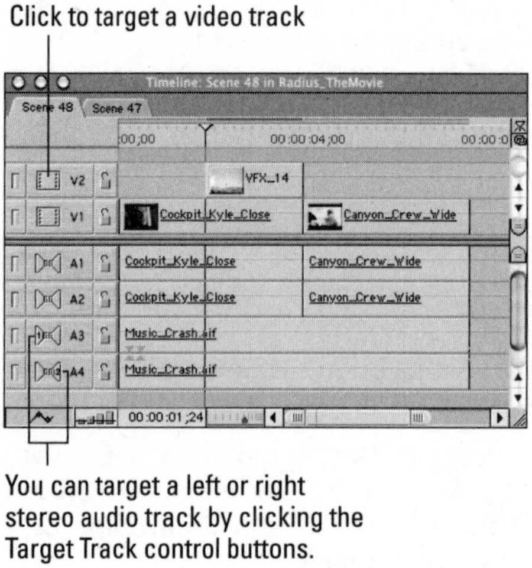

Click to target a video track

Figure 7-5:
The Target
Track
control
buttons for
video and
audio
tracks.

You can target a left or right
stereo audio track by clicking the
Target Track control buttons.

Adding and deleting tracks from the Timeline

Adding and deleting tracks while you build sequences of clips on the Timeline is natural. For example, you may want to add a video track to carry visual effects or titles for your movie or add a slew of audio tracks to hold different versions of your composer's musical score. (Having each version on the Timeline enables you to easily compare one revision with another.) At the same time, when you add tracks while you edit your movie, you may find reasons to toss out other tracks — maybe you decide not to use the clips on a track or two. Or you find that you have so many tracks that you can't keep them straight, so you decide to consolidate their clips to a more manageable number.

You may find yourself using a lot of audio tracks in your sequence to carry simultaneous dialogue clips, sound effects, music, and so on. Although Final Cut Express lets you add up to 99 audio tracks to the Timeline, it can't actually play all 99 tracks at the same time. Playing a clip of audio is no easy feat for your Mac; and when you ask it to play more than several at once, it cracks under the pressure. (Actually, it will play a repeating beep in place of the lush audio that you expect . . . no harm done, but you can't hear your audio.) The good news is that if you render the tracks first, you can play all those audio tracks together. When you render your audio, Final Cut merges all your audio tracks into a single audio clip, which it can play without breaking a sweat, but it does all this hocus-pocus behind the scenes without you having to worry about it. To render audio tracks, choose Sequence⇨Mixdown Audio. See Chapter 17 for more about rendering.

Adding a single track

If you want to add a track to the Timeline quickly, you have two options:

- Drag any clip (that is, a clip that's either already on the Timeline or that's currently in the Browser window) to the unused area above the last video track on the Timeline (for video clips) or below the last audio track (for audio clips).

 When you let go of the mouse button, Final Cut Express creates a new track on the Timeline and puts your dragged clip right in it. (Check it out in Figure 7-6.)

- Hold down the Control key and click anywhere in the track header, as shown in Figure 7-7. Then choose Add Track from the pop-up menu that appears.

 Final Cut Express adds a track directly below the track header that you clicked.

Unused area

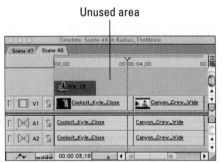

Figure 7-6: To add a video track, drag the clip to the unused area of the Timeline above the last video track.

Figure 7-7: The pop-up Add/Delete menu for tracks.

Adding multiple tracks

To add multiple tracks to the Timeline in one fell swoop, make sure that the Timeline window is active and then follow these steps:

1. **Choose Sequence➪Insert Tracks.**

2. **In the Insert Tracks dialog box, shown in Figure 7-8, type the number of video or audio tracks to add.**

   If you want to add video tracks but not audio tracks (or vice versa), you can deselect the check box next to either option to avoid adding any tracks (or just leave the number of tracks to add at zero).

Figure 7-8: The Insert Tracks dialog box.

3. **Choose where on the Timeline to insert them.**

   You have three options:

   - **Before Base Track:** This option inserts your new track(s) before the first video or audio track on the Timeline (that's your *base* track, which is called V1 for video and A1 for audio) and renumbers any existing tracks to make room for the new track(s). Suppose that you already have two audio tracks (A1 and A2) on the Timeline, and you add another two before the base. Your two new tracks become A1 and A2, and the original audio tracks become A3 and A4.

   - **After Target Track:** Final Cut Express inserts your new track(s) immediately after whatever track you've currently designated as a target track. For instance, if your target video track is V3, a new track added would be inserted as V4, and the track that was formerly V4 becomes V5. See "Designating your target tracks," earlier in this chapter, for more about target tracks.

The best number of tracks?

Final Cut Express lets you create up to 99 video tracks and 99 audio tracks in a sequence — in other words, a whole lotta tracks. But how many should you use? Can you gain anything by using more or fewer tracks?

My best answer is this: When you're building a sequence of clips, think about the theme of your clips and try to give each theme its own track. I know that sounds a tad abstract, so try this example on for size: my movie *Radius* has over 150 visual effects shots (plus a ton of conventionally filmed clips). While my editor edited *Radius,* she decided to keep the effects by themselves on a separate track. Why? She was constantly swapping in newer, more-polished

versions of each effect (as the artists went from prototypes to finished shots), and finding and replacing effects on a crowded Timeline was a lot easier when the effects were on their own track.

The moral of this story isn't "use fewer tracks" or "use more tracks;" it's "use the *right* number of tracks." Before you build your sequence, just stop and think about how you can effectively use tracks to organize your clips by theme (again, consider visual effects, music, dialogue for different characters, sound effects, title graphics, and whatever else) with an eye for how you might edit those themes down the road.

- **After Last Track:** Pretty straightforward: Final Cut Express slips your new tracks behind the very last video or audio track on the Timeline.

4. **Click OK to insert the tracks.**

Deleting a single track

The quickest, easiest way to delete a single track is to hold down the Control key and click anywhere in the track header (refer to Figure 7-7); then choose Delete Track from the pop-up menu that appears. Final Cut Express tosses out that track (along with any clips on it) and renumbers all the tracks after it.

Deleting multiple tracks

To give a group of tracks the old heave-ho, make sure that the Timeline window is active and then follow these steps:

1. **Choose Sequence⇨Delete Tracks.**

2. **In the Delete Tracks dialog box, shown in Figure 7-9, select the Video Tracks and/or Audio Tracks check box(es), depending on what kind of tracks you want to delete.**

3. **In Audio Tracks and Video Tracks, choose from these options:**

   • **Current Target Track(s):** Final Cut Express deletes whatever track (or two tracks, for audio) that you've currently designated as a target track. See "Designating your target tracks," earlier in this chapter, for more about target tracks.

   • **All Empty Tracks:** Selecting this option deletes all tracks that have no clips on them. (Perhaps you used these tracks as temporary staging areas to assemble clips before moving them to your main tracks, and you no longer need these tracks.)

   • **All Empty Tracks at End of Sequence:** This one's a bit more obscure: Select it to delete any empty video tracks that are *above* and any audio tracks that are *below* the outermost tracks that have clips on them. Say what? For example, suppose that you have six audio tracks, and Tracks A3, A5, and A6 are empty. Choosing this option deletes Tracks A5 and A6 but not Track A3 because it's followed by Track A4, which has clips on it.

4. **Click OK to complete the deletion.**

Customizing Your View of the Timeline

You can customize your view of the Timeline so that it shows tracks and clips in whatever way suits your work style. For example, if you're editing on a small monitor or laptop screen, you may want to show your Timeline tracks in Reduced view so that more of them fit on-screen. (This action saves you the time that you would have used scrolling up and down your tracks.) Or suppose that you're mixing all the audio for your movie together (that is, setting the volume levels relative to each other so that they're all nicely balanced). To make this a lot easier, the Timeline can show each volume level visually and even let you raise or lower the volume level with a simple click and drag.

When you customize your view of the Timeline, you can do it either for only your currently open sequence (so that you can have different settings for different sequences) or for all new sequences that you create from that point on.

To customize the Timeline for all sequences you create, choose Final Cut⇨Preferences and then click the Timeline Options tab. To customize the Timeline of only your current sequence, make sure that the sequence is active in the Timeline. (You know it's active when you see its contents on the Timeline.) Then choose Sequence⇨Settings.

Regardless of which way you chose to arrive at the Timeline Options tab, it gives you the choices shown in Figure 7-10. (This view is from the Sequence Settings dialog box.) Your options are as follows:

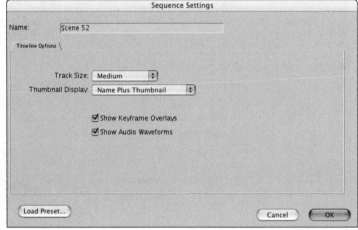

Figure 7-10: The Timeline options as they appear in the Sequence Settings dialog box.

✔ **Track Size:** You can set your tracks to be taller or shorter. If you're peering into a big monitor and the tracks are hard to see, make them larger here. If your screen real estate is cramped, consider going to Reduced view, which can fit a lot of tracks on even a modest iBook screen. (See the difference in Figure 7-11).

✔ **Thumbnail Display:** This option lets you decide how video clips display on their tracks. (Compare these views in Figure 7-12.) You can choose from the following modes:

  • **Name:** Shows only a no-frills clip name

  • **Name Plus Thumbnail:** Shows a clip name and a thumbnail image of its first frame

  • **Filmstrip:** Shows thumbnails for as many frames as can fit in the current zoom level of the Timeline

Personally, I like Name Plus Thumbnail the best. (Seeing the first frame of a clip helps keep me oriented.) Filmstrip mode makes my head spin.

✔ **Show Keyframe Overlays:** Selecting this option draws a horizontal line through any clips on your Timeline. This horizontal line represents opacity levels for video clips and volume levels for audio clips. What's great about this option is that you can click and drag these lines up and down to adjust your levels right on the Timeline without having to open another settings window. You can also set keyframes right here, which let you change a clip's opacity or volume level over time: Press the Option key and click anywhere on the levels line. (You can remove keyframes by Option-clicking them as well.) For more about keyframes, check out Chapters 11 and 13.

✔ **Show Audio Waveforms:** Select this check box, and any audio clips on your Timeline will show their waveforms, which use vertical lines to show the loud and soft areas of an audio clip. (The higher the waveform's vertical lines reach, the louder the audio is. See the audio levels in Figure 7-13.) This option is handy for syncing your video clips to events in dialogue, sound effects, or music. Usually, you can find these events in an audio clip by looking for spikes in the waveform, where the forms vertical lines reach higher, but be warned: Calculating all those waveforms on the fly can slow your Mac considerably.

Medium view   Reduced view

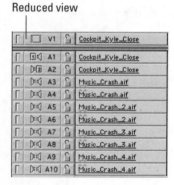

Figure 7-11: Reduced versus medium-sized tracks — major space savers.

By the way, you can quickly customize these aspects of the Timeline without visiting the Sequence Settings dialog box at all. You can click buttons directly on the Timeline to set your track size and show Keyframe Overlays (refer to Figure 7-13).

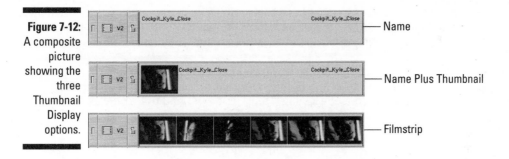

Figure 7-12: A composite picture showing the three Thumbnail Display options.

— Name

— Name Plus Thumbnail

— Filmstrip

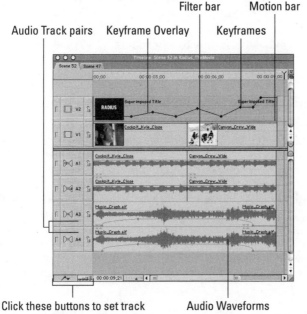

Filter bar   Motion bar

Audio Track pairs   Keyframe Overlay   Keyframes

Figure 7-13: Tracks with a variety of custom-ization options turned on.

Click these buttons to set track size, show Filter and Motion bars, or show Keyframe Overlays.

Audio Waveforms

Navigating the Timeline

When you're editing, you'll find yourself constantly moving the Timeline play-head from one place to another. (Think of the playhead as a record needle on your video — see Chapter 6 for more.) Sometimes you may move the play-head through a clip in search of the perfect frame to trim the clip to or make a cut on. Or you'll move the playhead to some edit point on the Timeline (where a clip ends or begins, or where two clips come together) so that you can adjust the edit in some way.

Final Cut Express offers a bunch of useful tricks that you can use to move the Timeline playhead wherever you want. I touch on some of these in Chapter 6, but now I'm laying them all out together so that you can see all your options.

For many of these options to work, you need to have either the Canvas or Timeline window selected. (Remember that these two windows mirror each other.) Sure, you may be saying "Duh!," but I just had to be official-like and say it.

Moving the playhead anywhere on the Timeline

To move the playhead instantly to any spot on the Timeline, use one of these methods:

✓ **Timeline ruler:** As shown in Figure 7-14, you can click anywhere in the Timeline ruler to move the playhead to that point in time on the Timeline.

✓ **Go to timecode:** You can also move the playhead directly to any timecode value on the Timeline (refer to Figure 7-14). Just type the value into the Current Timecode box, which you can find in either the Canvas or Timeline window. (Make sure that you don't have a clip currently selected, or Final Cut Express moves that clip instead of the playhead.)

Final Cut Express describes timecode values in terms of hours, minutes, seconds, and frames. (You can see the values listed in the Timeline ruler.) So typing the value **00:20:15;29** moves the playhead to the first hour, 20th minute, 15th second, and 29th frame of your Timeline sequence.

Markers   Timeline ruler

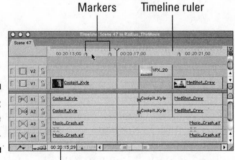

Figure 7-14:
The Timeline
ruler.

Current Timecode box

Moving the playhead linearly through the Timeline

In Chapter 6, I show you the easiest way to move the playhead linearly through the Timeline. But the following list gives my recommendations on which method to use to move the playhead. (Check out Figure 7-15 to see where these methods hang out.)

Figure 7-15: These Canvas controls move the playhead in different ways.

Jog control   Next edit

Previous edit   Shuttle control

✔ **Shuttle control:** To move the playhead back and forward at a variety of preset speeds, try using the Canvas window Shuttle control. You can click and drag this control all the way to the left or right for quick rewinds/fast-forwards, or you can set the control closer to its middle point to move the playhead slowly through your clips.

✔ **Keyboard shortcuts:** I find the quickest, most convenient way to move the playhead is by pressing J, K, or L on the keyboard. Press J to move the playhead back, K to stop it, and L to move it forward.

✔ **Click and drag:** If you really want to move the playhead along the Timeline in a hurry (often while scrolling a long sequence through the Timeline), just click in the Timeline ruler and drag it left or right.

✔ **Hand tool:** Select the Hand tool (hop ahead to Figure 7-17) from the Tool palette, click anywhere on a Timeline track, and drag left or right to scroll your view of the Timeline (or up and down to see tracks out of view).

- **Frame by frame:** You have two options to move the playhead frame by frame when you want to be very precise:

  - **The Jog control:** Use the Canvas window Jog control, which lets you slowly drag your mouse back and forth across the control, moving the playhead frame by frame.

  - **Arrow keys:** Pressing ← moves the playhead back in time by one frame and pressing → moves it forward by one frame.

- **Edit by edit:** Instead of moving the playhead to the next *frame*, you can move it to the next *edit point* (the start or end of a clip, as well as any In and Out points that you've set on the Timeline). To do so, click its Next Edit or Previous Edit buttons in the Canvas, respectively.

- **Marker by marker:** If you've set markers, you can move your playhead back to the previous marker by pressing Shift+↓ or forward to the next marker by pressing Shift+↑. More on markers in Chapter 8.

Zooming In and Out of the Timeline

Final Cut Express lets you zoom in on your Timeline, which shows you a smaller sample of time in your sequence and makes your clips larger so that you can resize, move, cut, or otherwise edit them with frame-by-frame precision (just like in Photoshop, where you can zoom in on a small portion of a photo to tweak individual pixels). You can also zoom out of the Timeline as well, making clips appear smaller and letting you get a bird's-eye view of your entire sequence. See Figure 7-16 for a quick comparison.

In Chapter 6, I touch on the easiest way to zoom the Timeline, which is by using the Zoom In and Zoom Out tools in the Tool palette, as shown in Figure 7-17. After you select either tool, just click it repeatedly on the Timeline to zoom in or out. (Holding down Option also toggles the zoom between in and out.)

But when you're in the thick of editing, choosing a separate tool just to zoom the Timeline is often a hassle. Instead, you want to do this seamlessly, and Final Cut Express offers a couple of different ways to take care of this matter:

- **The Zoom Control:** The Zoom Control (refer to Figure 7-16) is very straightforward. Click to the left of the control to zoom in and see more detail on the Timeline. (Whatever clips you see on the Timeline stay centered while you zoom in.) Click to the right, and you zoom out, seeing less detail but more clips in your sequence. You can also click and drag the control if that suits you.

✔ **Keyboard shortcuts:** To zoom in one level, press ⌘++. (Yes, that's really the Command key and a plus symbol). Press it repeatedly to keep zooming in. To zoom out, try pressing ⌘+- (minus sign). When you use your keyboard to zoom, Final Cut Express keeps selected clips centered on the Timeline; if none are selected, Express keeps the playhead centered. (Try it both ways, and you'll see the difference.)

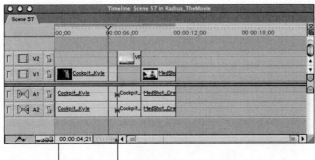

Current Timecode   Zoom Control

Figure 7-16:
The top figure shows 18 seconds (notice the timecode on the Timeline ruler), whereas the bottom figure shows only 9 seconds.

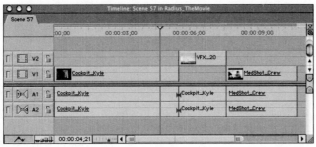

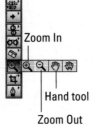

Figure 7-17:
The Zoom In and Zoom Out tools.

Zoom In

Hand tool

Zoom Out

Checking Out Some Last Details

By now, you know more about the Final Cut Express Timeline than you ever *wanted* to know. But having come this far, I may as well show you a few last icons and buttons that may come in handy. (Check out Figure 7-18 to follow along.)

Snapping control

Render Status bar

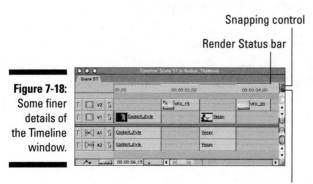

Figure 7-18:
Some finer
details of
the Timeline
window.

Linking control

▱ **Render Status bar:** This bar shows the render status of any clips on the Timeline. (See Chapter 17 for more on rendering.) When you need to render a clip on the Timeline before playing it, you see a red line in this status bar, drawn right over the needy clip. When you've already rendered a clip, the Render Status bar replaces the red line with a blue one. A green bar means that you don't have to render the clip to play a real-time preview, but you will need to render the clip before recording your program to tape or displaying it on a TV. Notice that Final Cut Express actually divides the render bar into two parts — the top line shows status for video clips and the bottom line for audio.

▱ **Snapping control:** By clicking this icon, you can quickly turn Snapping on and off. For more about the Snapping feature, see Chapter 6.

▱ **Linking control:** Normally, when you select a video clip that has audio clips linked to it (or vice versa) on the Timeline, Final Cut Express automatically selects all the linked clips together. (See Chapter 6 for more about linking.) But clicking this icon turns this linking off, so you can select just the clip that you click without all its dependents subclips.

Chapter 8

Editing Wizardry

*Y*ou already know enough about Final Cut Express to cruise through most projects on autopilot, but if you want to turbo-charge your editing work, this chapter has what you need. In fact, this chapter is very likely to have *more* than what you need. It all depends on the kind of work you're doing. My advice is to read the topics that are likely to apply to just about everybody — my coverage of advanced editing tools, for instance — and then skim through the rest of the chapter headings to see what else jumps out at you.

Going Beyond Insert and Overwrite Edits

In Chapter 6, you learned two different ways to edit a clip to the Timeline: insert and overwrite. You can either insert it (Final Cut Express scoots over any clips on the Timeline to make room for the new clip), or you can overwrite it (brutally erasing any clips or segments of clips that stand in the way of the new clip). But Express offers a few other options — such as replace edits, fit to fill edits, and superimpose edits — that can come in quite handy, depending on the situation.

Replace edits

A *replace edit* works like an overwrite edit but replaces a single clip on the Timeline with a range of frames from a different clip (your *source* clip) that you've opened in the Viewer window. (That range equals the number of frames used by the original clip on the Timeline, so the length of your movie doesn't change when you replace a shot.)

When you do a replace edit, Final Cut Express pays particular attention to where you've placed the playhead in the source clip (that is, the clip in the Viewer), and where you've placed the playhead on the Timeline (you'll see why in a moment). For a quick and easy way to do a replace edit, follow these steps:

1. **Find a clip on the Timeline you want to replace with a new one.**

2. **Position the Timeline playhead on the In point of the clip you want to replace.**

   Make sure the clip is on a Timeline track that is a target track. Remember that when you make edits on the Timeline, those edits affect whatever is on your current Target track. (See Chapter 7 for more about setting target tracks.)

3. **From the Browser, find the new clip that you want to add to the Timeline (this clip replaces the clip that's currently there), and open it in the Viewer window.**

4. **In the Viewer window, position the playhead on the frame that should be the clip's first frame to be moved on the Timeline.**

   It's like you're setting the clip's In point, but you do this simply by placing the Viewer playhead on that.

5. **Click and drag the clip from the Viewer to the Canvas window, and then select Replace from the Clip Overlay that appears, as shown in Figure 8-1.**

   Final Cut Express replaces the clip on the Timeline with the new clip in the Viewer. The first frame of the new clip is the frame you positioned the Viewer playhead on in Step 4. Express places the new clip's remaining frames (the frames to the right of the Viewer playhead) on the Timeline until they fill the same number of frames occupied by the original clip you're replacing.

   If you have any excess frames in the Viewer, Final Cut Express leaves them off the Timeline. For example, if the Timeline clip is 50 frames, Express adds only 50 frames from the Viewer, even if the clip in the Viewer contains 70 frames.

Figure 8-1:
Drag clips to the Canvas window and select the edit options from the Overlay.

Match Frame button

When doing a replace edit, you don't *have* to position the Timeline playhead at the *first* frame of the clip you want to replace — I just suggested doing that so that you can more easily see how replace edits work. In fact, you can position the Timeline playhead on *any* frame within a clip. When you do the replace edit, Final Cut Express centers the frame at the Viewer playhead to the frame at the Timeline playhead and fills in the Timeline clip with frames from both the left and right side of the Viewer playhead (sounds a bit complicated, but it becomes clear once you see this phenomenon in action).

If you get an `Insufficient Content for Edit` error message while replacing a clip (a likely scenario when you're getting used to this feature), Express is telling you that the source clip in the Viewer doesn't have enough frames to replace all the Timeline clip frames. (The source clip needs the same or a greater number of frames on *each* side of the Viewer playhead as the Timeline clip has on each side of the Timeline playhead.) For example, suppose a clip on the Timeline is 100 frames long. If you position the Timeline playhead in the middle of the clip, there will be 50 frames to the right of the playhead and 50 frames to the left. Now, suppose you have a 50 frame clip in the Viewer, and you position the Viewer playhead in the middle (so there are 25 frames to the left and right of the playhead). If you try to do a replace edit, it will fail, because the clip in the Viewer doesn't have enough frames on either side of its playhead (25 frames per side) to replace the frames on either side of the Timeline clip's playhead (50 frames per side). If you run into this annoyance, resize the Timeline clip so that it's smaller (and, therefore, has fewer frames to fill up) and then try your edit again.

The Match Frame feature

You can use a replace edit with the Match Frame feature to quickly synch up an event in a video clip with an event in an audio clip (for example, to synch a dancer's exaggerated step to a beat of music in a music video). Try these steps:

1. **On the Timeline, place your audio clip in an audio track directly below your video clip, so the two clips fall within the same time frame.**

   Don't try to synch the video and audio events yet — just make sure that your audio clip is directly below the video clip (it doesn't matter which track the audio clip occupies, however). It's okay if the video and audio clips aren't the same length, and therefore don't line up perfectly. You just want to line them up as best as you can.

2. **Position the Timeline playhead at the point where the audio event takes place.**

   For example, you may want to position the playhead on a beat of music. For greater precision, you may want to display the Timeline clips bigger and set them to show audio waveforms. (To do this, choose Sequence⇨Settings and make the appropriate selections.)

3. **Turn off targeting for all the audio tracks by clicking the speaker icons next to each of the audio tracks.**

   After turning the audio tracks targeting off, you should *not* see a little 1 or 2 in any of the icons. See Chapter 7 for more about track targeting.

4. **Make sure to "target" the Timeline track that carries your video clip.**

   The video track carrying your clip must be the target video track.

5. **Without moving the Timeline playhead, do a match frame by pressing F. Alternatively, you can click the Match Frame button in the Canvas window (refer to Figure 8-1).**

   In the Viewer window, Final Cut Express opens the original clip that the Timeline *video* came from. (It's as if you found that clip in the Browser, and double-clicked it to open it in the Viewer.) Notice that the Viewer playhead is positioned on exactly the same frame as your Timeline playhead. (In other words, the Viewer and Canvas windows should now show exactly the same frame because each playhead is on the same frame.) This, by the way, is how the Express Match Frame feature works — it looks at the frame where you've positioned the Timeline playhead and opens the original clip in the Viewer window, with the playhead positioned on that same frame.

6. **In the Viewer window, move the playhead to the video frame you want to synchronize with the audio event.**

   Remember that you positioned the Timeline playhead on that audio event in Step 2. You're now about to synch up the Viewer video frame with the audio from on the Timeline.

7. **Do a replace edit: Drag the clip from the Viewer to the Canvas window and select Replace from the Overlay that appears.**

   Final Cut Express replaces the current video clip on the Timeline with the Match Frame version in the Viewer (lining up the Viewer playhead frame with the Timeline playhead, which also happens to be positioned on your audio event). The video and audio should now be synchronized, provided that the Viewer clip had enough frames available on either side of the Viewer playhead to replace the Timeline video clip's frames on either side of the Timeline playhead. (See my warning about `Insufficient Content for Edit` errors in the "Replace edits" section.)

Fit to fill edits

Fit to fill is aptly named because that's exactly what this edit does: It literally forces a clip to fit any gap (range of frames) you set for it on the Timeline. Final Cut Express does this by speeding the clip up or slowing it down.

Suppose you've finished editing your movie, but you are waiting for a fancy animated opening title from a motion graphics artist. You've reserved a five-second gap in the movie for the title, but when you finally get it, it's only four seconds long! You can't edit the title into the Timeline as it is, so you use a fit to fill edit to add a second to the title so that it fits the gap you reserved for it. The result? Final Cut Express figures out how to play the four-second clip slower, so it actually fills its five seconds.

To do a fit to fill edit, follow these steps:

1. **On the Timeline, make sure you've targeted the track you want to receive the fit to fill clip.**

   The targeted track is where Final Cut Express places the fit to fill clip. See Chapter 7 for more about targeting.

2. **On the Timeline, select the range of frames you want to receive the fit to fill clip.**

   You do this by setting In and Out points on the Timeline. (The points you set are indicated in the Timeline ruler.) Just position the Timeline playhead at the start of the range, and press the I key. Then move the playhead to the last frame of the range and press the O key.

After you set this range, don't worry about where the Timeline playhead is. It can be anywhere. Unlike other edits, the fit to fill edit ignores the Timeline playhead, and focuses on the Timeline In and Out points you've set. Express fits your clip between these points.

3. **Open the clip you want to fit to fill in the Viewer window and set its In and Out points, if necessary.**

   You don't have to set In and Out points if you want to fit to fill the entire clip.

4. **Drag the clip from the Viewer to the Canvas window.**

   When you drag the fit to fill clip over the Canvas, the Overlay appears, displaying editing options.

5. **Select Fit to Fill from the Overlay (refer to Figure 8-1).**

   Final Cut Express adds the fit to fill clip to the Timeline, setting it to play at the appropriate speed.

6. **Render the clip by selecting it and choosing Sequence⇨Render Selection.**

   If the clip needs to play faster than normal (to fit a smaller space than it originally filled), Final Cut Express renders the clip so that it skips frames while playing. If the clip needs to play slower than normal, Express renders it with some duplicated frames. To see the speed the fit to fill clip now plays, you can select it on the Timeline and choose Modify⇨Speed.

Superimpose edits

When you superimpose a clip, Final Cut Express moves it to the Timeline but places it on the next available track *after* the current target track. If you need to stack multiple clips on top of each other (for instance, if you're about to composite many different images together into one shot or add all sorts of audio clips that will play simultaneously), a superimpose edit is a great way to get those clips on separate Timeline tracks quickly.

You perform a superimpose edit the usual way — that is, by opening a clip in the Viewer window, dragging it to the Canvas window, and selecting Superimpose from the Overlay that appears. But a superimpose edit is unique in one important way: Normally, when you edit a clip to the Timeline, Final Cut Express places it to begin where the Timeline playhead happens to be — but not this time! Instead, Express looks at the position of the Timeline playhead, and if a clip is already at that point in time on the targeted track, that clip's In and Out points on the Timeline become the In and Out points for the superimposed edit (as you can see in Figure 8-2).

Figure 8-2:
Three clips
super-
imposed
with the
Track
V1 clip,
matching its
In and Out
points on
the Timeline.

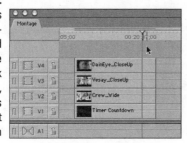

For instance, suppose you're superimposing a five-second video clip on the Timeline (it will wind up on Track V2), but you place the Timeline playhead where you already have a two-second clip on the V1 target track. When you superimpose the five-second clip — surprise! — only two seconds actually make it to Track V2 on the Timeline.

This strange functionality might seem like an annoying bug, but when you're in the superimposing mood, you usually want superimposed clips to match each other's durations, so this unique twist works in your favor. And if it doesn't, you can set your own In and Out points on the Timeline before superimposing a clip — in this case, Final Cut Express ignores the length of any clip on the target track and edits the new clip into the edit points that you set.

You can superimpose a group of clips together, each going to its own Timeline track, by selecting the group in the Browser window and dragging them to the Canvas window, where you can select the Superimpose option from the Canvas Overlay (refer to Figure 8-1).

Splitting Video and Audio Edits

When you edit DV clips that have video and audio linked together (either by setting In and Out points in the Final Cut Express Viewer window or by adjusting those points after the clips are on the Timeline), you're usually affecting both the video and audio segments of clips at the same exact point. In other words, when a video clip begins or ends, its audio does so too (or vice versa).

By doing a split edit, you can actually set different In and Out points for the video and audio segments of a clip. That is, you can end a video clip while letting its audio continue on (as you can see in Figure 8-3), or you can begin the audio first and then bring in the video a moment later.

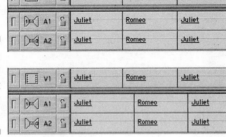

Figure 8-3:
Before and
after a split
edit on the
Timeline.

Pretend that you're editing a new-millennium take on *Romeo and Juliet*. You see Juliet standing on her balcony, calling out, "Romeo, hey, Romeo. Where are you, man? Your cell phone goes straight to voice mail, and your pager's off too!" But as Juliet calls out, you cut to Romeo, in the darkness below, to see his reaction as she continues to speak. (Translation: You've cut away from the video portion of the Juliet clip but let the audio keep playing.) That's a split edit in action, and you see them all the time in movies, television, and so on.

Splitting edits from the Viewer

You can set up split edit points in the Viewer. Doing so is almost as easy as marking simple In and Out points, but you can mark up to four points — In and Out points for video and In and Out points for audio.

1. **From the Browser, open a video clip that also incorporates audio in the Viewer window.**

   You have to select a clip from the Browser. Selecting a clip that's already on the Timeline won't work.

2. **Position the Viewer playhead on the frame where the video is to begin and set an In point by choosing Mark⇨Mark Split⇨Video In.**

   You can also press ⌘+Option+I to mark the video's In point.

   You've just told Express that the clip's video should start at this frame, but you still have to define the video's Out point as well as the In and Out points for the clip's audio.

3. **Repeat Step 2, but mark the Video Out, Audio In, and Audio Out points by choosing those options from the Mark Split submenu.**

   You can mark these points in any order. You can also skip setting an Out point for either the video or audio — if you don't, Final Cut Express just makes the last frame of the clip the Out point. (Express does just the reverse when you set Out points, but not In points, for video and audio.)

Also, if you want the video and audio to either start or end on the same frame (in many cases, you want to split either the beginning of a clip but not the end or vice versa), just place a simple In or Out point on that particular frame.

Figure 8-4 shows all Video and Audio In and Out points set.

Figure 8-4:
Split video
and audio
edits in the
Viewer.

Audio In point   Video In point   Video Out point   Audio Out point

4. Move the clip to the Timeline.

You can drag the clip directly to the Timeline or drag it to the Canvas window. After moving the clip to the Timeline, notice that Final Cut Express sets the video and audio points differently, reflecting how you split them in the Viewer.

When you've moved the split-edited clip to the Timeline, you can still adjust the clip's Video and Audio In and Out points by clicking and dragging them on the Timeline.

To clear split edit points, open the clip from the Browser window and choose Mark⊏▷Clear Split. The Clear Split submenu lets you clear each In and Out point or all audio or all video points together. Or, as a shortcut, press Control while clicking in the Viewer scrubber bar and clear your split edits from the pop-up menu that appears.

After you add a split-edited clip to the Timeline, you have limited ability to adjust the clip's split edits using the Viewer again. If you double-click the clip on the Timeline, it opens in the Viewer, but you can only re-adjust the clip's two In points (video and audio) together, as well as its two Out points (video and audio) together. The easiest way to adjust these linked points is to use your mouse to click them on the scrubber bar and drag them to a new location. But before you do this, read the next section, which shows you how to adjust (and re-adjust) split video/audio points directly on the Timeline.

Splitting edits on the Timeline

You can also create split edits to clips that are already on the Timeline. Personally, I prefer this approach because you can see not only the video and audio of the clip you're splitting (on the respective Timeline tracks), but you can also see neighboring clips that you'll eventually integrate with your split-edited clip. However, the decision to use the Timeline or the Viewer is up to you.

The easiest way to split edit a clip on the Timeline is to simply drag the edges of its video and audio to different points (the edges of a clip represent its In and Out points, of course). To do this, just hold down the Option key and drag the edge of the clip's video or audio to a new point. You'll see that the clip's video and audio stay linked (you can move the clip on the Timeline, and its video and audio portions stick together), but the clip's video and audio In/Out points are different.

You'll naturally use split edits to overlap the audio of one clip onto the audio of another clip. (For instance, remember the example — earlier in this chapter — of the Juliet dialogue continuing on, even though you've cut to the next video clip of Romeo in the bushes below her balcony.) When you're overlapping the audio of one clip onto that of another clip, putting each audio on a different audio track so you can hear each playing is not unusual. For instance, when you overlap the Juliet dialogue and the Romeo video, you still want to hear the audio for the Romeo clip — his breathing, the rustling of the bushes around him, and so on. And you do that by keeping the audio for each of the young lovers on two different tracks, as shown in Figure 8-5.

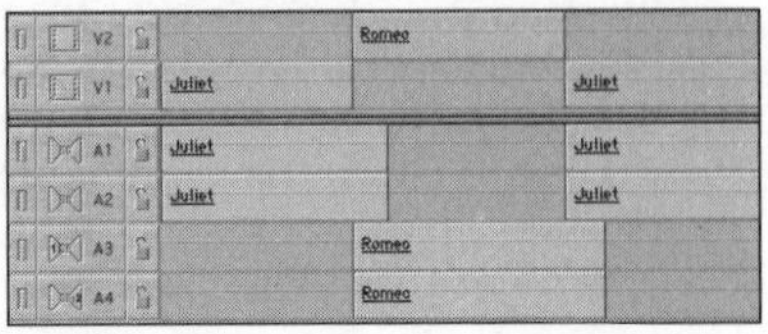

Figure 8-5:
Splitting
audio and
video on
overlapping
tracks.

Using Advanced Editing Tools

After you move media clips to the Timeline, most of your editing energy goes towards tweaking those clips so they cut smoothly from one to another. In Chapter 6, I introduced you to all the basic tools and techniques to do just that, but don't stop there! Final Cut Express sports a range of advanced tools — such as roll and ripple edits, or slips and slides — that let you edit in one simple step instead of two, three, or four steps (as can be the case when you're working with the more basic Express editing tools).

You use most of these power tools towards the end of your editing work, when you've already laid out your material and want to tweak a few clips (add a few frames here, cut a few frames there) without changing the length of the movie (or sequence). Why is preserving length so important? In the late stages of your work, you may have already laid down sound effects, music, and so on — all carefully synched up with your video. Or maybe your video just has to fit within an allotted time, like a TV commercial does. At any rate, these tools, with the exception of the Ripple Edit tool, all let you tweak clips but minimize the effects those tweaks have on other clips and your sequence in general.

You can do these advanced Final Cut Express edits in many ways, but the quickest and most intuitive approach is to simply select a new tool from the Tool palette, and apply it directly to clips you've already placed on the Timeline. Still, some of these tools and techniques can seem a bit confusing when you're reading about them the first time around. Don't get frustrated if you find yourself saying "Huh?" — just take the time to study the figures I provide and then try out this stuff on your own clips.

Editing clips often means making small, precise changes to them; but if you have the Final Cut Express Snapping feature turned on, you may find it hard to be as precise as you want because the mouse pointer keeps snapping to the edges of nearby clips instead of the frame you want to be on. If so, just press N on your keyboard to turn off Snapping. (You can even toggle Snapping while dragging a clip or its edges.)

Resizing clips with roll and ripple edits

Roll and ripple edits let you resize clips on the Timeline without having to separately move adjacent clips (that is, side-by-side clips) forward or back to accommodate changes. (For instance, you won't have to create a gap on the Timeline before extending a clip into that gap, and you won't have to close an unwanted gap after trimming a clip.)

Both of these edits affect how two adjacent clips join together on the Timeline. When you perform either a roll or ripple edit, you're either adding or taking away frames from the first clip (known as the *Outgoing clip,* which comes earlier in time) or the second clip (known as the *Incoming clip,* coming later in time), but you're maintaining their edit point — that is, the two clips stay connected, never leaving a gap in between.

Rolling edits

A *roll edit* lets you simultaneously move the edit point between two clips, making one clip longer and the other shorter, all in one fell swoop. (The clip that you're trying to make longer must have extra frames available to it that you haven't already edited onto the Timeline.) Say, for example, you have Clips A, B, C, and D on the Timeline, side by side, and you want to do a roll edit between Clips A and B. Check out Figure 8-6. The top image shows Clip A and B at the same size, before the roll edit. The next image shows a roll edit extending Clip B at the expense of Clip A. The bottom image is another roll edit in the opposite direction: extending Clip A at the expense of Clip B. No matter which way you move the roll edit pointer, Clips C and D stay the same.

When you do the roll edit, you're changing the Out point of Clip A and the In point of Clip B, but you're not changing the combined length of the two clips; therefore, you're not shifting any following clips (C and D) either forward or backward along the Timeline.

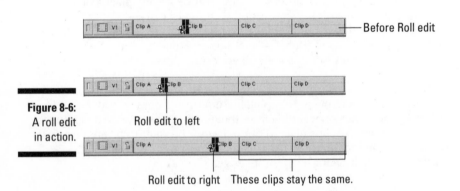

Before Roll edit

Figure 8-6:
A roll edit
in action.

Roll edit to left

Roll edit to right   These clips stay the same.

Why would you want to do a roll edit — besides to show off your Final Cut Express acumen to family and friends? A roll edit is great to use when you're trying to match the same action, as you cut from one clip to another. For instance, suppose you have the dubious distinction of editing *Rocky XXXIV,* and you want to cut from a medium shot of Rocky throwing his knockout blow to a close-up of his glove landing squarely on the jaw of his hapless challenger. In this case, you put these two clips side by side, trying to match the actions as close as possible, and then use the roll edit to fine-tune the edit point — looking for the perfect frame to exit out of the first clip and enter into the second clip.

Roll edits are easy to do right on the Timeline. Just follow these steps:

1. **Select the Roll Edit tool from the Final Cut Express Tool palette (as shown in Figure 8-7) or just press R (for roll).**

   The mouse pointer becomes a Roll Edit symbol.

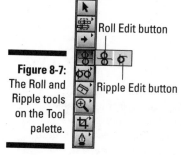

Roll Edit button

Ripple Edit button

2. **Click the Roll Edit tool on an edit point between two clips on the Timeline and drag the edit point either right or left (forward or back in time).**

   As you drag, keep an eye on the Canvas window: As shown in Figure 8-8, it goes into a two-up clip display — the frame on the left shows the last frame, or Out point, of the Outgoing clip (again, the clip to the left of the edit point), while the frame on the right shows the first frame, or In point, of the Incoming clip. When you release the mouse, the roll edit takes effect on the Timeline.

   And again, when you use a roll edit to extend an edit point by a certain number of frames, you're also shortening the adjacent clip by the same number of frames, so the two clips continue to share the same edit point. In other words, what you give to one clip, you take from the other (and vice versa).

   When you can't drag (that is, roll) the edit point any further along the Timeline, you've reached the last frame of either the Outgoing or Incoming clip. Because no more frames are available for either clip to give, that's the limit of the roll edit.

Figure 8-8:
The Canvas window becomes a two-up clip display.

Ripplin' with ripple edits

A *ripple edit* lets you resize a clip by moving its In or Out point on the Timeline — sounds simple enough, eh? But what makes ripple edits so cool — and probably the most handy editing tool you'll ever have — is that when you resize a clip, Final Cut Express automatically *ripples* that change through the rest of the Timeline sequence, moving clips forward or back in time (to make room for a clip you've extended or to close the gap left by a clip you've trimmed).

For instance, imagine that you've placed Clips A, B, C, and D on the Timeline side by side, but you decide to trim a few frames off the end of Clip B (the Out point) while *also* moving Clips C and D to the left so they fill the empty gap left by Clip B's trimmed frames, as shown in Figure 8-9. The top image shows the Timeline before a ripple edit. In the middle image, the ripple edit shortens Clip B and moves Clip C over to fill in the gap. In the bottom image, the ripple extends Clip B and moves Clip C out to make room. Normally, by using the steps described in Chapter 6, you'd trim Clip B and then have to manually move Clips C and D over to fill the gap — probably by using the Select Track Forward tool. But the Ripple tool does it in one easy step — ain't progress nifty?

Like the Roll Edit tool, the Ripple Edit tool is specifically designed to work with two clips — one on either side of an edit point (an Outgoing clip and an Incoming one). You can move either the Out point of the Outgoing clip (that is, the first clip) or the In point of the Incoming clip. To use a ripple edit on clips on the Timeline, follow these steps:

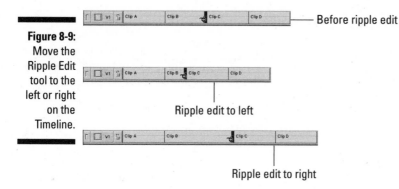

Before ripple edit

Ripple edit to left

Ripple edit to right

Figure 8-9:
Move the Ripple Edit tool to the left or right on the Timeline.

1. **Select the Ripple Edit tool from the Final Cut Express Tool palette (refer to Figure 8-7).**

   Alternatively, just press R *twice*. The mouse pointer becomes a Ripple Edit symbol.

2. **Click to the immediate left of an edit point with the Ripple Edit tool to select the Outgoing clip, or to the immediate right to select the Incoming clip.**

   Sometimes, you might wonder if you're selecting the Outgoing or Incoming clip at the edit point, because the two clips are right next to each other. But watch the Ripple Edit symbol's tail, which may look like a hook. It will always point towards the clip you're about to select.

   You're letting Final Cut Express know which of the two clips at the edit point you want to affect. Express responds by highlighting a thin slice of the clip next to the edit point. (Figure 8-9 shows Clip B selected in this way.)

3. **Click and drag the selected side of the edit point either forward or backwards in time to extend or trim it.**

   As you drag, keep an eye on the Canvas window: It goes into its two-up clip display — the frame on the left shows the last frame, or Out point, of the Outgoing clip (again, the clip to the left of the edit point), while the frame on the right shows the first frame, or In point, of the Incoming clip.

   When you release the mouse, Final Cut Express ripples the effects of the edit through all the following clips in the Timeline sequence. Seeing those clips shift in time can sometimes be disorienting (especially if you've extended or trimmed the edit point on the incoming clip), but go ahead and play the new edit in the Canvas window and you should see that all's well (if not, just choose Edit⇨Undo and try again).

   When you can't extend an In or Out point any further along the Timeline, you've reached the last frame of the clip, and no more frames are available.

Slip-slidin' clips

Slip Edit and Slide Edit are two other specialized tools in your editing arsenal. While you probably won't use them day in, day out (as you would the Ripple Edit tool), they definitely save you a few steps in certain scenarios.

Like roll and ripple edits, slips and slides are easiest when done directly on the Timeline, so that's what the next sections focus on.

Giving a clip the slip

A *slip edit* changes the In and Out points of a single clip, but not its duration or its position on the Timeline.

If this sounds a bit abstract, then try this example on for size: Suppose you open a clip in the Viewer, and it's 90 frames long. You decide to edit only its middle 30 frames (31–60) to the Timeline. After those frames are on the Timeline, you can use the Slip tool to change the 30 frames that clip shows — for instance, frames 1–30 or 15–45, and so on (as shown in Figure 8-10).

So now you're thinking, "Hmmm, pretty clever, but why on earth would I ever do that?!?" You can turn to the Slip Item tool when you've carefully edited a group of clips and need to change one clip in the sequence but don't want to affect any others. For instance, maybe you've meticulously synched some video to music beats or other sound events, but then you realize that one clip plays a bit awkwardly with the clips around it. If you don't want to extend or trim that clip (because that would change the duration of the sequence and throw off the synch with the audio), you can do a slip edit and try to find a better range of frames within the problem clip — without changing its position or length in the sequence.

But enough theory. To edit a clip using the Slip Item tool in the real world, follow these steps:

1. **Select the Slip Item tool in the Tool palette (as shown in Figure 8-11) or just press S (for slip).**

   Either way, the mouse pointer becomes a Slip Edit symbol.

2. **Click a clip on the Timeline and drag the mouse either left or right to slip its frames.**

   When you click the clip, Final Cut Express shows a rectangle frame that represents the total frames available to the clip. Drag left to move the latter frames of the clip into position or right to see its earlier frames.

   Also, keep an eye on the Canvas window — as you drag, it shows a two-up display of the new In and Out points for the clip (refer to Figure 8-8).

3. **Release the mouse when you're happy with those new In and Out points.**

4. **Play the slipped clip from the Timeline to see how it looks.**

Rectangle frame shows all frames available

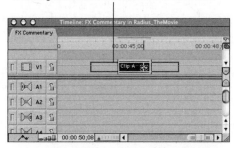

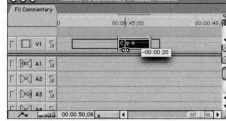

Figure 8-10:
Before and
after a slip
edit on the
Timeline.

Slip Edit tool

Slide Edit tool

Figure 8-11:
The Slip and
Slide tools
on the Tool
palette.

You can also slip a clip in the Viewer window (whether you prefer this approach just depends on your personal editing style). On the Timeline, use the standard Selection tool to double-click a clip that you want to slip. The clip opens in the Viewer; now, select the Slip tool (press S), and in the Viewer, drag either the clip's In point or Out point to a new location (you'll notice that the clip's In point and Out point move together, and therefore encompass a new range of frames — that's a slip edit in action!) The change you make in the Viewer will automatically be reflected on the Timeline as well.

Sliding a clip

The Slide Item tool is an unusual beast in that it moves an entire clip either forward or back on the Timeline, while *also moving* the edit points on either side of the clip. Translation: As you move a clip with the Slide Item tool, you are at the same time trimming or extending the clips to either side of it to accommodate the clip in its new location while keeping its edit points intact.

Say you've arranged Clips A, B, and C side by side on the Timeline (as shown in Figure 8-12), and each clip is 30 frames long. When you *slide* Clip B forward in time by 15 frames, you also trim the Clip A Out point by 15 frames and extend the Clip C In point by 15 frames. The result? Clip A is now only 15 frames long, Clip B keeps its original 30-frame length but will now be in a new position on the Timeline, and Clip C is 45 frames long (provided it had extra frames to extend out to, of course).

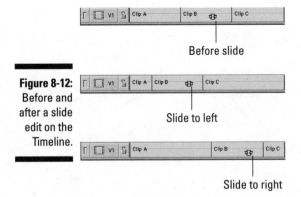

Before slide

Slide to left

Slide to right

Figure 8-12: Before and after a slide edit on the Timeline.

While you're not likely to use the Slide Item tool regularly, it can be helpful to move an important clip (usually to match a beat of music or some audio event) without changing the edit points of any other clips in the sequence. To use the Slide Item tool, follow these steps:

1. **Select the Slide Edit tool in the Final Cut Express Tool palette (refer to Figure 8-11), or just press S twice.**

   The mouse pointer becomes a Slide Edit symbol.

2. **Click a clip on the Timeline and drag the mouse either left or right to slide it forward or back in time.**

   The Canvas window switches to a two-up display (refer to Figure 8-8), showing the new Out-point frame of the clip to the left and the new In-point frame of the clip to the right.

   Also, a pop-up timecode box tells you how many seconds and frames you're sliding your clip away from its original location.

3. **Release the mouse when you think that you've moved the middle clip to a good spot.**

4. **Play the edited clips from the Timeline to see how they look.**

Using Markers to Highlight Important Moments

Markers are little signposts that you can place anywhere in a media clip or Timeline sequence to identify (or mark) frames that are important to you. You may need to mark a frame where you want to begin changing a clip's volume. Or you may want to place markers at a clip's existing In and Out points, so you'll always know where they were originally set (in case you plan to change those points, but want the option of going back to their original locations later on, if you don't like your changes).

In the next few sections, you find out how to use markers to their fullest.

Setting markers

You can set markers inside an individual clip or within a sequence on the Timeline. Set them in clips to flag important moments within that clip, and set them in a sequence to flag important moments in your edited story (for instance, a frame where you might want to insert additional clips, such as music, or possibly trim or extend a nearby clip to, and so on). You can set as many markers as you want — Final Cut Express just numbers them sequentially (Marker 1, Marker 2, and so on) until you rename them. (More on renaming markers later in this chapter.) Also, the Express Timeline can snap clips to markers (if you have Snapping turned on — press N to toggle it), which makes markers handy tools for lining up clips (or keyframes in clips) to other clips elements on the Timeline.

Setting markers within a clip

To set a marker within a clip (see Figure 8-13), try this:

Current Timecode

Figure 8-13:
Markers set
for a clip in
the Viewer
window.

Click to add a marker · A marker comment

Individual markers

1. **Open the clip in the Viewer window.**

2. **Position the Viewer playhead on the frame you want to mark and press M (for marker).**

   You can also click the Add Marker button in the Viewer window — refer to Figure 8-13.

Keep setting as many markers as you'd like. When you add the clip to the Timeline, you see those markers within the clip.

You can use markers to break up a clip into smaller subclips, which is a great way to quickly divide a long, unwieldy clip into smaller, bite-sized morsels. To take advantage of this cool little feature, open a clip by double-clicking it from the Browser window. In the Viewer window, set markers at each frame where you'd like a new subclip to begin. From now on, the Final Cut Express Browser identifies that marked-up clip with a little triangle next to its name. If you click the triangle, the Browser lists every marker you set in that clip (as shown in Figure 8-14), but your Browser has to be in its List view for this to work. (Choose Edit⇨Browser Items⇨As List.)

In fact, the Browser now treats each marker as if it's an individual clip (each of these new clips starts at the first frame you marked in the original clip and ends at the frame *before* the *next* marker you set). All the usual things you can do to clips apply to these subclips — you can rename them, open them in the Viewer window, set In and Out points for them, and move them to the Timeline. Cool, eh?

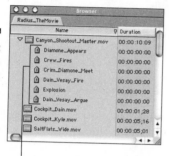

Figure 8-14:
A clip shows its markers in the Browser window.

Markers in the Browser window

You can actually set markers *while* Final Cut Express plays a clip in the Viewer (as opposed to stopping playback to set the marker). Just start playing the clip, and press M or click the Add Marker button anytime you want to place a marker on the fly. Granted, this method isn't highly precise (unless you've got incredible hand-eye coordination), but it's the best way to lay down a lot of markers in a hurry, or to beats of music.

Setting markers within a sequence

Setting a marker on the Timeline (that is, a marker that highlights a point in time, not a frame in a particular clip) isn't much different, as shown in Figure 8-15:

1. **Make sure that you haven't currently selected any clips on the Timeline.**

   To be safe, select the Timeline window, and then press ⌘+D to deselect any clips, or choose Edit⇨Deselect All.

2. **Position the Timeline playhead on the frame to mark and, you guessed it, press M to place the marker.**

Even if you're working in the Timeline, you can still set markers within a particular clip (as you would if you opened the clip in the Viewer). Just select the clip on the Timeline, position the Timeline playhead within that clip, and press M for marker. The marker appears within the clip itself (refer to Figure 8-15), not above it on the Timeline.

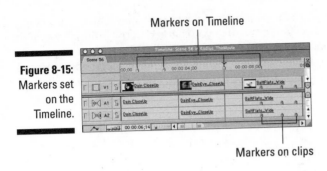

Markers on Timeline

Figure 8-15:
Markers set
on the
Timeline.

Markers on clips

Renaming and deleting markers

You can edit markers either from the Viewer window (for markers inside clips) or from the Timeline (for markers on the Timeline).

To rename markers, just follow these steps:

1. **In the Viewer or Timeline window, position the playhead directly on a marker.**

   Watch out: The screen may *look* as if you've positioned the playhead directly on a marked frame, but you may still be off by a frame or two. If the playhead is indeed on a marker, it changes color. For guaranteed results, you can also jump the playhead to the previous and next markers by pressing Shift+↑ or Shift+↓.

2. **Choose Mark⇨Markers⇨Edit or just press M.**

   Either way, Final Cut Express opens the Edit Marker dialog box.

3. **In the Edit Marker dialog box (shown in Figure 8-16), type a new name for the marker, and click OK.**

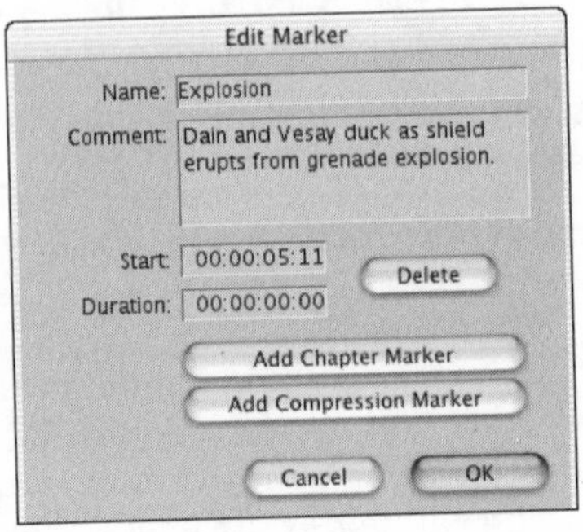

Edit Marker

Name: Explosion

Comment: Dain and Vesay duck as shield erupts from grenade explosion.

Start: 00:00:05:11   Delete
Duration: 00:00:00:00

Add Chapter Marker

Add Compression Marker

Cancel   OK

Figure 8-16:
The Edit
Marker
dialog box.

Naming markers something meaningful is helpful if you ever need to search for a marker by name (which I cover in the following section).

You can also type a comment for a marker (a habit that is helpful when, a few weeks down the road, you can't remember why you placed the marker in the first place).

If you want to delete a marker, follow these easy steps:

1. **In the Viewer or Timeline window, position the playhead directly on a marker.**
2. **Choose Mark⇨Markers⇨Edit or just press M.**
3. **In the Edit Marker dialog box, click the Delete button.**

Searching for markers

You can quickly search for markers you've set in either clips or a Timeline sequence. A word of advice, though: To get the most out of these searches, make sure you rename markers so they're more descriptive than the default names Final Cut Express gives them (Marker 1, Marker 2, and so on). See the preceding section for more about renaming markers.

To search for Timeline markers, follow these steps:

1. **Press Control and click the Current Timecode box in the Timeline (refer to Figure 8-15).**

    Alternately, you can also click anywhere in the Timeline ruler while holding the Control key.

2. **Select the marker from the pop-up menu.**

    Final Cut Express moves the Timeline playhead to that marker.

To search for markers within a clip, follow these steps:

1. **Open the clip in the Viewer.**
2. **Press Control, click the Viewer Current Timecode box (refer to Figure 8-15), and choose the marker from the Timecode pop-up menu.**

You can also search a Timeline sequence for markers by using the Final Cut Express Find command:

1. **Make the Timeline or Canvas window active.**

2. **Choose Edit⇨Find.**

   The Find dialog box displays, as shown in Figure 8-17.

Figure 8-17:
The Find
dialog box.
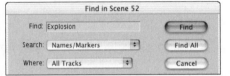

3. **Select Names/Markers from the Search pop-up menu and type part or the whole marker name in the Find text box.**

4. **Click the Find button.**

   Final Cut Express moves the Timeline playhead to the first clip or sequence marker that fits the description. Clips have to be on the Timeline for Express to find their markers. (You'll hear a beep if Express can't find any markers.)

5. **To move to the next marker that fits the description, choose Edit⇨ Find Again.**

From the Viewer, Canvas, or Timeline windows, you can quickly jump the playhead to the next or previous marker: Press Shift+↓ for Next and Shift+↑ for Previous.

Changing a Clip's Speed

Slowing down and speeding up video clips are great ways to add drama and suspense or frenetic action to your movie. When you slow down a clip, Final Cut Express is actually adding frames to the clip, so it takes more time for the clip to play at the DV 29.97 frames-per-second pace. Likewise, when you speed up a clip, Express just tosses frames out, making the action seem to go quicker. To add either effect, follow these steps:

1. **On the Timeline, select a clip you want to play slower or faster.**

   If you want to change the speed of only part of an existing clip, you have to separate that part of the clip from the rest (using the Razor Blade tool).

2. **Choose Modify⇨Speed.**

3. **In the Speed dialog box (as shown in Figure 8-18), type either a new percentage of speed or a new time duration for a clip.**

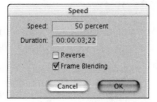

Figure 8-18:
The Speed
dialog box.

When you change the speed of a clip, you're also changing its duration. (A clip that plays twice as fast lasts only half as long, right?) Final Cut Express lets you set the speed either way, depending on your needs. For instance, if you're trying to fit the clip into a fixed amount of time, type a new duration value, down to the last frame. Or if you're just going by gut instinct, try using a percentage. (A percent lower than 100 percent makes the clip play in slow motion, and a higher value speeds the playing of the clip up.)

When you enter a new percentage for the speed, try to use whole, even numbers, which result in the smoothest looking video.

4. **Toggle Frame Blending on or off.**

This option is handy for slow motion clips. Ordinarily, Final Cut Express creates a slow motion effect by taking the original clip and duplicating some or all of its frames, once or many times. Repeating the same frames over and over again can create a stuttering effect; so when the Frame Blending option is turned on, Express tries to create entirely new frames that are blends of the original frames in the movie. For instance, instead of playing Frame 1 twice, Express would play Frame 1 once and then draw a new frame that is halfway between Frame 1 and Frame 2 (and so on). The result is a smoother, slow motion effect.

5. **Click OK and render the clip.**

When you click OK, you see that Final Cut Express has either lengthened or shortened the clip on the Timeline (as shown in Figure 8-19). Because you've basically created a new kind of clip, you have to render it before seeing the effect in action (just select the clip, and choose Sequence⇨Render Selection).

Final Cut Express slow motion versus the real thing

You may notice that your slow motion effects never look quite as smooth as those you see in big Hollywood videos. Why not? Hollywood film-makers ordinarily shoot their footage at 24 frames per second, but when they want to capture slow motion, they crank the frame rate of their camera higher, to maybe 50 frames per second, 75 frames per second or higher. This approach uses a lot of frames to capture an action, and when a movie projector plays those frames back at regular speed (24 frames per second), the result is a silky smooth slow motion

effect, where each frame is different from the last and captures a small bit of time and motion.

Now consider Final Cut Express, which usually duplicates frames to create a slow motion effect. Because you're seeing the same frames two, three, or more times instead of unique frames, the slow motion effect seems a lot choppier. Even when you use the Express Frame Blending option, the software has no way to invent new frames that look as good as a genuine unique frame shot by a camera.

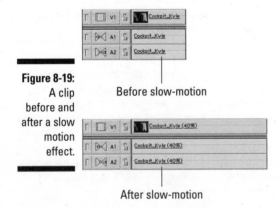

Figure 8-19: A clip before and after a slow motion effect.

Before slow-motion

After slow-motion

Playing a Clip Backward

Occasionally, you may find it handy to play a clip backward instead of forward. For instance, in my video *Radius*, I needed footage of a timer counting down to zero, but the timer prop could only count up, not down. No problem: The cameraman just filmed the timer counting up and then I reversed the footage after it was on the Timeline, so it seemed to be counting down. To reverse a clip, perform the following steps:

1. **On the Timeline, select the clip you want to reverse.**

   If you also want to keep a version of the clip that plays forward on the Timeline, duplicate the clip with the Final Cut Express Copy and Paste commands (under the Edit menu) and select one of the copies to reverse. Remember, you can also create copies of clips in the Browser window, and store them there for safekeeping.

2. **Choose Modify⇨Speed.**

3. **In the Speed dialog box (refer to Figure 8-18), select the Reverse check box, click OK, and render the clip.**

   Notice on the Timeline, that (100%) follows the clip name. This name change tells you that the clip is playing at 100 percent speed, but in reverse. Because you've created a new kind of clip, you have to render it before seeing the reverse in action.

Stopping Action with a Freeze Frame

In the course of a movie, you may want to suddenly freeze the action on a single frame of video and hold it for a moment. (This stylistic touch was hot in the '70s and is coming on strong again these days.) Final Cut Express lets you freeze frames easily by turning any frame in an existing clip into a still picture that lasts as long as you want. To freeze a frame, try the following steps:

1. **In the Viewer, open the video clip you want to freeze.**

2. **Move the Viewer playhead to the frame you want to freeze.**

3. **Choose Modify⇨Make Freeze Frame.**

   Final Cut Express opens that frame in the Viewer, treating it as a new clip of video. The frozen frame has a duration of ten seconds by default.

4. **In the Viewer, move the In or Out points of the frozen frame to change its duration (as shown in Figure 8-20).**

   You can see the frame's current duration in the Viewer Clip Duration box (in the upper-left corner of the Viewer). You can also, of course, trim or extend the freeze frame clip after it's on the Timeline.

5. **Move the freeze frame clip from the Viewer to either the Timeline or the Browser by clicking anywhere in the Viewer image area and dragging the freeze frame to its destination.**

Figure 8-20:
A freeze
frame in the
Viewer.

When you create the freeze frame in the Viewer, Final Cut Express doesn't automatically add the freeze frame to the Browser as a clip (as if you'd just imported a movie or still picture into Express). You don't have to add it to the Browser, but I recommend moving it there anyway, just so the freeze frame becomes a permanent clip in the project, and you can quickly reuse it if you need it again. Otherwise, move the freeze frame clip right to the Timeline and edit it into a sequence like any other video clip.

After a freeze frame is on the Timeline, you have to render it because you're essentially creating a new video clip from what was once just a single frame (select the freeze frame clip, and choose Sequence⇨Render Selection).

To save a bit of time, you can actually freeze a frame directly from the Timeline. Just position the Timeline playhead on a frame of video and choose Modify⇨Make Freeze Frame. You see that frame appears in the Viewer window, ready to be moved to the Browser or back again to the Timeline.

Nesting a Sequence into Another Sequence

Final Cut Express lets you assemble a group of clips into a sequence, but you can *also* assemble a group of sequences into *yet another* sequence (as shown in Figure 8-21). This process is called *nesting* sequences, and it's particularly handy because it lets you break down bigger projects into more manageable morsels. For instance, you can edit each movie scene (or act, or any other division you want to make) in its own sequence, and then edit those finished sequences together to assemble a full-fledged project.

Figure 8-21:
Nested
sequences
on the
Timeline.

In any event, to nest one sequence into another, follow these steps take a deep breath first; this is pretty tough:

1. **Double-click a sequence icon in the Browser to open it on the Timeline.**

   This sequence receives any other sequences you're nesting.

2. **Click and drag another sequence from the Browser window to the Timeline.**

   You've now nested the second sequence into the first, as if it were a single media clip — except it probably contains lots of clips, already pre-edited.

That's it!

After you've nested another sequence into the Timeline, Final Cut Express treats that nested sequence like any old media clip. You can apply the same effects to a nested sequence that you apply to individual clips — add audio and video filters, set volumes and opacity levels, and even animate them with motion settings. When you do so, the effects apply to all the video and audio in the nested sequence. As far as Express is concerned, the sequence is a single clip of media.

If you've nested Sequence A into Sequence B but then decide to edit Sequence A again (for instance, to get access to trimmed video and audio in your original media clips), you can quickly open Sequence A just by double-clicking it on the Timeline. This action opens the sequence on the Timeline, where you can edit its clips one by one (you can get back to the earlier sequence by clicking its tab at the top of the Timeline window). Added bonus: Any changes you make in Sequence A automatically appear in its nested version in Sequence B. Pretty cool, eh?

Customizing the Final Cut Interface

As you get comfortable working in Final Cut Express, you'll probably want to customize the layout of major Express windows and palettes to suit your work style. For example, if you're working on a Powerbook or iBook, you may want to shrink the Viewer and Canvas windows so that you can work with a larger Timeline and Browser or vice versa, as shown in Figure 8-22. Or if you have two monitors hooked up to the Mac (you lucky dog), you can put the Browser window on that second monitor, so you can spread it out and see all the available clips as large icons.

Final Cut Express comes preprogrammed with a handful of different window layouts. To use these existing layouts, just choose Window⇨Arrange and then pick one of the layout options in the Arrange submenu. Go ahead and check them out — some, like Wide, give you an extra wide Timeline.

And if those stock layouts don't cut it for you, you can create two custom layouts always available to you directly from the Window menu. To do your own thing, try this:

Figure 8-22:
An
alternative
window
layout.

1. **Drag the major Final Cut Express windows and palettes into a layout that works for you.**

   You can position and resize the Browser, Viewer, Canvas, and Timeline, as well as the Tool palette and Audio meters. Final Cut Express won't save alternate arrangements of other windows, such as Effects or Favorites.

2. **Hold down Option, choose Window⇨Arrange.**

3. **From the submenu that appears, choose Set Custom Layout 1 or Set Custom Layout 2.**

   You're assigning a window layout to one of two custom Final Cut Express layouts. Now, whenever you launch Express, it opens into whatever layout you set last. And you can always choose a different layout by choosing from the submenu in Window⇨Arrange.

As you scientifically contemplate the most precise, optimized layout for Final Cut Express windows, consider this: Not all those windows need to be visible at once! When you have limited screen space (for instance, if you're running Express on an iMac or laptop), you may want to overlap the Timeline, Viewer, Canvas, and Browser, so each window can be bigger when you're actually using it but disappear under another when you're not. The trick to making this work is using the keyboard shortcuts to call up the window you want to work with quickly — use ⌘+1 for the Viewer, ⌘+2 for the Canvas, ⌘+3 for the Timeline, and ⌘+4 for the Browser. With some practice, you can get quite good working this way.

Adding a Voice-Over to a Sequence

The Final Cut Express Voice Over tool lets you connect a microphone to a Mac and record your voice (or a narrator's) as Express plays through a Timeline sequence. The Voice Over tool provides a quick and easy way to add voice narration to any movie — maybe you're editing a documentary or training program, or adding directors' commentary to your latest block-buster, or just going hog wild with those vacation videos.

If you really want to push the envelope, you can even record ADR dialogue in your movie. (*ADR* stands for automatic dialogue replacement, where an actor has to lip synch lines recorded on set, but that aren't useable because the original recordings are too noisy or distorted.)

Having recorded your voice, Final Cut Express turns it into an AIFF audio clip (saved to your hard drive, naturally) and adds it to the Timeline on its own audio track. You can record a voice-over through the entire Timeline sequence or through just a part of it. You can also set the fidelity of the sound you record and the volume level for headphones attached to your Mac. By wearing headphones, you can listen to the voice recording as your Mac hears it. This isn't helpful if you're recording yourself — it's usually distracting to hear yourself as you speak — but it's handy if you're monitoring the sound quality of someone else doing a voice-over. Here's how to do it:

1. **Connect a microphone to the Mac.**

   Any microphone that's compatible with the Mac OS X operating system will do. You may have to install specific drivers for the mike, but hopefully not, because OS X is designed to work with many devices right out of the box. And remember, many Macs have built in microphones that you can use without having to buy extra gear. These mikes aren't high performance, but they work in a pinch.

2. **On the Timeline, position the playhead where you plan to begin recording the voice-over.**

   You can also set In and Out points on the Timeline if you just want to record a segment of the sequence.

3. **Choose File⇨Voice Over.**

   Final Cut Express opens the Voice Over dialog box, shown in Figure 8-23.

4. **In the Voice Over dialog box, type a name for the voice-over audio clip you plan to record in the Name text box.**

Review   Type the name of your clip here

Record button

Discard Last Recording

Figure 8-23:
The Voice Over tool comes in handy for documentaries, training videos, and director's commentaries.

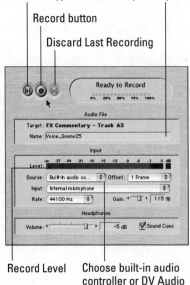

Record Level   Choose built-in audio
controller or DV Audio

5. **Click the Source pop-up menu to choose either Built In Audio Controller (use this for internal and external mikes) or DV Audio (in case you have a DV camera hooked up and are recording live through its microphone).**

   If you're using an adapter such as the Griffen iMic to connect a mike to your Mac, it may have its own option listed here as well.

6. **Click the Input pop-up menu to select the microphone.**

   Choose Internal Microphone if you're using the mike built into your Mac, or the External/Line In option if you're using a plug-in mike.

7. **Click the Rate pop-up menu to set the sample rate (that is, the quality) for your voice recording.**

   Choose the rate that matches your current Timeline sequence setting (you can see it by choosing Final Cut Express⇨Easy Setup and noting the audio rate listed next to Sequence Preset). If you can't match your sequence rate exactly, choose the option from the Rate pop-up menu that is closest to your sequence rate.

8. **Correct for any delays (known as *latency*) that occur between the time when the microphone picks up an audio signal and when the device capturing that signal actually records it by using the Offset pop-up menu.**

   Most USB capture devices suffer from a one-frame latency, so choose an offset of one frame to counteract that. If you're capturing audio from a DV camcorder, try an offset of three frames.

9. **To set the volume level for the recording, move the Gain slider to the left or right.**

   The higher the gain, the louder your voice recording will be.

10. **Set the volume level for the headphones by moving the Volume slider left or right.**

    Your range is from 0–60 decibels; keep volume low but still loud enough to hear the voice through the headphones.

11. **Select the Sound Cues check box.**

    When you select the Sound Cues check box, Final Cut Express plays a series of beeps a few seconds before recording begins and a few seconds before it ends. These beeps aren't recorded in the actual voice-over audio; they just help the person recording the voice-over gauge when to start speaking and when to stop.

12. **In the Voice Over dialog box, click the Record button to start recording.**

    Don't start speaking immediately: Final Cut Express first does a five-second countdown before recording. (You can see the countdown in the Recording Status box.) After recording does get under way, Express starts playing the sequence at whatever point you specified and starts another countdown in the Recording Status box. This countdown tells you how many seconds until it stops recording (that is, until it reaches the end of the sequence or an Out point you set on the Timeline).

As you record, keep an eye on the Voice Over tool Level meter and make sure that your recording levels aren't going into the red on the far right of the meter. (If so, you can reduce your gain by moving the Gain slider to the left and try again.)

Some people, when recording voice-overs, tend to move around a lot as they speak, which can create lots of variations in the volume and overall sound quality of your recordings. Try to keep your subject's movement (in relation to the microphone's position) to a minimum for consistent results.

Some voice narrators tend to vary the speed of their reading, and the pitch of their voice, without knowing it. You can help dodge these headaches by giving your voice-over subjects lots of time to practice in front of the microphone, so they become comfortable speaking into the microphone in a consistent manner.

 13. **Click Stop (this button toggles between Record and Stop) to stop recording at any point or continue recording until the Timeline playhead reaches an Out point or the end of the sequence.**

Final Cut Express places a new audio clip containing the voice narration on a new audio track on the Timeline.

 14. **Review your work and decide whether to keep it or give it the ol' heave-ho.**

Click the Voice Over tool Review button to play the sequence with its new voice narration. Click the Discard Last Recording button if you want to erase that narration clip from the Timeline.

Final Cut Express records the voice-over to whatever folder you set as the Scratch Disk (choose Final Cut Express➪Preferences, and click the Scratch Disks tab to see where that is). You'll find the recordings in that location, within a folder called Capture Scratch, and then again in a folder that shares the same name as the current project.

If you're trying to record a long voice narration, don't try to do it in one fell swoop, if you can avoid it. Instead, record narration for a small segment of a sequence, get it right, and then move on to the next.

When you finish a voice narration, Final Cut Express adds the new audio clip to the Timeline but not to the Browser window, meaning that you won't have a permanent reference of the narration clip. If you delete the narration clip from the Timeline, you'll have to track its AIFF file down in some obscure folder on the hard drive, and then import it again. I recommend dragging any narration clips you want to keep to the Browser window, where they become an official audio clip in the project.

Part IV
Adding Pizzazz

The 5th Wave   By Rich Tennant

ROOM 101

"I failed her in algebra but was impressed with the way she animated her equations to dance across the screen, scream like hyenas, and then dissolve into a clip art image of the La Brea Tar Pits."

In this part . . .

In Part IV, I explain how to use many Final Cut Express video transitions, which let you smoothly transition from one video clip to another. I also dive into all sorts of audio-related topics: how to set different volume levels for different clips, how to edit out scratches and pops in your audio, and how to use the numerous Express audio filters to create unique audio effects and spruce up audio that may be too loud, soft, or feature the hum of equipment in the background. I also look at the Express video filters, which let you change and enhance video clips in all sorts of stylish ways.

Finally, this part explains how to use the Express advanced effects engine to scale text, graphics, and video clips in size; change their positions on-screen; change their opacity; and composite different images together into a single shot.

Chapter 9

Transitions

· ·

· ·

*T*ransitions are special effects for shifting smoothly from one video clip to the next, rather than simply cutting away from one clip and starting another on the next frame. You are probably familiar with some of the more common transitions, such as the Cross Dissolve and the Wipe. The Cross Dissolve fades one clip out as it fades a new clip in, making the two seem to merge for a moment, whereas a Wipe slides one shot in over the other. (George Lucas uses these transitions a lot in his Star Wars movies.)

Final Cut Express places a dizzying and exotic array of transitions at your disposal, and you can apply them and customize them easily.

Exploring the Final Cut Express Types of Transition

The following list details some of the important transition types provided in Final Cut Express:

> ✔ **3D Simulations:** As the name implies, these six transitions imitate an action in three dimensions. You can use them to zoom in and out of video clips or to create spins, cube spins, and swings. These transitions have an animated, high-tech feel, and you often see them in commercials and news shorts.

The 3D simulations transitions are Cross Zoom, Cube Spin, Spin 3D, Spinback 3D, Swing, and Zoom.

✔ **Dissolves:** A *dissolve,* the most common transition, is an equal fading out of a clip over an equal fading in of another. These transitions morph the image into something else by gradually erasing what was there previously.

The dissolves available to you are Additive, Cross, Dip to color, Dither, Fade In Fade Out, Non-Additive, and Ripple.

✔ **Iris:** Like the view you see when looking through a telescope, an iris puts the focus on the center of the frame, and the edges change toward that center. You can manipulate an iris transition in dozens of ways.

Iris transitions include Cross, Diamond, Oval, Point, Rectangle, and Star.

✔ **Map:** By selecting or inverting specific channels, you can create dramatic, solarizing effects during a transition. *Solarizing* appears to burn out the edges of images, reminiscent of one of psychedelic effects from the '60s.

The Map transitions are Channel and Luminance.

✔ **Page Peel:** In a page peel transition, the first clip peels away to reveal the second. You can make many adjustments to this effect. Think about the relationship between the two images as one is peeled away. If you peel slowly top to bottom while talking heads are on each screen, you may find your audience laughing at what looks like Mr. Potato Head.

✔ **QuickTime:** The Apple QuickTime video format has its own set of transitions, which by any program that uses QuickTime (Final Cut Express included) can access. Some of these transitions are similar to the Express native transitions (such as Zoom), but QuickTime has some unique ones too — such as such as Radial, in which the first clip swings out in an arch like the hands of a clock to reveal the second.

The 12 QuickTime transitions are Channel Compositor, Chroma Key, Explode, Gradient Wipe, Implode, Iris, Matrix wipe, Push, Radial, Slide, Wipe, and Zoom.

✔ **Slide:** Your uncle's old slide projector could never move slides out of the way like this collection of transitions. Final Cut Express can push video frames around just about any way you can think of — from the top, bottom, or a split in the middle.

The Slide transitions in Final Cut Express are Band, Box, Center Split, Multi Spin, Push, Spin, Split, and Swap.

✔ **Stretch (and Squeeze):** The name says it all. These transitions are great for very exaggerated, fun, and psychedelic effects.

This set of transitions includes Cross Stretch, Squeeze, Squeeze and Stretch, and just Stretch, for those mellow days!

✔ **Wipe:** Wipes differ from dissolves in that wipes don't blend. They move one thing out of the way with another, but wipes give you more options than slides. Wipes are fun — for example, the Jaws wipe is a great way to amuse your friends when showing video from that fishing trip.

The 14 wipes available to you are Band, Center, Checker, Checkerboard, Clock, Edge, Gradient, Inset, Jaws, Random Edge, V, Venetian Blind, Wrap, and Zigzag.

One bit of stylistic advice: Don't get carried away with all the crazy transitions Final Cut Express offers you. Let the mood and emotion of your story dictate the kind of transitions you use. Just because you have access to a transition that makes people say "Wow!" doesn't mean it's the best transition for your project. Also, if your project requires transitions, try to keep the transitions you pick within the same family. That is, pick a type of transition (such as a Cross Dissolve) and stay with it so as not to distract the viewer with a variety of different transition styles.

Applying Your First Transition

Although Final Cut Express gives you tons of different transitions to use in your movies, you'll probably use a simple Cross Dissolve the most, fading one movie clip gracefully into another clip. However, before you can employ a Cross Dissolve, you need to trim the clips:

1. **In the Browser window, double-click first one clip and then the other to load them into the Viewer window.**

2. **For the first clip, mark an Out point about one second before the end of the clip.**

   Position the Viewer's playhead on the desired frame, and press O. See Chapter 6 for more about In and Out points.

3. **For the second clip (the later clip in the transition), mark an In point one second after the beginning of the clip.**

   Position the Viewer's playhead on the desired frame, and press I.

   This trimming is crucial because Final Cut Express uses the trimmed, unseen frames of a clip to create a transition from one clip to another. Untrimmed clips placed on the Timeline (that is, clips that show all their frames on the Timeline) don't have any unused frames for Express to use in creating the transition. See the sidebar, "Understanding unused frames," for more information.

Understanding unused frames

All transitions have one thing in common: handles. *Handles* are the extra frames (outside the In and Out points of the selected clip) that you need at the end of one clip and the beginning of the next clip in order for a transition to work.

A transition takes a specific amount of time to unfold. The Final Cut Express default for all transitions is one second (30 frames). If one clip disappears over the course of one second while another appears during that same one second, the transition involves a total of 60 frames — 30 frames from the outgoing clip (the earlier clip on the Timeline) and 30 frames from the incoming clip (the following clip). When the transition is half a second, you need the same amount of time present at the ends of both clips as extra frames for the transition. (*Note:* Express always tries to create a transition with all the extra

frames available to it. When Express doesn't have many extra frames available, the transition occurs very quickly and isn't very smooth.)

The way to deal with handles is to *always* leave enough extra footage (frames outside the clip's In and Out points) so that you have a handle. The simplest way to leave handles on clips is to use the Viewer window to mark the In point a bit into playing the clip (as opposed to the very first frame of the clip) or mark the Out point a few seconds earlier than the end of the clip. (You don't have to create handles at both the beginning and end of a clip — just the part of the clip that you want to incorporate into a transition.) You can also create handles by trimming clips after they're on the Timeline. See Chapters 6 and 8 for more information about trimming from the Timeline.

Now that you have trimmed the clips, you can try out a Cross Dissolve:

1. **Place two trimmed clips side by side in the Timeline, as shown in Figure 9-1.**

2. **Click the cut point (where the two clips meet on the Timeline) to select it.**

3. **Choose Effects⇨Video Transitions⇨Dissolve⇨Cross Dissolve.**

   The Video Transitions submenu has transitions galore. Subcategories include dissolves, iris, wipes, and lots more, but for now stick with the basic Cross Dissolve. Final Cut Express responds by placing a transition over the edit point between the two clips (refer to Figure 9-1).

4. **Play the transition on the Timeline.**

   If you have a Mac with a newer G4 processor and if you're not watching video through a television hooked to a DV camera, then you should be able to play the transition in real time. Place the Timeline playhead before the transition and press the space bar so that you can see the transition play in the Canvas window.

   If you're using a Mac with a G3 or older G4 processor, you may have to render the transition before playing it (Final Cut Express warns you by drawing a thin red line over the transition in the Timeline). To render a Cross Dissolve, click the transition in the Timeline to select it and then choose Sequence⇨Render Selection (or just press ⌘+R).

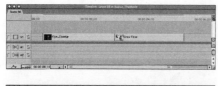

Figure 9-1:
A transition
in progress.

Looking at the Many Ways to Apply Transitions

Final Cut Express usually offers more than one way to accomplish a task, and transitions are no exception. The following sections describe some alternative methods you can use to apply transitions.

Dragging from the Browser to the cut point

One of the quickest ways to create a transition is to drag it from the Browser to the cut point. Just follow these steps:

1. **In the Browser, click the Effects tab to display the Express effects, grouped by category into bins.**

2. **Click the little triangle next to Video Transitions, for example, to see all the transition families (also in bins) available to you (as shown in Figure 9-2).**

3. **Open a transition bin, and drag a desired transition to a cut point on the Timeline (in other words, where two clips meet).**

Figure 9-2:
The Effects
tab in the
Browser
window tab
stores all
transitions.

If you hate to dig through all those bins to find your favorite transitions each time, drag the transitions to the Favorites bin in the Browser (or anywhere else in the Browser for that matter). Express makes a copy of the transition in this new location, leaving the original where it belongs. Now you can use this copy and not jump through too many hoops each time you need a transition.

Dragging from the Browser to the Canvas

Sometimes you may find moving the transition from the Browser and the Canvas an easier method to use. To do so, follow these steps:

1. **Select the edit point between two clips in the Timeline, clicking the area where the two clips join.**

2. **Drag the transition from the Effects tab in the Browser window to anywhere in the Canvas window.**

   This process is just like editing a shot into the Timeline, except that this time you're adding a transition.

Using the keyboard shortcut

You can apply Final Cut Express Cross Dissolve transition (which is considered its default transition), with a keyboard shortcut. What could be simpler? Just follow these steps:

1. **Select the edit point on the Timeline where you want to add a transition.**

2. **Press ⌘+T (T for transition, of course).**

Copying and pasting a transition

You can copy and paste a transition from one edit point to a new edit point that you have prepared. This method is handy if you have a custom transition at the 2nd edit point and want to apply it at the 20th edit point in the sequence (more about custom transitions a bit later). To copy and paste a transition, follow these steps:

1. **Make sure you have handles at the new edit point!**

2. **Click an existing transition on the Timeline to select it, and then press ⌘+C to copy it.**

3. **Move the Timeline playhead exactly between the two clips where you want to copy the transition.**

   The Express Snapping feature can be very helpful at this point. To toggle Snapping on and off, press N. Or press the Up and Down arrows on your keyboard to jump the Timeline playhead between clips.

4. **Press ⌘+V to paste the transition.**

   Alternatively, you can Option+drag-and-drop the transition from one edit point to another to make an exact copy of the transition in the new location.

Editing Clips and Adding Transitions

In Chapter 6, I explain how to insert or overwrite a clip from the Viewer window to the Timeline. But you can also perform these edits while automatically adding the default Express transition (the trusty Cross Dissolve) to the clip you're editing, without having to manually apply the transition. Follow these steps to edit two clips together and, in the process, perform an insert edit with a transition:

1. **Double-click the first clip into the Viewer and set an In and an Out point.**

   Remember that you can press I and O to set the points. Make sure Final Cut Express has enough extra frames past the Out point to accommodate the transition time.

2. **Edit this clip into the Timeline by dragging it into the Canvas window and choosing either an Overwrite or Insert edit.**

   Note that you can also drag the clip directly into the Timeline, but make sure that you have positioned the Timeline playhead at the end of the edited clip. It's very important that the playhead be positioned right after the clip you just edited.

3. **Double-click the second clip in the Viewer to open it in the Browser and again set In and Out points.**

   Make sure Final Cut Express has enough extra frames before the In point to accommodate the transition time.

4. **Drag the clip from the Viewer to the right side of the media area in the Canvas window.**

   Final Cut Express reveals a set of options, as shown in Figure 9-3.

5. **Drop the clip into the Insert with Transition section in the Canvas window.**

   You can also choose to overwrite the clip as well. Either way, Final Cut Express adds the clip to the Timeline, but with a Cross Dissolve already attached at the beginning of the clip, so it transitions seamlessly with the clip before it.

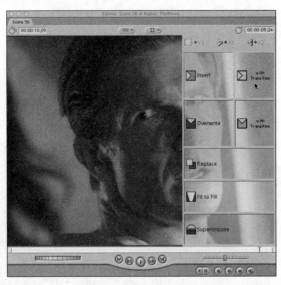

Figure 9-3:
Dragging a clip to the right side of the media area in the Canvas reveals Overwrite and Insert options.

Rendering Transitions

After you've placed a transition, you may have to render it before you can see it. (You'll see a thin red line over any clip on the Timeline that needs rendering.) *Rendering* is the process in which Final Cut Express calculates how to visually merge two transitioned clips and then writes a new video clip (which incorporates the new frames the transition uses) to the hard drive.

In the stone age of video editing (in other words, a couple of years ago), you had to render any transition you created before you could play it, but Final

Cut Express offers real-time previews of some major transitions, meaning a fast G4 Mac (usually 667 MHz and above), should be able to play the transition on the Timeline without rendering. (The Timeline shows a green line over the transition if it can be played as a preview.) These real-time capabilities definitely save a lot of time, but they have some limitations too:

- **Previews don't work for all transitions:** Real-time previews work only for a handful of transitions, such as Cross Dissolve, some wipes, and all the iris transitions. Final Cut Express displays these lucky transitions using bold text in the Browser window.

- **You must watch all previews on the Canvas:** Real-time previews work only when displayed in the Final Cut Express Canvas window and not on a TV you've hooked up through a DV video camera.

- **Real-time previews are temporary.** If you want to record a Final Cut Express movie to DV tape, you'll have to render them.

- **Preview quality may be poor:** Sometimes Final Cut Express stutters (usually because of some CPU or hard drive bottleneck) when it attempts to play real-time previews of transitions that you should be able preview. When this stuttering occurs, you need to render the transitions so they play smoothly.

The point is that, sooner or later, you must render transitions the old-fashioned way, so the following sections take a look at the ways you can play the rendering game. (Check out Chapter 17 for more about rendering in general.)

Rendering a single transition

To render a single transition in the Timeline, follow these steps:

1. **Select the transition in the Timeline.**

   Just use the Selection tool to select the transition.

2. **Choose Sequence⇨Render Selection.**

   Alternatively, you can press ⌘+R.

   The rendering process begins, and a render status bar shows the progress. Click Cancel in the status bar or press Esc to cancel the rendering.

Rendering multiple transitions

You can also choose to simultaneously render more than one transition in the Timeline by following these steps:

1. **Select the transitions in the Timeline.**

   Select the first one by clicking it, and then hold down ⌘ and click to select additional transitions in the Timeline.

2. **Choose Sequence⇨Render Selection.**

   Alternatively, you can press ⌘+R.

   The rendering process begins, and a render status bar shows the progress. You can cancel anytime by clicking Cancel in the status bar.

Rendering all transitions in a range

If you have very many transitions to apply, you may want to just apply them all in the Timeline without rendering them one by one. Using the method outlined here, you can render everything in the Timeline in one go after you're finished applying transitions:

1. **Select or open a sequence in the Timeline window.**

2. **Choose Sequence⇨Render All.**

   You can also use the Option+R shortcut to begin rendering everything in the Timeline.

Modifying Transitions

More often than not, after you have applied, rendered, and played a transition, you're not immediately satisfied. You want to modify it. Final Cut Express enables you to modify transitions in numerous ways. You can change the duration of transitions, change their alignments in respect to the edit point, or simply move them around.

Changing the duration of a transition

You can use a few different methods to modify the duration of a transition. One of the most common methods is the following:

1. **Control+click the transition in the Timeline.**

   Make sure you're clicking the transition itself, not the edit point between the two transitioned clips.

2. **Choose Duration from the pop-up menu that appears, as shown in Figure 9-4.**

   The Duration dialog box appears.

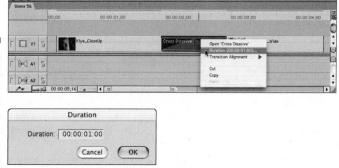

Figure 9-4:
Use the
Duration
dialog box
to alter the
duration of a
transition.

3. **In the Duration dialog box, type a new duration and click OK.**

Another way to change the duration of a transition is simply to drag the ends of the transition (as shown on the Timeline) to change its overall duration:

1. **On the Timeline, click and drag either end of the transition.**

    A timecode pop-up tip appears, as shown in Figure 9-5.

2. **Drag the edge of the transition and watch the timecode change.**

    With a little practice, you can change the duration of fades on the fly. What's really cool is that Final Cut Express displays the impact of this customization in the Canvas window as you drag.

You might want to zoom in your view of the Timeline, which makes each clip on the Timeline appear bigger and makes it easier to edit your transition with precision. You can select the Zoom In tool from the Express Tool palette (or just press Z), and click the Zoom In tool on the Timeline to zoom in (click repeatedly to zoom even more). To zoom out, use the Zoom Out tool in the same manner (or press Z twice).

Changing the alignment of a transition

By default, Final Cut Express centers transitions on an edit between two clips. That is, the transition straddles the edit point equally on both sides — half of the transition on the outgoing clip and the other half on the incoming side.

However, after you've placed a transition and previewed it, you may want it to occur earlier or later. For example, you may want the transition to start immediately *after* an edit point, instead of occurring squarely in the middle of the edit. On the other hand, you may want a transition to begin and end before it even reaches the edit point between two clips. Fortunately, Express allows you to quickly change the alignment of a transition, so that it occurs immediately before or after an edit point.

Figure 9-5:
Modifying
the dura-
tion of a
transition.

You can change the alignment of the transition by following these steps:

1. **Control+click a transition and choose Transition Alignment from the pop-up menu that appears.**

   Make sure you're not clicking the edit point between the two transitioned clips.

2. **Using the submenu that appears, choose to either start, center, or end the transition on the edit point between the two Timeline clips.**

   Figure 9-6 shows the method of transition alignment selection and their results.

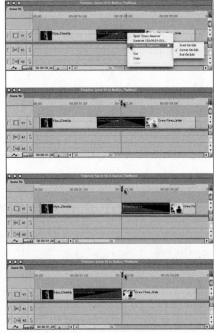

Figure 9-6:
Control+
click a
transition
and
select an
alignment
from the
Transition
Alignment
submenu.

If you find yourself changing the alignments of transitions frequently, you may want to use the keyboard shortcuts to perform this function. Select a transition and press Option+1 to start the transition at the edit point between the two clips. Pressing Option+2 centers the transition on the edit point, and pressing Option+3 ends the transition at the cut point.

Moving transitions

In Final Cut Express, you can move a transition from one edit point to another. This process removes the transition from the first edit point and moves it to the new one. If by any chance, you have a transition at the next edit point, Express replaces it. To move a transition, click and drag it from its current location to the new edit point.

Note that you can even align the transition to center, end, or start on the edit point. As you drag the transition to the new edit point, you can feel the transition snap to the edit point (center, beginning, or end).

Replacing and removing transitions

Many times you may be unhappy with your choice of a transition. In that case, you can easily replace the current transition on the Timeline with another one. Final Cut Express keeps the duration of the previous transition as well as the alignment to the edit point and simply applies a different type of transition. To replace a transition, follow these steps:

1. **On the Timeline, select the transition you want to replace.**

   Just use the Selection tool to select the transition.

2. **Choose Effects⇨Video Transitions and choose another transition from the submenu options.**

   The new choice replaces the older transition. Unhappy with this one too? Well, keep replacing it until you get the effect you're searching for.

If you decide not to use a transition you've already applied, just select it with Selection tool, and press Delete. Simple!

Fading In and Outs

Fading into or out of a clip in Final Cut Express couldn't be easier. You can use a transition at one end of the clip, and you automatically get a fade in or fade out. The transition most commonly used for this purpose is a Cross Dissolve, but you can choose any transition to create a fade.

To fade into or out of a clip, follow these steps:

1. **Edit a clip into the Timeline.**

   Make sure that no clip is adjacent to this clip, on either its left or right side. It's important that the clip touches no other nearby clip on the Timeline.

2. **Drag a Cross Dissolve transition from the Effects tab in the Browser window and drop it at the beginning of the clip (see Figure 9-7).**

   This step gives you a fade in from black into the clip.

3. **Drag another Cross Dissolve transition from the Effects tab in the Browser to the end of the clip.**

   This step gives you a fade out to black from the clip.

4. **Render the transition if your Mac isn't generating a real-time preview.**

   As shown in Figure 9-7, you have just created a fade in and fade out for the clip. And remember, you can lengthen or reduce the time that these fades last by clicking the ends of the Cross Dissolve and dragging to make them longer or shorter.

Figure 9-7: Fading in and out on a clip in the Timeline.

When you're creating a fade in or fade out, click and drag the transition from the Browser to a clip's edit point on the Timeline, and then press the ⌘ key to force the transition to land at the start or at the end of a clip's edit point. This way, you don't have to precisely position the transition yourself — Express does it for you.

Saving and Organizing Custom Transitions

You will soon find, as most editors do, that you use certain transitions more than others. What's more, often these transitions have different durations than the one-second default that Final Cut Express offers.

Using the following steps — which assume that you have a few transitions applied in the Timeline that have been modified to your preferred duration — you can save transitions and rename them as you see fit:

1. **Drag the Effects tab out of the Browser window so that it is a separate window.**

2. **Press ⌘+B to create a new bin in the Browser window.**

3. **Name this bin something intuitive (Custom Fades, for example) by clicking it once to highlight it, and then clicking a second time to edit its name.**

4. **Drag and drop the new bin into the Favorites bin in the now separate Effects window.**

5. **Drag a transition from the Timeline where you applied it and into the new bin that you just created.**

   This step saves the name of the transition as well as its duration.

6. **Rename the transition according to its purpose so that you'll remember what it does.**

   To rename the effect, double-click its name and type a new name for it. Editors commonly rename transitions to indicate their duration as well. For example, `Cross Diss10fr` means a Cross Dissolve with a ten-frame duration.

Using the Transition Editor to Customize a Transition

The Transition Editor window provides a number of tools and options for a more precise control over transitions. These customizing features increase in number, depending on the complexity of the transition you're using. The advantage is obvious: You can set up a special transition for repeated use (maybe a 3D cube spin for a short commercial or a very precise type of Cross Dissolve for a movie project) and then save it for repeated use.

You can load a transition into the Transition Editor window (see Figure 9-8) one of two ways: either by double-clicking a transition in the Timeline or by double-clicking a transition on the Effects tab of the Browser window. Each method allows you to change and modify transitions. However, when you double-click a transition from the Timeline, you modify only that existing transition on that particular sequence; you don't modify all transitions of that type.

The follow list presents some of the tasks that you can accomplish in the Transition Editor window:

Duration Timecode

Clip handle

Alignment buttons

Drag Hand

Playhead

Recent Clips menu

Figure 9-8:
You can
use the
Transition
Editor
window
to accom-
plish some
precise
tweaking of
transitions.

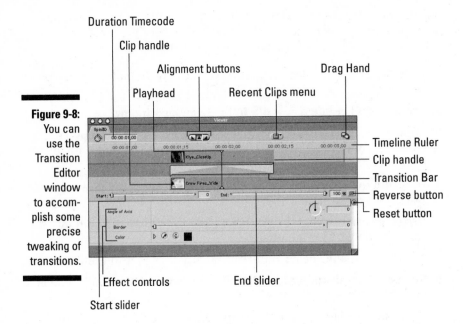

Timeline Ruler

Clip handle

Transition Bar

Reverse button

Reset button

Effect controls

End slider

Start slider

✔ **Change the duration of a transition:** Enter a new duration in the time-code field in the upper-left side of the window (refer to Figure 9-8) to change the duration of a transition.

✔ **Drag a transition:** Using the Drag Hand icon, you can either drag the transition into the Timeline to apply to a cut point, or drag it back to the Browser into the Favorites bin, which is on the Effects tab.

✔ **Reverse a transition:** Click Reverse to reverse the direction of a transition.

✔ **Change the start and end percentage:** Use the Start and End sliders to change the starting and ending percentages of a transition. This method is especially useful during some wipes in which you may want the transition to start out at 50 percent (halfway through the transition) for any reason.

✔ **Changing the edit point around the transition:** Another neat trick you can do in the Transition Editor window is to change the edit point under the transition. For example, you can drag at the ends of the two clips shown in the window and change the location of the edit point between the clips. The transition automatically moves to the new location of the edit point.

Chapter 10

Adding Text to Your Videos

*N*ot long ago, you needed a big piece of dedicated, expensive electronics hardware to add simple titles to video. Now you can accomplish the task of adding text to your video with Final Cut Express.

Final Cut Express allows you to create text for all kinds of occasions. You can create title cards to open and close your movie, and you can also create captions, subtitles, and logos to superimpose over video. You can animate *crawls*, which are like the running news ticker tape at the bottom of any CNN broadcast, or scrolling credits. You can go conservative with any of this, playing it cool with respectable typefaces or creating treatments so wild that they make your eyes hurt.

What you do with the Final Cut Express text tools depends entirely on your vision. This chapter is designed to show you how to pull off whatever that vision may be.

Formatting Text for Display on a TV

One of the first things that you should know when thinking about text and titles in y our videos is that because computer displays and TV sets work differently, text that looks good on a Mac monitor (or liquid crystal display [LCD] screen) may not look so hot when displayed on a television set. This isn't important if you never expect your video to be seen on a TV, which may be the case if, for example, you're just making videos for your Web site or for a CD-ROM. However, if you expect someone to watch your movie on a TV, you should keep some things in mind.

If you expect your movie to end up on a TV, make sure that you test and preview all the text that you're creating on a TV to make sure that everything looks good. (See Chapter 2 for how to hook a TV up to your Mac via FireWire.)

Selecting the right font size

Tiny print doesn't cut it in video. Small print, whether used for closing credits or the fine print of a copyright notice, may look good on your Mac's screen but probably appears fuzzy and illegible on a television because a TV's resolution isn't good enough to clearly display the small, thin little lines that make up small text. (See the sidebar "Text can look bad on a TV but good on a computer" for more information.) So how do you know what font size *will* work? Selecting font size is as much art as science, so unfortunately I can't give you any hard and fast rules. Fonts vary in size between faces. Saying that 12 points is the smallest size font that you should use isn't necessarily true for all font faces; you may be able to get by with 10 points in some fonts. However, I don't recommend getting too far below 10 points, no matter what the typeface. The bottom line is to test small font sizes on a decent TV before you commit.

Avoiding thick and thin

For best results on a TV, try to avoid fonts with thick and thin parts to each letter. For example, take a closer look at the Times font — the font face that you're reading right now. Take a look at the letter O, and notice how its vertical lines are thick, but the horizontal lines that form the top and bottom of the letter are much thinner.

In addition to having thicker and thinner parts of letters, Times has little turns, or *serifs*, such as the ends of the top of a capital *T*. Fonts with these little curlies at their ends are called by their family name: *serif fonts*. The narrow lines of the serifs on these fonts can *buzz* (flicker) or disappear altogether on a television (at least at smaller font sizes). For example, the *e* may look like a *c* or an *o*. *Sans serif* fonts, such as Arial, Helvetica, and Futura, don't have these serifs, which makes these fonts easier to read on a TV. For easy readability, stick to the sans serif family of fonts. In fact, a proverbial Cult of Helvetica exists in the television business. This cult is made up of people who use nothing but endless variations on the Helvetica font. Hey, it works!

Text can look bad on a TV but good on a computer

TVs and computer screens (both monitors and LCDs) work differently. Standard NTSC video images, the video signal standard for North America (it's PAL in Europe), are made up of horizontal lines (*scan lines*) that are drawn across a screen at a very high rate of speed. Scan lines create a video frame on the screen about every $\frac{1}{30}$th of a second. (Technically, the frame rate for NTSC video is 29.97 frames per second, so I just round it up to 30 frames, okay?)

When a computer displays an NTSC image, it shows all the scan lines that make up a frame of video together — in one fell swoop. When a television set shows an NTSC video frame, however, it actually creates the frame by quickly displaying two semi-frames called *fields;* the TV flashes one field for $\frac{1}{60}$th of a second and then flashes the next field for $\frac{1}{60}$th of a second. Each of these two fields that make up a frame are

slightly different; one shows only the odd-numbered scan lines that make up an image (lines 1, 3, 5, and so on), and the other shows the even-numbered lines (2, 4, 6, and so on). These two fields are said to be *interlaced;* it's like their even- and odd-numbered scan lines are laced or meshed together to create an image. Anyway, your TV flashes these two fields so quickly that your eye and brain can't really tell the difference and accepts them as one frame.

In fact, these two *interlaced* frames don't really match up perfectly. The brightness and position of the lines vary slightly, which isn't a problem when the screen displays a large object. A thin line, however, which is what small text is made up of, doesn't fare so well. Because of those fields, small text can appear to vibrate or buzz, especially a light vertical line on a dark background.

Using textures and colors sparingly

As you'll see, Final Cut Express gives you the capability to do some amazing things with a font face, such as creating bizarre shapes or applying colored, patterned textures to the lines that make up a font. (You may also be tempted to use some third-party, text-effect applications, such as TypeStyler, to make fancy type for your videos.) However, when these effects are viewed on a TV, you can run into the same buzzing and legibility problems that occur with a serif font: Thin, precise lines may fuzz out, bright vibrant colors may buzz, and darker colors may seem to disappear when superimposed over video that's also on the darker side. The key, again, is to view the final output on a TV monitor so that you know you're safe!

To avoid flickering artwork on final video output, avoid using artwork with lines thinner than 1 pixel. If you're using Photoshop or Adobe Illustrator files, be sure to make the lines in the artwork about 2 to 3 pixels thick.

Getting Started with a Text Generator

The first step when building a text title is to select a text generator for the text clip. In Final Cut Express, a *text generator* is the main tool for creating text. A generator is just like any effect except that unlike an effect, which can be applied only to a clip, Express treats the generator like a clip. Express can add the generator to the Timeline like any other media that you have.

Final Cut Express offers a number of text generators, which do different things, such as create static text, create scrolling or crawling text, and so on. I cover those topics shortly, but the important thing to know now is that you can select a text generator in one of two ways:

✓ **Generator pop-up menu:** You can choose a text generator from the generator pop-up menu located in the lower-right corner of the Viewer window (see Figure 10-1). When you make your choice, this text generator opens into the Viewer (like any other clip opens into the Viewer), and you can then edit the text.

✓ **Effects tab:** Alternatively, you can locate the text generators on the Effects tab of the Browser. Click the Video Generators bin to open it and in the Text bin, double-click the text generator of your choice to open it in the Viewer. (You can also just drag the text generator from the Browser's Effects tab directly into the Viewer to edit it.)

Figure 10-1:
Text generators are located in the generator pop-up menu in the Viewer window (left) or on the Effects tab (right).

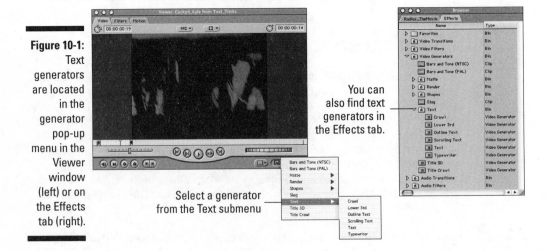

You can also find text generators in the Effects tab.

Select a generator from the Text submenu

Creating Text

The best way to get a feel for how to create text is to look at the process from start to finish. The following section explains how to choose the most common Final Cut Express generator, open it in the Viewer, and use the Viewer Controls tab to tweak the text to your liking. I then describe how to apply the text to the Timeline in two different ways so that it appears over a solid colored background (good for opening title cards) or superimposed over a clip of video (good for things like captions, subtitles, and so on).

If you mess up any of these steps, don't worry about it! You can always undo an action with the ⌘+Z shortcut.

Creating and adding text to a video

These steps use the Final Cut Express generator called Text, which is the quickest, easiest way to get basic, static text up on the screen. However, these steps work the same way if you want to apply other generators, which I look at a bit later in the chapter:

1. **Open the Viewer window by choosing Window⇨Viewer.**

   You can also use the ⌘+1 shortcut to open the Viewer.

2. **Click the Effects tab in the Browser window.**

3. **Twirl down the small triangle next to the Video Generators bin and open the Text sub-bin, which contains the text generators.**

4. **Double-click the generator called Text (which looks like a small clip with some color bars on it) to open it in the Viewer.**

   After you open the Text generator in the Viewer, you can see white text that reads SAMPLE TEXT on the Viewer Video tab, and the Viewer window also sports a new tab titled Controls.

5. **Drag the Viewer Controls tab outside of the Viewer so that it opens in its own window (see Figure 10-2).**

   This new Controls tab window lets you type text and edit it, but the Video tab in the Viewer is where you see what the text actually looks like while you finesse it. By dragging the Controls tab outside of the Viewer (so that it's in its own window), you can tweak the text and see it displayed in the Viewer's Video tab at the same time.

6. **On the Controls tab (now in its own window) replace the SAMPLE TEXT and make changes to your text.**

To do so, highlight SAMPLE TEXT in the Text field on the Controls tab window and replace it with your own text. For example, you may want to type **The End**.

Figure 10-2:
You can
change
attributes
for the Text
generator
on the
Controls tab
of the
Viewer
window.

7. **Tweak the other settings on the Controls tab if you want.**

   The other settings in the Text generator Controls tab work like a basic word processor. For example, you can change the font by using the Font pop-up menu. You can also change the location where your text appears on-screen by clicking the Origins cross hair in the Controls tab. Your mouse pointer becomes a cross-hair symbol, and then you can click your mouse somewhere in the Viewer window to reposition your text at that spot. See the section "Understanding the options on the Controls tab" for details on modifying these settings and many more.

   Unfortunately, the Achilles heel of the standard Final Cut Express Text generator is that it doesn't let you apply different settings to different parts of the text. All the text has to be the same font, size, and style. If you need more flexibility, see the sidebar, "Let Boris turbocharge your titles," later in this chapter.

   When you make changes, you should see them reflected in the Viewer Video tab. If not, click the Viewer window once, and this should wake it up so that it shows changes while you make them. Then go back to the Controls tab window and tweak away!

8. **Change the duration of the generator's text.**

   By default, all generators create a clip of text that lasts for ten seconds (after you add to the generator's text to your Timeline). If you want to change this setting, highlight the timecode in the Duration field (located in the upper-left side of the Viewer Video tab) and type a new duration, such as **5:00** for a duration of five seconds. Of course, after you place your text on the Timeline, you also can adjust the text clip's length by dragging its edges, just like any other media clip.

9. **Move the generator's text to the Timeline to superimpose it over an existing video clip or to make the text appear over a black background:**

   • **Superimposed over video:** If you want to superimpose the text clip over a video clip (to display the name of a person who's currently on camera, for example), first move your video clip to the Timeline, making sure that the Timeline playhead is over this clip. Next, drag the generator's text from the Viewer to the Canvas window and then select the Superimpose option from the Edit Overlay that appears over the Canvas. The Superimpose edit places the text in a new video track, above your video clip. What's more, Final Cut Express automatically adjusts the duration of your text to match that of the underlying video clip. Figure 10-3 shows a Text clip superimposed in the Timeline over a video clip.

   • **Black background:** If you want the text to appear over a black background (for instance, if you're designing an opening title card), you can drag the text from the Viewer Video tab down to a video track in the Timeline.

Figure 10-3: A Text generator clip on the Timeline by itself creates a title card. When placed on top of another clip on the Timeline, the Text generator clip is superimposed.

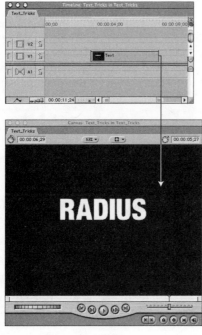
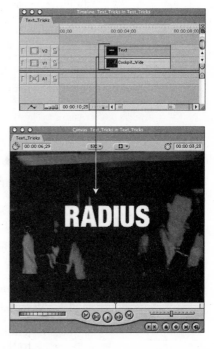

10. **If necessary, render the text and play it on the Timeline.**

    If Final Cut Express is set up for real-time previews of effects (see Chapter 17 for more), you won't have to render the text to play it. If you see a thin, red bar drawn over the Text generator clip in the Timeline, the text clip does need rendering, and you need to select the Text generator clip on the Timeline and then choose Sequence⇨Render Selection. After Express completes the rendering, place the playhead just before the Text generator clip in the Timeline and press the space bar to play through the text.

    If Final Cut Express is set up to show real-time previews of text without rendering, the Timeline will show a thin, green bar over the text clip. The text quality that you see playing from the Timeline may seem a bit soft or otherwise rough because Express is showing you a lower resolution preview of the text. When you finally print the movie to tape or export it to a QuickTime digital file (see Chapters 15 and 16), Express will render the text. To see how clearly the text clip will appear when really rendered, just select it on the Timeline and choose Sequence⇨Render Selection.

11. **Make further adjustments to the text generator by double-clicking it on the Timeline.**

    Like any clip, the generator opens in the Viewer window, and you use its now-familiar Controls tab to make tweaks.

After altering any of the text generators, you can drag the text from the Viewer Video tab back to the Browser and rename it the same way that you rename any old clip. (This way, you have a copy of the clip to apply elsewhere in the project.) Later, you can drag this text as many times as you like into the Timeline. This tip is handy when you need to reuse the same title more than once.

Understanding the options on the Controls tab

After you open any text generator in the Viewer window (see a rundown of different generators in the section "Touring the text generators"), the Controls tab appears in the Viewer. On the Controls tab, you can find the various options that you can tweak for that text generator.

Discussing each setting for every text generator is beyond the scope of a *For Dummies* book, but that's okay because many of the controls are common among all the generators, and they're pretty intuitive as well. The following list outlines some of the most common settings that you see when using the Final Cut Express text generators:

✔ **Text:** The Text pane in all text generators contains the text SAMPLE TEXT by default. To add your own text, highlight the default text and then type the new text that you require. Some text generators, such as Lower 3rd, have two separate areas for text entry: one for the top line and one for the bottom.

✔ **Font:** Select the font from the drop-down list. Final Cut Express uses all the TrueType fonts loaded in your system. (Again, if you have Adobe PostScript fonts installed on your Mac, you won't be able to use 'em in Express. Sorry.) After you select a font from this list, the Text pane updates the font to show you what the font looks like.

✔ **Size:** To select the font size, click in the Size text box and then type the size (in points). By the way, you can also use the slider to change the font size.

✔ **Style:** Use the drop-down list to select the style that works for your project. Options include Plain, Bold, Italic, and Bold/Italic. Italicizing a font is generally not a good idea for video because it can create flickering on the screen.

✔ **Color:** The color pane offers really cool features, as you can tell by the detail of the color options shown in Figure 10-4. (Refer to Figure 10-2 to see where the Color pane is on the Controls tab.)

Click triangle to reveal HSB sliders

Eyedropper for color selection

Hue direction

Color swatch

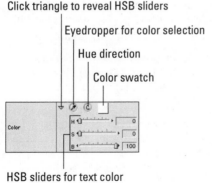

Figure 10-4:
The Color pane of the Controls tab.

HSB sliders for text color

You have three ways to select the color of your text:

• **Eyedropper:** The Eyedropper button is right next to the little drop-down triangle. Clicking the Eyedropper button changes the cursor to an eyedropper. Click anywhere in the Canvas window with this Eyedropper tool to select any color that you like from the video displayed in the Canvas. Presto! The color selection is now in the color swatch to the right of the Eyedropper button back on the Controls tab. And Final Cut Express applies this selection to the text.

- **Color Picker:** Click the small, square color swatch located to the right of the Eyedropper tool, and the Color Picker wheel opens. The Color Picker displays many small squares of various colors. You can click any color to select it. The Color Picker also displays the RGB values for the selected color. (*RGB values* are numeric descriptions of color relating to the amounts of red, green, and blue in that color.) You can modify any of the preset colors by fiddling with their values. If you happen to know exactly what the values are for the color that you want, you can type them in the Color Picker. When you're finished in the Color Picker, click OK to close it.

- **Hue, Saturation, Brightness:** Not enough options for you yet? Click the little triangle text to the Eyedropper tool, and down drops a menu with the HSB sliders. The *H* stands for Hue (or tint), *S* for Saturation (the intensity of a color), and *B* for brightness. Changing these sliders changes the color of the small color swatch and gives you direct feedback about your color choices. Close the menu by clicking the triangle.

✔ **Spacing or Tracking:** *Spacing* refers to the space between the letters. When you drag the slider to the right, the spacing between the letters in a word increases. Be careful, however, because you don't have to move the slider so far that your audience can no longer make sense of the words crawling across the screen. Note that for tight spacing, you can type negative numbers in the text box to the right of the slider. Some headline fonts bunch up when you use negative values.

✔ **Leading:** Leading controls the space between lines of text. You can type a percentage or use the slider to affect this setting. The higher the percentage, the bigger the space between lines of text.

✔ **Origin or Center:** You can set exactly where text appears on-screen (lower-right corner, upper-left, and so on). Click the cross hair in the Controls tab, and the mouse pointer becomes a cross-hair symbol. Click the mouse anywhere in the Viewer Video tab (where you can see your text) to position the text at that point. (Final Cut Express centers it at the point.) You can also offset text horizontally and vertically, respectively, by typing values (positive and negative) in the two text boxes to the right of the Origin cross hair.

✔ **Location:** You can choose where you want the text to appear on-screen. The higher the number, the lower the text is on the screen.

✔ **Direction:** In the case of a Crawl generator, select either Left or Right from the drop-down list. Left means that the crawl heads for the left side of the screen, which is almost always the best option. A crawl that heads right makes your audience go nuts. In the case of a Scroll, the choices in the Direction menu are Up or Down, which indicate whether the text scrolls up or down.

✔ **Auto Kerning:** Kinda sounds like the name of a World War I field general, doesn't it? When you turn on Auto Kerning by selecting this check box, the general lines up the characters in an automatic and precise way so that they're all nice and tidy. Some fonts don't respond well to the general's commands, so sometimes you may just want to send him packing.

Note that the Auto Kerning setting affects the Spacing setting as well. If you have the Auto Kerning setting selected, you can use the Spacing slider. Turning off the Auto Kerning setting causes the font to use its default spacing, and the Spacing slider has no effect.

Touring the text generators

Again, Final Cut Express offers a number of text generators with different characteristics, purposes, and features to appreciate (and some hazards to watch out for as well). Some of these may be handy; others, you'll never touch. The following sections give you a rundown of all the text generators available in Express and what their features and benefits are.

Crawl

The Crawl generator in Final Cut Express produces a line of text that moves horizontally across the screen. It emerges like a ticker tape from the side of the screen. In this generator, you also select the font, size, style, spacing, color, and vertical location of the text.

✔ **Typical use:** Having text crawl is a common device on TV news to warn viewers of breaking news. This consists of just a single line of text crawling across the bottom of the screen from right to left.

✔ **Feature notes:** You can do virtually anything with the Crawl text generator, including all the usual text variations. You can also use it with the myriad of filters, such as drop shadow and blur.

If you installed the Boris Calligraphy generators from your Final Cut Express CD, you'll also have a supercharged Text Crawl generator available called Title Crawl. It's better than the standard Express Crawl generator in that you can apply a deflicker treatment to text, and you can also easily set a Mask that lets the text crawl across only part of the screen instead of the whole thing. The Boris generator also enables you to set a Blend value, which makes text appear to gently fade in and fade out while it crawls on and off the screen.

Let Boris turbocharge your titles

Final Cut Express also ships with two bonus text generators that can turbocharge your titles. The generators are called Title 3D and Title Crawl by a company called BorisFX, and you can choose to install them from your Final Cut Express CD. If you've installed them already, you can find them in the Effects window Video Generators bin. If you don't see them there, dig up your Final Cut Express CD, load the installer program, and look for an option to install Boris Calligraphy plug-ins.

Both of these generators give you more control over titles, but the Title 3D generator really steals the show. For starters, it enables you to mix and match fonts, sizes, and styles in a single title (see the figure in this sidebar), which is something that you can't do with the Final Cut Express default Text generator. For instance, you might have the movie title in a big, bold 90 point font but its subtitle in italics 50 point and its copyright text way at the bottom in lil' ol' 12 point. What's more, the Title 3D generator enables you to do such crazy and downright unnatural things to text that you're bound to break the law in some states.

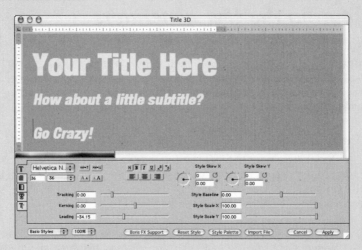

You can spin, skew, scale (separately on X- and Y-axis) and "tumble" letters or words. You can customize drop shadows with five unique parameters. You can set margins for text wrapping. You can design the kind of outline that appears around text and apply a slew of predesigned styles to text. (For instance, a USA style fills text with a color gradient that goes from red to white to blue.) The Title 3D generator also has a nice Deflicker feature that can help minimize the glow that you'll see on TV text, especially at smaller sizes.

Anyway, I recommend exploring the Title 3D generator if you want to take your titles a bit further than most. You can apply it (or Boris' Title Crawl generator) the same way that you apply all the other Final Cut Express text generators. That is, open the generator in the Viewer, click the Controls tab, type the text, and start fiddling with all the sliders and dials and check boxes that you see. Enjoy!

More handy tips about text generators

Use video filters. You can apply any of the Final Cut Express video filters to a text generator. (For instance, you might add a Wind Blur filter to text to make it seem out of focus.) See Chapter 12 for more about filters and how to apply them to clips, including generators, because hey! they're clips, too.

Animate text. You can animate text (make it grow bigger and smaller or move all over the place) by using some settings found in the Final Cut Express Motion tab and its motion keyframes.

See Chapter 14 for how to animate clips, including the text generators.

Use only TrueType fonts. Final Cut Express works only with fonts in the TrueType format. Mac OS X already ships with a lot of TrueType fonts built in, but thousands of fonts in the PostScript format (also known as Type 1) won't work. The good news is that if you have a PostScript font that you just have to use, you can get a shareware program like TransType (www.fontlab.com), which will convert fonts from one format to another (even between Macs and PCs).

Lower 3rd

As the name of this text generator suggests, it enables you to draw two lines of text in the lower-third portion of the screen. Like in most other text generators, you can select all aspects of the type, including the font, style, size, tracking, and color.

- ✔ **Typical use:** This text generator displays text that identifies the name and organization of a news feature personality or interviewees in a documentary. This is a common device during news shows in which an interviewee is being identified. Of course, as an alternative, you could also use another text generator and simply change its Origin value to position it anywhere on-screen.

- ✔ **Feature notes:** Using a bit of a drop shadow when using this text effect can make the text stand out from the background image.

Outline Text

The Outline Text generator in Final Cut Express creates an outline around the letters; for example, you can create black text with a white outline or vice versa. It dresses the text for greater on-screen visibility.

- ✔ **Typical use:** Outlining makes text easier to read over a busy background.

- ✔ **Feature notes:** The Outline Text generator has the basic features of text editing software, such as changing the font, the size, and so on. These features make Final Cut Express a tool of choice for creating outlined text. The Express sliders and other tools enable you to create an outline text clip quickly. Best of all, clip controls for text and line graphics enable you to fill either the text or the outline with an image of a clip that you apply, not just a solid color.

Practicing safe text

Home televisions use a cathode ray tube to display the images of a video. Many of these tubes have a slight overscan, where certain items closer to the edges are cropped off and are not seen by the viewer. The overscan on televisions varies from TV to TV. Over the years, engineers have come up with a safety area grid that allows editors to ensure that their text won't be cropped off on some TVs.

The safety area grids are called Title Safe and Action Safe, as shown in the following figure, and they're available to you via the Final Cut Express Overlays. To select an Overlay, click the Video tab in the Viewer. Next choose View⇨Overlays (so that it's turned on) and then choose View⇨Title Safe so that menu option is on, too. You see two aqua-colored rectangles in the Viewer window. The inner rectangle is the Title Safe grid; do not lay any text outside the edge of this inner rectangle. The outer grid is the Action Safe grid; do not place any action of importance outside the outer rectangle. In short, when shooting a video, don't place the most critical element outside the Action Safe grid; otherwise, many home viewers may never see the critical element.

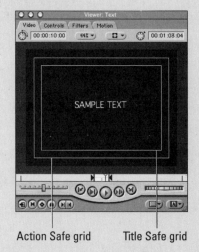

Action Safe grid   Title Safe grid

When laying out any titles in Final Cut Express, be sure to have these Overlays turned on and make sure that no text is laid outside the Title Safe grid.

Oh, and one more thing: If you like working with Title Safe Overlays, you can also apply them to the Canvas window. Just select the Canvas and follow the same steps above for turning on the Overlays.

Scrolling Text

The Scrolling Text generator creates titles that run bottom to top as if on a scroll. You can also flip-flop them to run from the top down.

✔ **Typical use:** Scrolling is commonly used for displaying credits at the end of a video.

✔ **Feature notes:** The length of the clip to which you apply this text effect determines how fast the text goes by. When you have long text credits but the generator that you place on the Timeline is only a few seconds long, the credits flash by. When you have only a few text credits but the credit's generator lasts a minute on the Timeline, the credits go by really slowly. You have to experiment with the amount of text and the length of the text's clip before you find what works in your project. Layout, spacing, type style, font, and even the color influence the effectiveness and legibility of the scroll. You have control over all these and more in this Final Cut Express text generator.

Text

I cover this generator earlier in this chapter, so you're probably familiar with it. For starters, the Text generator creates static text in the center of the screen. (You can adjust the generator's Origin value to move it later to anywhere else in the screen.) Like a full-featured word processing or a good drawing program, this text generator enables you to control virtually everything about the text, such as the font, size, and color of your text. The only real limitation is you can't mix and match fonts, sizes, or styles together — whatever settings you have affect all the text in the generator. If this text generator is too limiting, see the sidebar "Let Boris turbocharge your titles" in this chapter.

- ✔ **Typical use:** The Text generator creates text on-screen between scenes, like in those reruns of *Law & Order* or *The X-Files*.

- ✔ **Feature notes:** You can get beautiful, detailed text by using the Subpixel feature. (Refer to Figure 10-2 to see this setting in the Controls tab.) The Subpixel feature in this text generator calculates the text drawing down to a very minute and refined (hence *subpixel*) level. This type of calculation is important if the text needs a polished, refined look. The text takes longer to render when the Subpixel feature is enabled, but it's worth it. Don't miss the Use Subpixel check box, which is at the bottom of the Controls tab and easy to overlook. The default view leaves the check box hidden at the bottom of the Controls tab.

Typewriter

Although typewriters have become boat anchors and doorstops for most people, they're still the perfect metaphor for words presented one letter at a time. That's what this little generator does; it creates one letter at a time any way that you want.

- ✔ **Typical use:** This text generator mimics an old Teletype by displaying a tape and a letter at a time on the screen or splattering letters and words in a wave. Maybe you're doing a *film noir* detective film set in 1939 Los Angeles, and you want to indicate the time and place in a style evocative of the time period. You can do it with Typewriter text generator. Keep in mind that getting carried away with this generator can kill readability.

- ✔ **Feature notes:** When used, the Typewriter text generator defaults to a timing of ten seconds. The text that you type in the text generator takes ten seconds to type onto the screen. Be aware that when you first apply this generator, you don't see any text. You have to play the effect to see the text type. Press the space bar to play the Typewriter text generator in the Viewer window.

Creating titles on colored backgrounds

If you add a text generator to the Timeline without superimposing it on another clip, the text will appear against a black background (refer to Figure 10-3). If you want to change the color of text's background, you can use another generator called Color to create a *matte*:

1. **Open the Effects window.**

   You can choose Windows⇨Effects or click the Effects tab in the Browser window.

2. **Open the Video Generators bin and then open the Matte sub-bin.**

3. **Double-click the generator called Color to open it in the Viewer.**

4. **Set the generator's color, which will be used the text's background.**

   Click the Viewer Controls tab and use the color controls to set the color that you want.

5. **Move the generator from the Viewer to the Timeline.**

   Clicking the Viewer Video tab and then dragging the generator directly to the Timeline is a quick approach. By doing this, you're creating a colored matte on the Timeline. (The matte just displays a single color on-screen.)

6. **Move a text clip (containing the title that you want) to a track directly above the matte that you just placed on the Timeline.**

   You're basically superimposing the title on top of the colored matte. Refer to Figure 10-3 for a view of how the two clips look on the Timeline. Make sure that the text uses a color that works well with the color of the matte. You can change the text color by following steps outlined earlier in the section "Understanding the options on the Controls tab."

7. **If necessary, render the two clips on the Timeline to see how they look.**

   Select one of the clips and then choose Sequence⇨Render Selection.

Instead of superimposing the text over a solid color matte generator, you could use a different generator, such as Gradient or maybe Custom Gradient, to create colored backgrounds that involve a range of custom colors instead of just one solid color. You can find these generators in the Final Cut Express Effects window, in the Video Generators bin, and then in that nested Render bin.

Building Your Collection of Custom Titles

When you create titles, you'll probably find instances where you want to start collecting your favorite ones so that you can easily apply the same kind of title to different projects as time goes by. Start by creating a new Final Cut

Express project, and name it something like *Favorite Titles*. Now, when you generate a title that you might want to save for later use, copy and paste it from the Timeline into your new Favorite Titles project. (You can paste it into the Browser window of this new project, and organize the collection of titles into bins.) This way, when you decide to use a favorite title, you can just open up this Favorite Titles project and then copy and paste the desired title clip into whatever new project you happen to be working in. (Again, you can paste into the new project's Browser window or straight to its Timeline.)

Using Titles and Text Created Outside Final Cut Express

You can create titles and text in other programs and import that text into Final Cut Express. However, overlaying such text over video (where the video will be seen behind the text) can create special circumstances and needs.

Many software packages are available that can help you design cool type treatments, and an entire library of books has been written on creating and manipulating images in these various programs. But one product, Adobe Photoshop, is recognized as the leader in this field, letting you do some incredible things with type (and logos, not to mention images and graphics of any sort) that you could never do with Final Cut Express alone. The details of working in Photoshop are outside the scope of this book. Refer to *Photoshop 7 For Dummies*, by Deke McClelland and Barbara Obermeier (Wiley Publishing, Inc.) for an excellent guide for learning the many features in Photoshop.

Working with Photoshop and Final Cut Express

Photoshop and Final Cut Express work well together, but they're still different applications. When you move between the two, you may experience some bumps along the way. Remember these important points about creating files in Photoshop and bringing them into Express:

✔ **Pixel type:** DV video (the Final Cut Express native format) uses rectangular *pixels* to describe an image (remember, DV uses 720 horizontal pixels and 480 vertical pixels to describe a frame of NTSC video), whereas photo and graphics programs, such as Photoshop, use square pixels. This means that even though you create an image in Photoshop that's 720 x 480 pixels (perhaps to fill a full video frame), when you import it into Final Cut, it will look distorted because Express takes those 720 x 480 pixels and converts them into DV's rectangular pixels, whereas the image was initially designed with square pixels. Don't worry, though: There's a fix for this, and I talk about it in a moment.

✔ **Colors:** DV video doesn't work well with certain colors that you might create in Photoshop, rendering those colors in a way that makes them appear too bright or washed out. Fortunately, Photoshop will display a yellow exclamation icon (!) in its Color Picker when the color that you select exceeds the video spectrum that's safe for DV. When selecting colors in Photoshop, avoid this warning by toning down the colors.

✔ **Editablility:** Final Cut Express can't change text and images imported into it from Photoshop. To edit them, you must open the original files in Photoshop, edit, and then reimport them into Express.

Preparing Photoshop text for Final Cut Express

This section outlines how to prepare text files created in Adobe Photoshop that are headed for a DV project in Final Cut Express. While you go through these steps, bear in mind that the frame size for DV is 720 x 480 pixels. But in Adobe Photoshop, you need to start out working with an image size of 720 x 534 pixels. You need this odd size to prevent Photoshop images (which use those square pixels) from becoming distorted when you import them into Express (which, thanks to the DV format, uses rectangular pixels).

The following provides you with steps and tips for bringing text created in Photoshop into Final Cut Express:

1. **Create the text as an image in Photoshop (refer to *Photoshop 7 For Dummies* if you need help).**

   The image should have the following dimensions: a width of 720 pixels, a height of 534 pixels, and a resolution of 72 pixels per inch.

2. **When you're finished with your creation, save the file.**

   Make sure that you save the file as a Photoshop file, with the .psd extension. In the Save As dialog box, you can choose Photoshop from the Format pop-up menu.

3. **Make a copy with the same name as the original but add *version 2* or *import* to the filename.**

   You can make a copy by choosing File➪Save As in Photoshop. By entering a different name than the original file, you're creating a copy. Again, make sure you're saving as a Photoshop file with the .psd extension.

4. **Working with the image copy, choose Image⇨Image Size.**

   The Image Size dialog box opens.

5. **Deselect the Constrain Proportions check box.**

6. **In the Pixel Dimensions area, change the height from 534 pixels to 480.**

   Remember these numbers; you need them every time that you want to prepare a text in Adobe Photoshop for use in Final Cut Express.

   Figure 10-5 shows the Photoshop file before and after the height change. The O's appear distorted, but importing them into Final Cut Express corrects the distortion automatically.

Before the size change, the Os are okay.   After the size change, the Os look distorted.

Figure 10-5:
Before and after shots show that text prepared for Express looks distorted.

7. **Be sure to select Resample Image.**

   Whoa! Someone flattened the image! But rest assured that's just the way it should look to look good in Final Cut Express.

8. **To make sure that the colors in the Photoshop image will look good in video, choose Filter⇨Video⇨NTSC.**

9. **Save the file.**

   Again, make sure that the file is saved with a Photoshop extension (.psd). If not, do another Save As to add this extension to the name.

10. **Open the Final Cut Express project that will receive the Photoshop file.**

11. **In Final Cut Express, choose File⇨Import⇨Files and then locate the Photoshop file.**

12. **In the Choose a File dialog box, select the Photoshop file and then click Choose.**

The Photoshop file is imported into the Final Cut Express Browser. Use this Photoshop still as a clip anywhere in the Timeline. Final Cut Express automatically compensates for the distortion that you created in the text, and the text appears correctly proportioned.

Chapter 11

Audio Excellence

· ·

· ·

A udio is one of the most devalued and underestimated aspects of film-making. Video is a visual medium, so it's easy to get excited about great shots and well-edited sequences, whereas recording and editing good audio aren't nearly as "sexy." And yet audio can significantly affect the ultimate impact your movie — mediocre audio (such as uneven volume levels or distortion and hiss) is the quickest way to make a video seem amateurish.

Fortunately, Final Cut Express gives you plenty of latitude for designing a quality audio experience. You can set the volume levels for just a clip, part of a clip, or even a part of a frame of a clip. By selectively setting volume, you can mix all the audio elements of your movie — that is, multiple dialogue tracks, music, and sound effects — so that they all blend smoothly together. This process ensures that no one element overpowers the other unless you want it to. Additionally, by setting a clip volume with super-precision (by increments as small as $\frac{1}{100}$ of a frame), you can edit out minor distortions (such as the occasional pop of a microphone) or obvious audio annoyances (such as actors breathing excessively or someone's cell phone ringing on set while the camera's rolling).

You can also use audio transitions to smooth cuts from one audio clip to another, just like you use a Cross Dissolve video transition to gracefully blend one video clip into another. See Chapter 9 for more on dissolves.

You can even use audio filters to add special effects to the audio, such as echoes or distortion, or to enhance the dynamic range of like the audio. These filters can also help you cut out unwanted noise, the hum of a noisy camera on set, or the dull murmur of traffic on the street outside.

I cover a variety of audio issues throughout the previous chapters of this book. If you want to revisit some key audio topics, try these:

- ✔ **Chapter 2:** Establishing the sequence audio settings with Easy Setup

- ✔ **Chapter 3:** Capturing audio (along with video) from a DV camera or tape deck

- ✔ **Chapter 4:** Importing different audio files (and converting audio into formats that work best with Final Cut)

- ✔ **Chapter 6:** Opening and editing audio clips in the Viewer and Timeline windows

- ✔ **Chapter 6:** Getting audio out of and back into sync

- ✔ **Chapter 7:** Creating, managing, and deleting audio tracks on the Timeline

- ✔ **Chapter 8:** Using split edits to edit audio separately from its associated video clip

In this chapter, I focus on some important topics that I don't cover elsewhere.

Understanding Stereo and Mono Audio

Final Cut Express can work with mono or stereo audio clips, but what's the difference between the two? Mono audio came of age in the early days when radios, record players, and televisions used just a single speaker. In the stereo world of today, audio plays through *two* speakers (a left and a right speaker), and elements of the overall audio play differently on either one (louder on one speaker, softer on the other). The result is that stereo audio sounds much fuller and richer than mono because stereo has more of a 3-D spatial quality.

Final Cut Express can work with audio clips recorded in mono or stereo. Both mono and stereo clips appear as a single clip in the Browser window, but Express treats them a bit differently when you move them to the Timeline:

- ✔ **Mono:** A mono audio clip is referred to as *one channel;* in Final Cut Express, it occupies only one audio track on the Timeline.

- ✔ **Stereo:** A stereo audio clip is referred to as *two channels;* in Express, it takes up two Timeline tracks. Final Cut Express places the left and right channel of the clip on separate Timeline tracks, as shown in Figure 11-1.

You don't have to tell Final Cut Express specifically whether you're working with mono clips or stereo clips — it can figure that out for itself.

Figure 11-1:
A mono
clip versus
stereo
clips on the
Timeline.

Paired audio track labels

A stereo clip takes up two tracks.

A mono clip takes up one track on the Timeline.

When you import stereo audio to the Timeline, the two clips that make up the audio are referred to as *stereo audio pairs*. Final Cut Express links these two, paired clips together, and they essentially act as one — that is, moving, resizing, or cutting one has the same effect on the other. If you ever want to break the link these paired clips share, just select them on the Timeline and choose Modify➪Stereo Pair. For example, you may want to apply an effect like a pan to just one mono clip from the stereo pair — more on panning in the section, "Changing Pan and Spread," later in this chapter.

Capturing and Maintaining High-Quality Audio

Express lets you tweak audio in all sorts of ways, but the quality of the audio quality is largely determined before you do any of this. For the most part, the battle for good audio is won or lost when you actually record it (or mix it), so here are a few tips to help you record audio that sounds top-notch . . . and keep it that way:

> ✔ **Find a good microphone.** When shooting audio with a DV camera, I seriously, seriously suggest buying or renting a separate microphone for the camera (built in camera mics often pick up the hum of your camera gears and electronics). Even buying a consumer add-on model (typically $50–$100), which sits directly on your camera, can significantly improve the audio that you get from the internal mics on most cameras. Also, if you're recording audio outdoors, you can minimize the sound of wind and other background noise by getting a "wind sock" for the microphone.

✔ **Always work with high-quality audio.** Whether you're capturing audio from CDs or videotapes or getting digital files from a composer or sound designer, keep the audio in a high-quality format. Audio that's recorded at settings of 48 kHz, 16-bit stereo is as good as you can get, but 32 kHz, 16-bit will do fine as well. Fortunately, DV cameras and decks, as well as dedicated audio gear, can deliver one or the other of these formats, but just make sure that you've set them to record or capture at these levels (and that you have set the Easy Setup of your project to accommodate these audio levels — see Chapter 2 for more).

✔ **Get a good pair of headphones.** If you can't design and mix audio in a studio that has high-grade speaker systems and good room acoustics, a great, relatively inexpensive alternative is to buy a good pair of headphones. You can find them for about $100, and they make a big difference.

If you've set a Timeline sequence to work with 48 kHz audio, the sequence can also accept clips at 44.1 kHz (or vice versa). But if you bring in audio that's significantly different from the sequence settings (for example, if you import a 32 kHz audio clip into a 48 kHz sequence), Final Cut Express may play those clips with distortion.

Rendering Audio

You may run into a few instances (or many, depending on your project) where Final Cut Express can't play the audio until you've rendered it. Rendering is necessary when Express doesn't have the processing power to play an audio clip in real time, so you have to let Express calculate how the clip should sound before actually playing it. You may have to render the audio in these instances:

✔ If you import audio that's been compressed (for instance, with an audio codec such as IMA or MACE), you have to render the audio first. (See Chapter 2 for more about compression codecs.) Fortunately, you're not likely to come across compressed audio too often unless you're downloading it from the Internet.

✔ If you add an audio filter to a clip, you have to render the clip before hearing the filter effects.

✔ If the Timeline sequence tries to play several audio clips *at the same time* (that is, clips that are stacked together on different tracks), your Mac may not have the processing power to keep up, so you'll have to render the clips first.

You know that audio needs rendering when Final Cut Express plays a series of beeps instead of whatever you're expecting to hear. (You also see a red, horizontal line drawn over the clip in the Timeline Render status bar, as shown in Figure 11-2.) To render that audio, just select it on the Timeline and then choose Sequence⇨Render Selection (or press ⌘+R).

A red line indicates that
a clip needs rendering

Figure 11-2:
The Timeline
Render
status bar.

Setting Volume Levels

When you import an audio clip, Final Cut Express sets its volume at 0 decibels, but you can change that level to as high as 12 decibels (louder) and as low as –60 decibels (dead silence). You can make these changes either in the Viewer window or directly on the Timeline. Which route should you take? It's a matter of preference, but in general, using the Viewer is easier for fine-tuning audio (for instance, if you're setting lots of precise keyframes). Using the Timeline is usually quickest, however, and it also lets you see the volume of a clip relative to all the other clips around it.

When you're setting the decibel level of a clip in Final Cut Express, you should know that the decibel values are all relative from clip to clip — that is, just because you set two clips at the same decibel level *doesn't* mean that they actually play at the same volume. That's because clip volume actually depends on two factors:

✔ The decibel level used in the original recording of the clip (by a microphone, or a composer's or sound editor's computer, and so on)

✔ The decibel level that you set for the clip when you bring it into Final Cut Express

It may seem strange that Final Cut Express sets a clip at 0 decibels of volume when you first import it (zero, it seems, should mean silence), but that actually means Express plays the clip at the volume level used in its original recording without adding or taking away any decibels. That's why clips that have the same decibel value (zero or any other value) may still not play at equal volumes.

Changing audio clip volumes in the Viewer

When you adjust audio clip volume in the Viewer, you can set a new level for an entire clip or for just a part of it, thanks to keyframes.

The highs and lows of dynamic range

When you set the volume levels for audio clips (dialogue, music, effects, and so on), you're establishing the *dynamic range* of the soundtrack — that is, the range between the softest and loudest volumes used in your movie.

Dynamic ranges vary widely, depending on the content: For example, a couple arguing and then reconciling could go from yells to whispers — a wide dynamic range. On the other hand, your garden-variety heavy metal rock anthem probably has a more narrow range because it's likely to blare from start to finish.

Make sure that the dynamic range gives your content the room it needs but without getting too extreme. A good test for range is to play the soundtrack on whatever TV or computer sound system that you believe most of your audience has. Usually aim for modest equipment instead of sexy top-of-the-line sound hardware that few people can afford. Also, if you intend to compress the soundtrack so that your movie can play over the Internet or on CD-ROM, export a test track of the audio using whatever compression codec that the final product will use and then test that sample dynamic range. (See Chapter 16 for more on exporting your movies.) If the audio sounds clear and you don't need to adjust volume while listening to it (turning up soft parts or turning down the loud ones), you're in good shape. But if you hear sound distortions (usually a sign of things getting too loud) or you can't hear some parts, you need to narrow the range by finding the troublesome audio and adjusting its volume. (You can also apply some audio filters for greater control — see the "Exploring Audio Filters" section in this chapter.)

Changing the volume for an entire clip

To change the volume for an entire clip, follow these steps:

1. **Open the audio clip in the Viewer window.**

   You can double-click the audio clip from the Browser window or from the Timeline if you've already placed the clip there.

   Either way, the Viewer displays the clip as an audio waveform. If your audio clip is already linked with a video clip, you may have to click the Viewer Audio tab to see the waveform.

2. **Change the clip volume in one of three ways (as shown in Figure 11-3):**

   • Drag the Level slider left or right.

   • Type a new decibel value in the Viewer Level text box (anywhere between –60 and 12 will do) and then press Return.

   • Click and drag the red Level Overlay line up or down.

Changing the volume for part of a clip

You can change the volume in only part of a clip instead of the whole enchilada. You may want to use this technique to do things like briefly lower your music's volume so that a key line of dialogue can be heard more clearly. To do this, you'll set *keyframes* within your audio clip, which are like little markers that define a different volume level for your clip at that point. You set a keyframe in your clip, give that keyframe a volume level, and then set another keyframe elsewhere in the clip and give that keyframe a different volume. The result is that while Final Cut Express plays your audio clip, it smoothly increases or fades the clip's volume across the range of keyframes that you set. Follow these steps to try this technique:

1. **Open the audio clip in the Viewer.**

2. **Position the Viewer playhead on the frame where you want the volume change to begin.**

You're often likely to set keyframes on or near noticeable events in the audio (such as a beat of music, a pop of a microphone, or an unusually quiet moment). You can pinpoint these events by studying the clip's audio *waveform*, which is a visual representation of the clip's loud and soft moments. Spikes in the waveform indicate loudness, and dips indicate quiet moments.

Sometimes the waveform will seem so compressed (its lines will be scrunched together) that you can't really make out its detail, making it hard to place a keyframe on the perfect frame. To increase the waveform detail (effectively stretching it out across the Viewer window), just drag the Zoom control to the left (check out Figure 11-4). On the other hand, you can shrink the view of the waveform (to see more of it at once in the Viewer) by dragging the slider to the right.

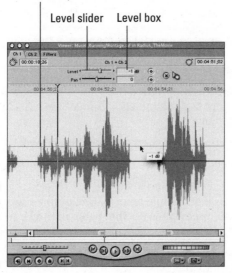

Level Overlay

Level slider   Level box

Figure 11-3:
An audio
clip in the
Viewer.

3. **Place a keyframe by clicking the Insert/Delete Keyframe button in the Viewer, as shown in Figure 11-4.**

   You can also press Control+K (for keyframe) on your keyboard. Either way, Final Cut Express places a volume keyframe at that frame of audio, setting the volume to the current volume level of the clip.

Reset Keyframes button

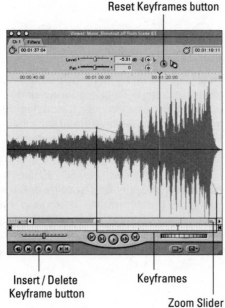

Figure 11-4:
Setting
keyframes
in the
Viewer.

Insert / Delete   Keyframes
Keyframe button
                       Zoom Slider

4. **Move the Viewer playhead to the last frame where the volume change should end.**

   For instance, if you want to smoothly dip the volume from 0 decibels to –20 decibels across 90 frames, move the Viewer playhead 90 frames ahead to the frame where the volume should finally reach –20 decibels and therefore stop dipping.

5. **Set a keyframe at that point and then set its volume level.**

   Remember that you need at least two keyframes to change a clip's volume over time.

   Again, you can set keyframe volume level by one of three ways: Drag the Level slider left or right, type a new decibel value in the Level text box, or drag the Level Overlay line up or down.

   In the Viewer, you can see the Level Overlay rise or fall from the first to the second keyframe that you set.

6. **Play the clip to listen to the volume change.**

   You can listen to the audio clip right in the Viewer, of course. But you may want to go back to the Timeline and play the clip from there so that you can listen to it while watching your movie's video and also hear any other audio that may be on the Timeline. This gives you a good idea of how your volume change works with other elements in the movie.

   You can also set keyframes in the Viewer by selecting the Pen tool in the Final Cut Express Tool palette and clicking at any point on the clip Level Overlay. Use this quick way to set many keyframes.

   If you want to fine-tune your work, you can go back to the Viewer and set more keyframes or adjust the ones that you already set.

Moving, changing, and deleting keyframes

Final Cut Express makes it easy to change keyframes that you've already placed. With the keyframed audio clip open in the Viewer, try the following:

✔ **Change a keyframe Level value (making it louder or softer):** Click and drag the Keyframe icon (the little diamond symbol on the clip Level Overlay) either up or down to increase or decrease its value, respectively. While you drag, watch the keyframe value change in the Viewer Level text box (refer to Figure 11-4). Just be careful not to accidentally drag the keyframe left or right because this will change the keyframe's location in time.

✔ **Set a new volume level for two adjacent keyframes:** Click and drag the Level Overlay line between the two keyframes up or down.

✔ **Move a keyframe forward or back in time so that it affects volume earlier or later in the clip:** Click and drag the Keyframe icon to the left or right.

✔ **Delete a keyframe altogether:** Option+click (hold down the Option key and click) an existing Keyframe icon. (The mouse pointer changes to a pen symbol.)

Subframe editing in the Viewer

You can set keyframes even more precisely within an audio clip — instead of setting keyframes frame by frame in the Viewer — you can set them every $\frac{1}{100}$ of a frame! This kind of precision is helpful if you want to edit out little pops that you may hear every once in a while. (Such sounds often occur at the In or Out points when you cut from one clip to another.) You can correct these little hiccups by setting keyframes around them and dropping the volume level for those keyframes:

1. **With the clip open in the Viewer, magnify the view of the audio waveform as much as Final Cut Express allows.**

You can use the Viewer Zoom slider, Zoom control, or the shortcut ⌘++ (⌘ and the plus key) to magnify the view.

When you've zoomed in all the way, you see that the Viewer playhead highlights a single frame at a time. A single frame is indicated by the dark shadow of the playhead, as shown in Figure 11-5.

2. **Hold down the Shift key and slowly drag the playhead to the part of the clip waveform that indicates a pop.**

   This allows you to move the playhead by fractions of a frame instead of a frame at a time.

3. **Set a few keyframes around the pop and lower their volume levels to silence the pop.**

4. **Follow the steps outlined earlier in "Changing the volume for part of a clip."**

   Four keyframes usually work best, as shown in Figure 11-5.

Subframe keyframe

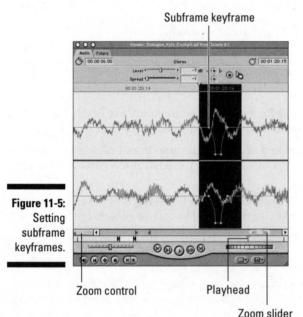

Figure 11-5:
Setting
subframe
keyframes.

Zoom control   Playhead

Zoom slider

Adjusting clip volumes on the Timeline

Sometimes changing clip volumes directly on the Timeline is easier than using the Viewer window (provided that the clips are already on the Timeline).

Clean up audio distortion with audio meters

When you're setting a clip volume, you want to make sure that it never gets loud enough to distort. (Not only does distortion sound bad, but also it can damage your speakers.) Contrary to your first instincts, the best way to measure volume levels is *not* to listen to your audio on nice speakers or headphones because although the audio may sound great on *your* own equipment, it can easily distort on someone else's hardware (computer, television, headphones, or what have you). The best way to gauge a clip or movie volume is to use the Final Cut Express Audio meters (seen in this sidebar's figure). Choose Window➪Audio Meters if your meters aren't already on-screen.

Using those meters is easy. Just play a clip from the Viewer or play your movie from the Timeline, and watch the left and right vertical bars on the meter jump up and down while the audio plays. The bars represent the decibel level of the left and right channels of stereo audio, and if either bar goes into red (that is, reaches about the –3 decibel mark), you know that the audio is distorting. (Again, you may not *hear* it, but it's happening nonetheless!) If you want to check the levels frame by frame, you can just position the playhead on a given frame and check the meter reading.

So, what are you to do if the volume creeps into the red zone? Well, you might first just ignore it. If the bars are just creeping into the red every once in a while, chances are that the distortion occurring won't register on human ears (even though the distortion is technically there). But if the your audio bars are going higher into the red (especially hitting the top 0 mark), here's a simple solution: Lower the volume by moving the clip or movie to a lower decibel level or by using keyframes or audio filters (such as the compressor/limiter filter — see "Exploring Audio Filters") to lower only the spots that peak on the meters. Each method has consequences: By lowering the entire clip/movie volume, you may make already-soft areas *too* soft. On the other hand, if you just lower the volume for the loud parts, you may find that the difference between the soft and loud areas of the audio isn't great enough anymore. (This is a case of shortening the dynamic range — see the nearby sidebar called "The highs and lows of dynamic range.") The route that you ultimately choose is up to you and depends on your priorities.

Although using the Timeline isn't as precise as using the Viewer, it's quick and enables you to more easily match the volume changes to the video:

1. **Click the Clip Overlay button in the Timeline (see Figure 11-6).**

   Final Cut Express shows a thin, horizontal line (called the *level overlay*) through each audio clip on the Timeline. This overlay represents the volume level of each clip — the higher the line is within the clip, the louder the clip plays.

Figure 11-6:
The Clip
Overlay
button helps
you see an
audio clip's
volume on
the Timeline.

Clip Overlay button   Overlay

A pop-up box indicates the decibel level

2. **Use the Selection tool to raise or lower the volume for the entire clip or just part of it.**

   To change the volume for the entire audio clip: Click and drag its Level Overlay line up or down to raise or lower volume, respectively.

   To adjust the volume for only part of the audio clip: Set different keyframes on the clip's level overlay. (See the section "Changing the volume for part of a clip" earlier in this chapter, where I explain the concept behind keyframes.)

   - **Set a keyframe:** To set a keyframe, first make sure that the Final Cut Express Selection tool is active. Then Option-click the audio clip's level overlay (the mouse pointer becomes a pen symbol when Option is held), and Final Cut adds a Keyframe icon at that point on the overlay (the icon looks like a diamond).

   - **Adjust a keyframe:** To adjust a keyframe, click and drag the Keyframe icon on the audio clip level overlay to the left or right in order to change the keyframe location in time or up and down in order to adjust the keyframe volume.

   - **Adjust the volume for two keyframes at once:** You can click the Level Overlay line between two keyframes and move it up or down to adjust the volume for both keyframes at once.

   - **Delete a keyframe:** To delete an unwanted keyframe, Option-click the keyframe. A little minus sign appears next to the pen pointer when it hovers over the keyframe.

Final Cut Express can show the audio waveforms of a clip directly on the Timeline, which helps you set keyframes more precisely (as shown in Figure 11-7). The quickest way to toggle waveforms on and off is to press ⌘+Option+W, but you can also turn waveforms on by choosing

Sequence⇨Settings. If you want to see those waveforms as large and clearly as possible, choose the largest track size by clicking one of the taller bars within the Track Size button on the Timeline (again, as shown in Figure 11-7).

If you try to set volume levels for a stereo audio clip on the Timeline, you may find that you have to set each of the clip's two channels (left and right) separately. (For example, you may set the volume for the part of the clip on the A1 track and then have to set it again for the part of the clip on the A2 track.) This can get annoying and time consuming and lead to inconsistent volume levels between a clip's stereo channels. The solution is to link the stereo clip's two channels together so that they're treated as one. Just select the clip on the Timeline and then choose Modfiy⇨Stereo Pair.

Figure 11-7:
The Time-
line with
waveforms
and key-
frames
displayed.

Track Height button

Drag keyframes on the Timeline to adjust volume

Changing Pan and Spread

If you've never worked with audio before, you may never have heard of *pan* and *spread*. Setting and changing these elements enables you to design a more sophisticated stereo audio experience. You use both pan and spread to move your movie's audio from one speaker to another. For example, imagine editing a scene in which a character speaks offscreen. To make the charac-ter's voice seem to come from the right or left (instead of front-and-center), you can pan the voice clip so it plays on only one speaker or the other. Or imagine that your character's caught in a fierce storm; you can use spread to move howling stereo wind from one speaker to another, thus heightening the sense of movement.

Panning and spreading have similar effects, but controlling spread works only on audio clips that are in stereo, and panning works only on mono clips. If this sounds a bit abstract, don't worry. The next sections explore both pan-ning and spreading in depth.

Spreading that audio around

If an audio clip is in stereo (that is, has left and right channels), you can adjust the *spread*. Adjusting the spread lets you swap the channels — and therefore the speakers — that the stereo pairs play through. For instance, if you want a clip that's playing through the left stereo channel/speaker to play through the right channel/speaker, you adjust its spread.

Changing audio clip spread is easy: Open the clip in the Viewer and use the Spread slider or Spread text box to enter a value between the following three ranges, as shown in Figure 11-8:

✔ The value –1 plays the left channel through the left speaker and the right channel through the right speaker. (This setting is the Final Cut Express default.)

✔ The value 0 plays the left and right channels equally on each speaker. (You're essentially playing the stereo pairs in a mono format because each plays at the same volume on each speaker.)

✔ The value 1 swaps the channels so that the left channel plays on the right speaker and vice versa.

You can enter spread values in very small increments (such as 0.80 or –0.65), which will play an audio channel mostly on one speaker but partially on the other.

From time to time, you may import a stereo audio clip only to notice that it's playing through only one of two stereo speakers. This situation usually means that although the clip is in stereo, no audio data appears in one of its stereo channels. (Maybe the clip was originally recorded in mono and then converted to stereo, or a technical glitch occurred during recording and only one channel was captured.) To fix this, just set the clip spread to 0. Final Cut Express then plays its single working channel on both speakers, making it essentially mono.

Panning left and right

When you're working with a stereo audio clip, you can adjust its spread. When you're working with a mono clip, you can adjust its *pan* — that is, you can play the mono clip equally on both stereo speakers or play louder on one speaker and softer on the other.

A stereo clip opened in the Viewer automatically features a Spread slider, but a mono clip automatically features a Pan slider. To control a clip pan, just open a mono clip in the Viewer and adjust the Pan slider or type a value in the Viewer Pan text box:

  ✔ The value –1 plays the clip on the left speaker only.

  ✔ The value 0 plays the mono clip equally between the left and right
     speakers (that is, with no pan).

  ✔ The value 1 plays the clip on the right speaker only.

Using a value between 0 and 1 or 0 and –1 favors one speaker without playing
completely silently on the other.

Spread slider   Spread box

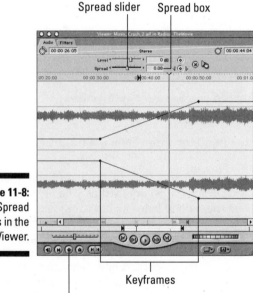

Figure 11-8:
Spread
levels in the
Viewer.

Keyframes

Insert / Delete Keyframe button

Remember, you can pan only a mono audio clip — not a stereo, paired clip. If
you want to pan a stereo clip, break it into two mono clips by selecting it on
the Timeline and then choosing Modify➪Stereo Pair. You're breaking the pair
into two separate clips and can now pan either one to your heart's content.

Creating Audio Transitions

You can use the Final Cut Express cross fade transitions to smooth over awk-
ward or obvious cuts in the audio (that is, when one audio clip ends and the
next begins). You have two cross fades to choose from — each one essentially fades out the volume for the outgoing clip while fading the incoming
clip in (as you can see in Figure 11-9), but they do it a little differently.

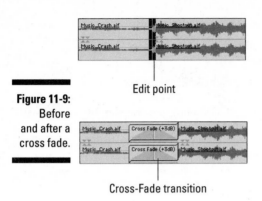

Edit point

Figure 11-9:
Before
and after a
cross fade.

Cross-Fade transition

Applying an audio transition is easy. Just follow these steps:

1. **Select an edit point between two adjacent audio clips.**

2. **Choose Effects⇨Audio Transitions.**

3. **Choose either Cross Fade (0 dB) or Cross Fade (+3 dB) from the Audio Transitions submenu.**

   What's the difference between the Cross Fade (0 dB) and Cross Fade (+3 dB)? It's subtle, but Cross Fade (0 dB) briefly dips volume while the first clips fades out and the second fades in, but Cross Fade (+3 dB) keeps volume steady through the whole transition. But don't fret much over which cross fade to use: Give each a try, and use the one that sounds best. You can easily replace one transition for another by selecting the transition on the Timeline and then choosing a new Transition from the Audio Transitions submenu. Or you can press Delete to toss the selected transition.

If you get an error message that reads `Insufficient content for edit` while you try to apply a cross fade, consider this: To do a fade between two audio clips, each clip needs to have additional frames available to it beyond its Timeline edit points. The default cross fade lasts one second. Therefore, the first clip (the outgoing clip) needs an additional 15 frames beyond its Out point, and the second clip (the incoming clip) needs an additional 15 frames available before its In point. The cross fade uses these extra frames to make a smooth transition between the two clips.

After you've applied a cross fade, you can customize it to play over more or fewer frames on the Timeline — just drag the transition edges to stretch or shrink it. When you resize a cross fade, you can save it as a Favorite in case you ever want to apply a transition of that size somewhere else. To save a cross fade as a Favorite, follow these steps:

1. **Open the Final Cut Express Effects tab in the Browser window (see Figure 11-10).**

Either choose Windows⇨Effects or click the Effects tab in the Browser window.

2. **Click and drag the customized transition from the Timeline to the Favorites bin in the Effects tab to add it there.**

   It's a good idea to rename the transition now (like you would any clip in the Browser window — see Chapter 5), so that you can recognize it later. After you name it, you're free to use that exact transition any time you like; just open up the Effects tab and drag the transition from the Favorites bin to any new edit point (between two clips) on the Timeline.

Figure 11-10:
The
Favorites
bin in the
Effects
menu.

Working with Audio Filters

When you bring audio into Final Cut Express, you may want to change the sound in some way — for instance, to add a little reverb to a big sound effect, to add an echo on a character's voice, or to tone down the hum of some electrical equipment that your microphones picked up on set. Good news: You can do it all, thanks to the Express library of 16 audio filters, which you can apply to clips on the Timeline and tweak to your heart's content.

Granted, if you're new to audio tweaking, figuring out the Final Cut Express audio filters can be a little daunting. For starters, most of them use not-so-user-friendly names like DC Notch, High Shelf Filter, and Parametric Equalizer, leaving the uninitiated with absolutely no idea as to what each does. Secondly, most of these filters give you a number of technical parameters to adjust — settings such as Frequency, Threshold, Ratio, and Attack Time — making the filters even more daunting.

But don't fret! After you get past this initial bewilderment, getting a grip on the Final Cut Express audio filters isn't so difficult. You just need to take a little time to understand the purpose for each filter — and what controls you can use to fine-tune it.

Describing each filter in detail is beyond the scope of a *For Dummies* book, but later in this chapter, I cover the major categories of the 16 Final Cut Express filters, and I tell you how they work. This understanding will give you a good foundation to build on. In the meantime, the next sections tackle how to apply and work with audio filters in general.

Applying and rendering an audio filter

You can apply a filter to an audio clip in a variety of ways, but the following steps outline the easiest, most straightforward approach:

1. **Select an audio clip on the Timeline, choose Effects⊅Audio Filters and then choose a filter from the Audio Filters submenu.**

   Final Cut Express draws a red, horizontal line over the filtered clip in the Timeline Render status bar, meaning that you have to render the clip before hearing how it sounds.

2. **To render the clip, first make sure that the clip is still selected; then choose Sequence⊅Render Selection.**

   Alternatively, you just press ⌘+R on the keyboard.

3. **Play your rendered audio clip.**

   If you don't like it, you can always choose Edit⊅Undo, and Express will return your filtered clip back to its unrendered form.

You can also apply a filter to an audio clip on the Timeline by dragging filters from the Effects window:

1. **Open the Final Cut Express Effects window (as shown in Figure 11-11).**

   You can click the Effects tab in the Browser window or choose Windows⊅Effects.

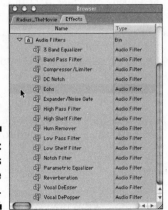

Figure 11-11:
Audio filters
on the
Effects tab.

2. **In the Effects window, drag any filter in the Audio Filters bin to an audio clip on the Timeline.**

Tweaking filter parameters

A handful of filters don't have parameters, but most do. After you've applied a filter to a clip, you may want to tweak whatever parameters that the filter offers. Just follow these steps:

1. **Double-click a filtered clip on the Timeline to open it the Viewer.**

2. **Click the Viewer Filters tab (as shown in Figure 11-12).**

   You can now see any filters that you've applied to that clip as well as any sliders or other controls that you can use to tweak the parameter values.

3. **Move the sliders for each parameter and tweak away.**

   You can also type values into each parameter's field.

4. **When you finish your tweaking, make sure that you still have the filtered clip selected on the Timeline and then render the clip.**

   Choose Sequence➪Render Selection to render it.

5. **Play the clip on the Timeline and listen to the filter effects on it.**

   If you don't like the results, you can undo both the render and the filter values that you created by choosing Edit➪Undo as many times as necessary to get back to the state that you want. Alternatively, you can go back to Filter tab in the Viewer and further tweak your settings; then render your clip again.

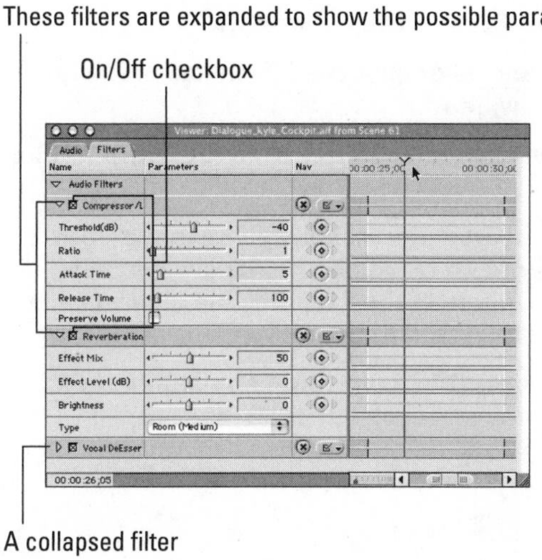

These filters are expanded to show the possible parameters

On/Off checkbox

Figure 11-12: Three filters applied to a clip, seen from the Filters tab of the Viewer.

A collapsed filter

When you apply more than one filter to a clip, you see them stacked in the Filters tab (again, check out Figure 11-12); the top filter is the first one that you applied, followed by the second, and so on. This order is important to keep in mind when you render all the filters together — Final Cut Express renders the audio with the first filter, renders the *rendered* clip with the second filter, and then renders *that* rendered clip with the third filter, and so on. In other words, the order in which you apply the filters can seriously affect how a clip sounds when Express finally finishes all the rendering. With that in mind, you can rearrange the order of the filters within the Filters tab by clicking and dragging them up and down.

Disabling and deleting filters

If you want to turn off a filter temporarily — without losing any of its settings — you can toggle it off and back on again by selecting the little check box next to the filter name (refer to Figure 11-12).

To delete a filter altogether (and lose whatever settings you've adjusted), just click its name to select it and then press the Delete key.

Getting quick access to your favorite filters

If you take the time to tweak filter settings and you know that you want to apply those same custom settings to another audio clip, you can save that filter as a Favorite by following these steps:

1. **Open the Final Cut Express Effects window.**

   Choose Window➪Effects or click the Effects tab in the Browser window to open the Effects window.

2. **Click and drag the customized filter from the Viewer Filter tab to the Favorites bin in the Effects window.**

   Technically, you can drag the filter anywhere in the Browser, but custom filters will be easier to find if you know you always keep them in your Favorites bin. Also, filters in the Favorites bin are available to all your Final Cut Express projects, not just the current one.

3. **Rename the filter now (like you would any clip in the Browser window) so that you can recognize it later.**

   That's it!

Now you can apply the filter to any clip on the Timeline by choosing Effects⇨Audio Filters⇨Favorites and then choosing the custom filter from the Favorites submenu.

Exploring Audio Filters

The previous section explains how to apply and edit audio filters. In this section, I take a look at the different kinds of filters that Express offers and how you can use them to both improve and/or stylize your movie's audio. I group the filters into four major categories:

- ✔ Equalization filters
- ✔ Echo and reverberation filters
- ✔ Compression and expansion filters
- ✔ Noise reduction filters

Equalization filters

Equalization filters (that's *EQ filters* for short) enable you to raise or lower the volume not of an entire clip but of individual sound frequencies within that clip. Having that capability is incredibly useful because sound is made up of a wide range of frequencies, and each frequency determines the *pitch* (the highness or lowness) of the sound. For instance, the deepness of man's voice is on a different frequency than the higher pitch of a woman's voice, and the low rumble of a car engine in the distance is on a different frequency than the hiss of recording tape.

You may want to use audio that's been marred by some unwanted element — for instance, the buzz of an old fluorescent lights or the hum of traffic. Fortunately, you can use an EQ filter to isolate a certain frequency within the audio and lower its volume so that it's less noticeable.

That's the good news about EQ filters. Now for some bad news: First, don't expect these filters to solve *major* problems with the audio because the filters make subtle shifts (not much help if your crew recorded a quiet, touching scene while a neighbor ran his leaf blower all day long). Second, getting good results from these filters takes a lot of trial and error — if you're not careful, you can end up distorting the audio. Experience helps with solving the problems.

At any rate, Final Cut Express sports three equalization filters that specialize in working with different ranges of frequencies, and each filter offers different parameters that you can tweak. If you want to explore each of these, I suggest that you search out a more comprehensive book, such as *Final Cut Pro 2 Bible* by Zed Saeed and Keith Underdahl (Wiley Publishing, Inc.).

Echoes and reverberations

You can use the Final Cut Express Echo and Reverberation filters to better match sound to the physical setting of your movie. Reverb in particular is useful to match the acoustics found in a wide variety of enclosed settings — for instance, a sprawling auditorium. Because Echo is a bit more extreme, use it to match the sound of a big outdoor setting such as a huge canyon.

Both filters let you set the following parameters so that you can hone your effect to perfection:

- **The Effect Mix slider:** This sets how much of the original, unfiltered sound Final Cut Express mixes together with the effect that the filter creates. The higher the number, the more affected the sound will be.

- **The Effect Level slider:** This one sets the volume of the affected sound in decibels (as opposed to the volume of the original, unaffected sound).

- **The Brightness slider:** Brightness gives the effect more punch (without changing its volume). Experiment with this parameter to get a feel for its effects.

If you're using Reverb, click the Type pop-up menu to set the style of reverb that you want, depending on the kind of environment that you're trying to acoustically match (a tunnel, a medium-sized room, a long hallway, and so on).

For the Echo filter, you can also use its Feedback slider to set how long each echo lasts; use its Delay Time slider to set the time between each echo.

Compression and expansion filters

Sometimes you want to expand or limit a *dynamic range,* which is the range between the softest and loudest volume of a clip. (See the sidebar, "The highs and lows of dynamic range," elsewhere in this chapter, for more information.)

By choosing the Compressor/Limiter filter, you can *compress* (that is, shorten) the dynamic range of a clip by lowering the volume on only the loudest points. You may want to use a filter like this when working with a dialogue track in which a character goes from speaking softly to shouting in short order, and you want to drop the volume on the character's shouts. (You can always try adjusting the clip volume by setting *keyframes* — as I cover earlier in this chapter — but a filter can do the same thing with a much more subtle touch, and you can apply the filter to many clips quickly.)

On the other hand, you could use the Expander/Noise Gate filter to increase a dynamic range by raising the volume on only the parts that are too soft — for instance, if the actor goes from whispering to shouting, and the shouts are at a perfect volume, but the whispers are barely audible.

When you use either of these filters, you have four different controls to fiddle with:

✔ **The Threshold slider:** Sets how low, in decibels, a clip volume can go before the filter does its thing (in the case of the Expander) or how high the clip volume can go before the filter does its thing (for the Compressor)

✔ **The Ratio slider:** Sets the amount of compression or expansion that you do to the clip after its high or low volume passes the threshold

✔ **The Attack Time slider:** Sets how quickly the filters react to changes in the volume of the clip

✔ **The Release Time slider:** Sets how slowly the filter eases out of its volume change

Noise reduction filters

These three filters help reduce unique kinds of noise that you recorded accidentally . . . or maybe a microphone not being tuned right or some electrical conflicts in your recording setup. Remember, too, that you can use an equalization filter to reduce other kinds of noise (such as the dull hint of traffic outside or the hum of fluorescent lights on set and so on):

✔ **The Vocal De-Esser:** This filter eases any heavy *S* sounds that your microphone picked up while an actor speaks.

✔ **The Vocal De-Popper:** This filter cuts down the harsh pop of spoken *P* sounds picked up by an overly sensitive mike.

✔ **The Hum Remover:** This filter is a little more obscure. (Well, actually, it's a lot more obscure.) Use it to cut down on the hum from electrical equipment in the background. (You can't hear these hums on set, but your recording equipment picks them up nonetheless.) Just make sure that you have good headphones — you'll need them to pick up and adjust the subtleties of hum.

Copying and Removing Audio Attributes

After you set the volume level, pan or spread, or audio filters of an audio clip, you may want to copy those attributes and then apply them to a bunch of other clips — without wasting time manually establishing the same settings for every single clip. For instance, you may have dozens of audio clips of a voice narration on the Timeline. After you set the volume level for one of those clips, how efficient would it be to copy that setting to all the other clips? Fortunately, Final Cut Express makes doing so a breeze.

Follow these steps to copy and paste audio attributes:

1. **Select an audio clip on the Timeline.**

   It doesn't matter whether the clip is linked to a video clip.

2. **Manually set the volume level, pan, and spread of a clip and then apply (and tweak) any audio filters to it that you want.**

   Use the techniques discussed earlier in this chapter. You can tweak all these settings or just one.

3. **Make sure that you still have the audio clip selected on the Timeline and then copy it.**

   You can press ⌘+C or choose Edit➪Copy. It doesn't matter whether the audio clip is linked to video.

4. **Select all the other audio clips on the Timeline to which you want to apply the copied settings and filters.**

   See Chapter 6 for all the ways that you can select multiple clips on the Timeline, but a quick option is to use the Selection tool and hold down the ⌘ key while selecting each clip.

5. **Choose Edit➪Paste Attributes.**

   The Paste Attributes dialog box appears, as seen in Figure 11-13.

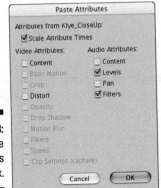

Figure 11-13:
The Paste
Attributes
dialog box.

6. In the Audio Attributes list of the Paste Attributes dialog box, select the check box next to whatever attribute you want to paste from the first clip to the selected clips.

If you want to paste just volume levels from the original, copied clip, make sure that you select the Levels check box. If you want to paste the filters from the copied clip as well, select the Filters check box. By selecting these attributes, you decide which attributes from the original, copied clip Final Cut Express applies to the selected clips on the Timeline. If there are attributes from the original, copied clip that you don't want to copy to your new clip (such as video attributes, in case you copied a clip that had video as well), simply leave the check boxes next to those attributes unchecked.

If the copied clip used keyframes in its volume settings, Final Cut Express applies those keyframes to new clips (provided that you select the Levels check box in the Audio Attibutes list). You may or may not want this, but if so, also selecting the Scale Attribute Times check box scales the distances between those keyframes to fit the larger or smaller clips that the keyframes are pasted to.

7. Click OK when you're done.

The clips that you selected on the Timeline now have the desired attributes from the original, copied clip.

You can also selectively remove audio attributes from multiple clips by using the same approach. Just select whatever clips you want to affect on the Timeline and then choose Edit➪Remove Attributes. In the Audio Attributes list, select the check box next to whatever attribute you want to remove from the selected clips and then click OK.

Pasting to and removing attributes from a large number of clips can make you nervous that you'll somehow make a mistake and apply or remove the wrong attributes, but you can always undo your actions by choosing Edit➪Undo.

Chapter 12

Special Effects and Corrections with Video Filters

Seems like someone has taken the "special" out of special effects these days: What was once strange and wonderful on the screen has become commonplace. For example, applying a vast array of color filters and treatments to a video was once considered cutting edge and required the services of an expensive post-production shop. Now you can do it all in spades — from your desktop! Indeed, Final Cut Express hands the video nut a bag of tricks that would make Houdini bug-eyed with envy.

In this chapter, I cover the video filters and other tools available to help you create special effects. You can think of a *filter* as an effect that modifies the clip in some way, such as adding a color or blur to it. You discover how to use filters to control the look, color, and consistency of a movie. You also acquire some tricks for enhancing or fixing the color in clips (to create a mood or match the look of lighting from one shot to another).

In fact, the word *color* comes up a lot in this chapter. No doubt about it: Color *is* a deep subject, and some people spend their lives learning about it. One of the cool features of Final Cut Express is that it offers tools for controlling color at many levels *without* requiring a Ph.D. on the subject. Yet, as easy as the tools are to use, these same controls and tools satisfy the expert as well. Try out the steps in this chapter on a clip or two and play with your new magic wands. Color has never been so easy or just plain fun to control.

You'll need to render any clips you apply filters to in Final Cut Express. Chances are, you're already well acquainted with rendering by now, but if not, check out Chapter 17.

Shooting Video with Effects in Mind

Before shooting video for a project, try to plan ahead. Think about the look you want the movie to have before you ever take out your trusty camera. If you're doing an artsy short in *film noir* (that dark, shadowy look that Hitchcock and others made so popular in the '30s), high-contrast lighting and appropriate camera settings can do a lot more for the project than any filter in Final Cut Express. If you want a high contrast clip that emphasizes primary colors, say, for an instructional video for children, make sure that you shoot with lots of light. Giving you a rundown of all the considerations for shooting footage is outside the scope of this book, but you can check out more in *Digital Video For Dummies*, 2nd Edition, by Martin Doucette (Wiley Publishing, Inc.).

Special effects video filters and controls in Final Cut Express can do some amazing things, but they definitely have limits. Post-production isn't the place for turning lead into gold. If the video is ugly to start with, chances are it will be ugly after you edit it.

Making a Colored Clip Black and White

A great place to start with this whole color thing is getting rid of it. That's right. Go black and white. Although many, if not most, of today's cameras offer the option to shoot in black and white, rarely does that actually happen. Why? The color shot contains so much information that you'd be silly not to take advantage of it, even if you plan to drop the color in the post-production process.

So why go black and white? Removing color is a way to give punch to a video, resurrect *film noir,* create a background for a color object or text, or go retro. Going black and white is easy to do. Just follow these steps:

1. **In the Viewer window, open the clip you want to convert to black and white.**

   You can also double-click the clip in the Browser to load it into the Viewer.

2. **In the Browser window, click the Effects tab and then click the little triangle next to the Video Filters bin.**

3. **In the Video Filters bin, click the little triangle next to the Image Control bin to open it.**

   In the Image Control bin, you can find the Desaturate filter, as shown in Figure 12-1.

4. **Click and drag the Desaturate filter from the Browser to anywhere in the Viewer window.**

   The clip immediately becomes black and white because the Desaturate filter is applied at a 100 percent strength by default. To *desaturate* means to take away the color.

5. **Click the Filters tab in the Viewer window.**

   On the other hand, you can drag the Filters tab outside the Viewer window so that you can make adjustments to the filter while seeing the effects on the video clip in the Viewer window.

6. **Use the Amount slider (refer to Figure 12-1) to control the level of desaturation to your liking.**

   Placing the slider in the middle creates a value of zero, or no change. Dragging the slider to the left creates negative values and super-saturates the color in the clip. If the value is all the way to the right (and has a numerical value of 100), all the color is removed and only a black and white image remains. Experiment with several values: Sometimes, just removing a little but not all of the color from an image can create a unique effect.

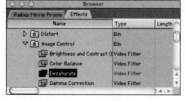

Figure 12-1: The Desaturate filter creates a black and white clip or sequence.

7. **Drag the clip from the Viewer to the Canvas window and drop it on the Overwrite overlay, which appears over the Canvas window.**

   Final Cut Express sends the clip to the Timeline. Alternatively, you can just drag the clip from the Viewer to the Timeline if you feel comfortable with that approach.

8. **Select the clip in the Timeline and choose Sequence⇨Render Selection.**

9. **After Final Cut Express renders the clip, position the playhead just before the clip in the Timeline and press the space bar to play the clip.**

Getting That Old, Grainy Video Look

Getting people's attention is hard in a media-crowded world. Not everyone or every project needs to go high-tech with videos that look like something from the 22nd century. Some projects make more sense looking old or oddly out of fashion. A video with a different look — if it fits the video and its message — can get the right kind of attention from the viewers.

Suppose an old video you caught on cable TV really inspires you. How did the video get that gritty, grainy look? Who knows, really, but you can use a Noise generator in Final Cut Express to get the same or similar effect. Just follow these steps:

1. **Drag a clip from the Browser to the Timeline into a video track.**

   See Chapter 6 if you need a refresher on how to put clips in the Timeline.

2. **Click the Effects tab in the Browser window.**

3. **Click the triangle next to Video Generators to open it and then click the triangle next to Render to open it.**

   In the Render bin, locate the Noise generator.

4. **Drag the Noise generator to the track above the clip in the Timeline.**

   Generators work just like clips in that you can place them directly on the Timeline.

5. **Drag the ends of the Noise generator so that the clip stretches out to cover the entire clip or sequence on the tracks beneath it. (See Figure 12-2.)**

   If the Noise generator on the Timeline track is so long that you have to scroll to find its start and end points (which can be disorienting and a bit time consuming), go back to Step 4 and double-click the Noise generator from the Browser. Final Cut Express brings the Noise generator up in the Viewer window (like any other clip), and from there, you can set narrow In and Out points before dragging the generator to the Timeline.

6. **In the Timeline, drag the playhead over the Noise clip.**

   You see the Noise generator noise in the Canvas window.

Figure 12-2:
Drag the
Noise
generator
from the
Effects tab
to the track
above the
clip on the
Timeline.

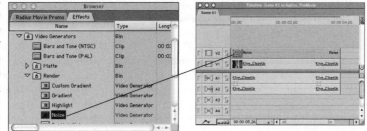

7. **Double-click the Noise generator clip in the Timeline so that it loads into the Viewer window.**

8. **In the Viewer window, click the Motion tab and click the little triangle next to the Opacity setting.**

9. **Move the Opacity slider, as shown in Figure 12-3, to get the grainy look you want.**

   The Canvas window shows this effect as you move the Opacity slider. Keep moving the slider until Final Cut Express generates the amount of grain you want.

10. **Select the Noise generator clip in the Timeline and choose Sequence⇨Render Selection.**

11. **After Final Cut Express completes the rendering process, move the playhead just before the clip in the Timeline and press the space bar to play the clip.**

Figure 12-3:
In the
Motion tab,
you can
modify the
opacity of
the Noise
generator
clip to
create a
grainy look
for a
project.

After the Noise generator is on the Timeline, a quicker way to adjust Noise levels is to click the Overlays button on the Timeline (refer to Figure 12-3), and then simply drag the opacity line of the Noise clip up and down.

Noise looks considerably different on a little Canvas preview window than it does on a TV. You need to experiment with the final product to find the right opacity setting to get the effect you want. Having a TV hooked up to your Mac is a big help here — if you need help doing that, see Chapter 2. Also, if you're generating a movie for the Web, skip the noise if you can. Web-destined video has to be compressed, but noise doesn't compress well and tends to *pixelate* (develop a checkered pattern) when you scale down your Web video's frame size.

Changing Colors

Changing the colors in a clip can be incredibly handy and really easy. But first a note of caution: This section is *not* about color correction. You can find info on that topic later in this chapter. This section is about giving a colored look to a clip or a project and about shifting colors to match a particular look and feel. These tools give you the power to change the color of the sun. Really. That golden hot-sun-autumn-washed-out look in *Oh, Brother, Where Art Thou?* isn't far from your reach. You can also make an ever-so-subtle change in a clip to warm it up or cool it down.

I discuss video generator matters and the RGB Balance filters in this section. Later in the section "Checking Out More Handy Filters," I tackle a third tool, the Tint filter.

Using mattes

An easy way to create a color change effect is to simply add a *filter,* something like a digital version of those tinted, plastic, color filters that you may have clamped over the lens of a 35mm camera. But the Final Cut Express filter is much easier to use, and you have all the colors of the rainbow at your disposal! In Express, a filter can be an effect that alters the clip in some way, such as adding a sepia tint or a glow to it. This type of filter is called a *matte.* Specifically, if you want to have a glow over a particular clip, as if the subjects were in a kind of golden fog, follow these steps:

1. **Drag a clip from the Browser to a video track on the Timeline.**

2. **Click the Effects tab in the Browser window.**

3. **Click the small triangle for the Video Generators bin to open it and then click the Matte triangle to open the Matte bin.**

4. **In the Matte bin, find the Color matte.**

5. **Drag the Color matte to the track above the clip in the Timeline**

   Again, generators work just like normal clips on the Timeline.

6. **Drag the ends of the Color matte so that the matte clip stretches out to cover the entire clip on the track beneath it. (This is similar to Figure 12-2.)**

7. **In the Timeline, place the playhead anywhere on the Color matte so that you can preview the effect.**

   If you do this, then you can later see changes you make to the Color matte in the Canvas window.

8. **Double-click the Color matte in the Timeline and then click the Controls tab in the Viewer window.**

9. **In the Color parameters area of the Controls tab, click the triangle to reveal the color controls, as shown in Figure 12-4.**

   Final Cut Express offers a few ways to select a color:

   - **Color swatch:** You can click the small square color swatch and select a yellowish color from the Color Picker selection box that pops up (refer to Figure 12-4).

   - **Eyedropper tool:** You can click the Eyedropper tool. After the cursor turns into an eyedropper, you can click any color you like in the clip, as displayed in the Canvas window. The Color matte then picks up the color that you selected with the Eyedropper tool.

     Sliders: You can use the sliders labeled H, S, and B to alter the Hue, Saturation, and Brightness settings of a color. You can preview any changes you make in the square color swatch and applied to the Color matte.

10. **Click the Motion tab in the Viewer window and click the little triangle next to Opacity.**

11. **Move the slider in the Opacity pane until the transparency of the Color matte is just right.**

    Note that when the playhead is located over the clips in the Timeline, the Canvas window shows you an update of the final color effect.

12. **Select the Color matte clip in the Timeline and choose Sequence⇨Render Selection.**

13. **After Final Cut Express renders the clip, position the playhead just before the clips in the Timeline and press the space bar to play the clip.**

Click the color swatch to access the Color Picker

Eyedropper tool

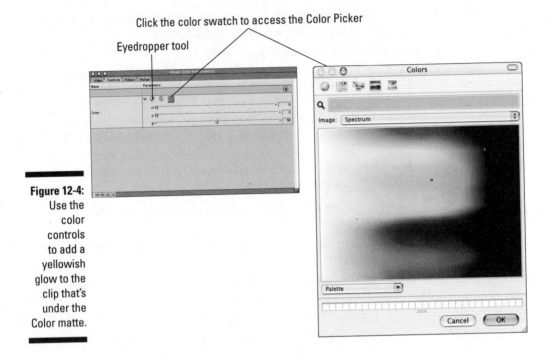

Figure 12-4:
Use the
color
controls
to add a
yellowish
glow to the
clip that's
under the
Color matte.

Using the RGB Balance tool

Rather than using an Overlay or a low-opacity matte, you can actually change the color of any given part of the spectrum in the video by using the RGB Balance tool. The controls are precise, and the numbers next to the sliders let you track and record edits. To change color with RGB Balance filter, follow these steps:

1. **Drag a clip from the Browser to a video track in the Timeline.**

2. **In the Timeline, drag the playhead anywhere on the clip so that later you can see a good preview of the effect in the Canvas.**

3. **Double-click the clip.**

   This step opens the clip in the Viewer window.

4. **Click the Filters tab in the Viewer window.**

5. **Click the Effects tab in the Browser window.**

6. **Click the Video Filters bin to open it, and then click the Color Correction bin.**

7. **Find the RGB Balance filter in the Color Correction bin and drag it onto the clip on the Timeline.**

   Just so you know, you could avoid Steps 5–7 by choosing Effects⇨Video Filters⇨Color Correction and then selecting the RGB Balance filter. It's just another way to do things.

8. **On the Filters tab in the Viewer, use the RGB Balance parameters to adjust the colors and thus achieve the look you want.**

   Any video image is made up of three color channels: Red, Green, and Blue. The Red set of sliders, for example, works on changing the amount of red in the highlights (whites), midtones (grays), and blacks of the image. So you have individual control of the amount of R, G, or B in either the highlights (whites), midtones (grays), and blacks. To create a golden glow, you increase the highlights and mids for both Red and Green. Red plus Green equals Yellow and tweaking just the highlights makes the overall look lighter, giving the clip a sunny, yellow feel.

   Figure 12-5 generally points out areas of highlights, midtones, and blacks in a clip.

   The tiny sliders are a pain, but they have one redeeming feature: Those tiny, tiny arrows at the ends of each slider enable you to change the numeric color values one at a time. Use the numbers to keep track of where you were and where you are. If you mess up, the tiny Reset button at the top (marked with a red X, as shown in Figure 12-5) resets everything to default.

9. **Select the clip in the Timeline and choose Sequence⇨Render Selection.**

Figure 12-5: RGB Color Balance provides controls to change the Red, Green, and Blue color balance in blacks, whites, and midrange (grays) values.

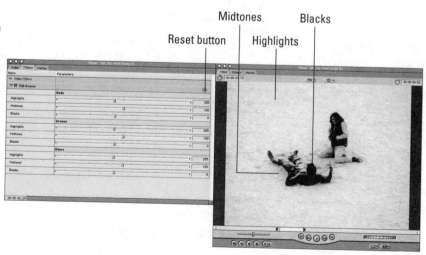

10. **After Final Cut Express completes the rendering process, position the playhead just before the clip in the Timeline and press the space bar to play and view the clip.**

If you have used Adobe Photoshop, you'll feel right at home with the RGB Balance controls. The RGB Balance tool in Final Cut Express is in many ways identical to the Color Balance tool in Photoshop.

Working with Color Correction Tools

Final Cut Express gives you surprisingly powerful color correction tools that were available only on very high-end editing systems (or from dedicated post production shops) only a few years ago. You will find the Express Color Corrector filter, in particular, helpful for improving the look of DV video. For instance, you can use the filter to lighten up shots that are too dark, and change orange, blue, or green tints caused by shooting in lighting conditions that the DV camera was not expecting (usually, the white balance of a camera needs to be set for shooting in different lighting situations, such as sunny daylight, cloudy daylight, indoor light, and light cast by fluorescents found in many offices).

Keep in mind that the Final Cut Express Color Corrector can't make badly shot video look perfect. There's no substitute for knowing what you're doing with a video camera. In other words, make sure scenes have adequate light and are exposed properly, and anticipate the kind of light you're shooting in by adjusting the white balance of a camera. However, the Express Color Corrector can definitely push "bad video" into "okay video" territory and can turn "okay video" into "polished video."

Before you start, note that it's best to view the output on a television or professional video monitor. (For the details on setting this up, see Chapter 2.) An RGB monitor or LCD display isn't the best monitor to base color corrections on (unless you expect the finished movie to be seen only on a computer — for instance, a video you may post only on your Web site).

Now you're ready to get started with some basic color correction. Just follow these steps:

1. **Drag a clip from the Browser to a video track on the Timeline.**

2. **Position the Timeline playhead anywhere on the clip so you can see the clip in the Canvas window.**

3. **Select the clip on the Timeline, and apply the Color Corrector filter to it.**

You can choose Effects⇨Video Filters⇨Color Correction⇨Color Corrector. Alternately you can find the filter in the Effects tab of the Browser window, and drag it to your clip on the Timeline.

4. **Double-click the clip on the Timeline to open it in the Viewer.**

   A new Color Corrector tab appears in the Viewer window.

5. **In the Viewer window, click the Color Corrector tab.**

   The Color Corrector filter defaults to the Visual view (as seen in Figure 12-6). If you find yourself in the Numeric view (with just numbers and sliders), click the Visual button in the upper-left corner.

6. **Click the Auto Contrast button for the filter (see Figure 12-6).**

   This step maximizes the range from black to white in the clip, which is the starting point for any color correction for the clip. Notice that the Blacks, Mids, and Whites sliders automatically move to achieve the best overall luminance distribution in the image. An image is essentially made up of dark tones (blacks), light tones (whites), and tones in between (grays, or "mids").

   If a video clip seems dark, clicking Auto Contrast can make a big improvement, and you can then fine tune things by adjusting the Whites, Blacks, and Mids sliders further. For instance, you might increase the Whites and Mids of a dark image. If the clip gets too washed out, then increase the blacks a bit to compensate.

   You can quickly compare the corrections against the original, uncorrected image by selecting the On/Off check box for the filter (refer to Figure 12-6).

7. **Click the Select AutoBalance Color button.**

   This button looks like a tiny eyedropper on the Balance color wheel.

   When you select this button, the pointer turns into an eyedropper when placed over the Canvas or the Viewer window.

8. **In the Canvas or Viewer window, click an area of the picture that is supposed to be pure white with the eyedropper cursor.**

   You're looking for an object that *should* be pure white (or close) but may have a color tint due to poor lighting or white balance problems in the camera. Be very careful and don't select an overexposed area, such as a highlight or a white blown out light source. Select a well-exposed surface.

   When you click the white in an image (or what you want to be white), the Color Corrector filter analyzes the RGB mix of colors in areas that share that color throughout the image and adjusts the center knob of the Color Balance wheel to offset the mix of colors that are tinting the whites.

   In most cases, you immediately see a change for the better in the whites. If they were green or bluish before, they are closer to white after this step, even if they're not altogether pure white.

Blacks Select Auto-Balance button

Blacks Balance color wheel

On / Off check box

Whites Balance color wheel

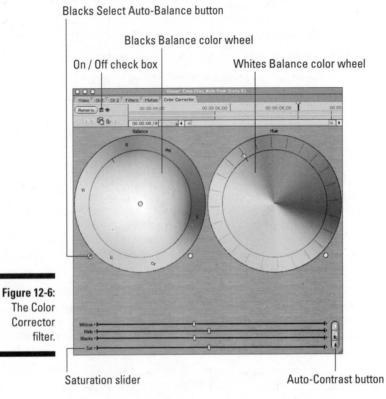

Figure 12-6:
The Color
Corrector
filter.

Saturation slider

Auto-Contrast button

9. **Tweak the Color Balance and Hue to make additional, small adjustments to color.**

Both of these controls effectively let you change certain colors in an image into new ones. You can adjust Color Balance by dragging the little circle in the middle of the Color Balance dial from the middle area towards a surrounding color, like red, magenta, cyan, green, and so on. To speed up the dragging, hold down the ⌘ key while you drag across the colors. Whites become whatever color you drag towards.

Similarly, you can change the *Hue* (which essentially means, the color of an image by dragging the Hue dial around to a new color value, for instance, green).

Chances are, you won't want to make big adjustments with these tools (unless you're going for a completely unrealistic look in the color). They're more for nudging color a bit here and a bit there to give it a bit of punch, or calm it down slightly.

In any event, if you make some adjustments that you don't like, you can reset any changes by clicking the Reset circle to the lower right of the Color Balance and Hue controls (refer to Figure 12-6).

10. **Adjust the saturation by using the Saturation slider in the Color Corrector.**

    You may want to adjust the Saturation (which makes colors appear a bit more vibrant). I've found it helpful in some cases — for instance, to bring out the red in someone's cheeks, or to ever so slightly punch up the color of a shirt or the blue of the sky. But be subtle with these saturation adjustments. Otherwise, the scenes and subjects may appear to glow!

11. **To see how the newly color corrected clip plays, select it on the Timeline and choose Sequence⇨Render Selection.**

If you apply a color corrector to a clip but then decide not to use the filter, you can remove the filter entirely from a clip. Switch the Color Corrector filter into Numeric mode (click Numeric at the top left of the filter pane), and then select the filter as it's listed in Video Filters, and press Delete.

Fixing or Adjusting Exposures

Occasionally, you'll come across a situation in which you aren't happy about the exposure of some video you're working with. (*Exposure* refers to the range of bright to dark values in the image.) Perhaps it is a bit too dark (see Figure 12-7) or too bright because the camera (or camera operator) used to shoot it didn't do a good job of setting the exposure level for the given scene. On the other hand, the video exposure may look decent when viewed by itself, but when you try to mix it with footage taken from another camera, the two don't match. One camera recorded things a bit brighter than the other, which can be a bit jarring for viewers.

Figure 12-7:
An under-exposed shot: before and after treatment in Final Cut Express.

Of course, Final Cut Express can help you adjust the video exposure to help compensate for these headaches. With one obvious filter and another that is somewhat obscure, you can make serious strides in fixing problem video clips.

Be aware, however, that extreme exposure problems can't be fixed. Glaring errors in exposure have to be prevented when you're actually shooting the video — for more on how to regulate exposure while shooting, see *Digital Video For Dummies*, 2nd Edition, by Martin Doucette (Wiley Publishing, Inc.).

Two effects filters can help in this correction process: Proc Amp and Brightness and Contrast. Proc Amp sounds like the opening band at a rock concert. (It actually stands for process amplifier.) The Proc Amp filter enables you to adjust aspects of exposure during the editing process. (If you're a Photoshop user, you'll notice that Proc Amp is similar to PhotoShop Adjust Hue/Saturation control.)

Follow this step-by-step guide to editing exposure levels in a project:

1. **Drag a clip from the Browser to a video track on the Timeline.**

2. **Position the Timeline playhead anywhere on the clip so you can see the clip in the Canvas window.**

3. **Select the clip on the Timeline, and apply the filters called Brightness and Contrast, and Proc Amp to it.**

   You can apply the filters by choosing Effects➪Video Filters➪Image Control. Alternately, you can find the filters in the Effects tab of the Browser window (in the Image Control bin), and drag them to the clip on the Timeline.

4. **Double-click the clip on the Timeline to open it in the Viewer.**

5. **In the Viewer window, click the Filters tab.**

   You should now see the two filters you just applied to the clip on the Timeline (as shown in Figure 12-8).

6. **On the Filters tab, adjust each of the filters you just applied.**

   Move the filters' sliders or repeatedly click the little arrowheads at the end of each slider until you get the desired results. Alternately, you can type in numeric values into the filters' fields.

   The Brightness and Contrast controls are pretty self-explanatory. The Proc Amp controls aren't as easy to figure out, so this list describes what these controls do:

   • **Setup:** Changes the black level in a clip. Blacks should be deep and dark with no grays in them. Look for blacks in hair or dark areas of the shot.

- **Video:** Affects the whites in an image. Adjust this slider until the whites start to glow in the image and then back off a bit till they're just below that glowing level.

- **Chroma:** Affects the color level or saturation. Be sure to check on a NTSC or PAL video monitor for a final decision on the amount of color you want to add to the clip.

- **Phase:** Gives you control over the hue in a clip (again, the hue is essentially its color). Whether you want to make the colors greener or redder, the Phase control can help.

7. **To see how the newly color corrected clip plays, select it on the Timeline and choose Sequence⇨Render Selection.**

A handy reference to use is another shot in a movie whose exposure and colors you like. Compare the two shots and make adjustments until you like what you see.

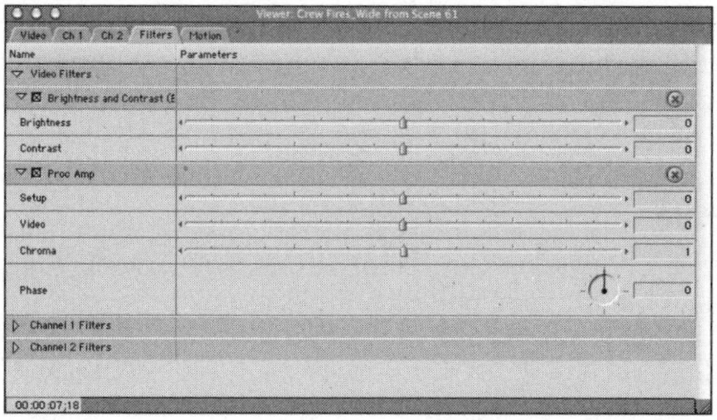

Figure 12-8:
The Brightness and Contrast filter and the Proc Amp filter help you fix clips with exposure problems.

Checking Out More Handy Filters

In this section, I discuss more cool filters and other special effects that can help give a video a unique look. To apply them, use the steps covered earlier:

1. **Place a video clip on the Timeline.**

2. **Position the Timeline playhead over the clip so you can see it in the Canvas window.**

   This way, you can preview the changes in the Canvas.

3. **Double-click the video clip to open it in the Viewer.**

4. **Click the Viewer Filter tab.**

5. **Click the Effects tab in the Browser window, and drag any desired effects to either the Viewer window, or the selected clip on the Timeline.**

   Each filter and its controls appear in the Viewer Filter tab.

6. **Adjust the controls for each filter in the Viewer window, while watching their effects in the Canvas.**

Just a dash of any of the following filter combinations can set your project apart. And of course, remember that these are just the tip of the iceberg: Final Cut Express offers many other filters that, with some tweaking and combining, may give you exactly the look you're looking for.

- ✔ **Tint, Sepia, and Desaturate:** Combining these three filters (found in the Image Control filters bin) at once can create some interesting effects.

  The Sepia filter tints a clip with a sepia tone, the yellowish-brown color often seen in old photos. You can change the color of the tint by clicking a color picker or using two sliders (labeled Amount and Highlight) to control the amount and the brightness of the tint you apply. The Tint filter is less useful than the Sepia filter because you can only select the color and the amount. You may want to switch between the Tint and the Sepia filters and see which effect you find to be more pleasing. And again, the Desaturate filter allows you to take out some color from the image. At the highest settings (100), the image becomes completely back and white.

- ✔ **Channel Blur, Channel Offset, Color Offset, and Invert:** You can find these filters in the Channel bin. Blurring on a color channel (by adjusting just one of the RGB blur sliders in the Channel Blur effect) and leaving the rest alone can take a poorly focused shot and give it a deliberate soft focus in one or more parts of the color spectrum. The Channel Offset filter shifts one color layer over to one side, creating a double-exposure look that can work as a dream effect. The Color Offset filter alters the color values in the Red, Green, and Blue channels with sliders, while Invert looks like something out of an old science-fiction movie; it inverts all colors to their complimentary colors.

- ✔ **Sharpen and Edge Detection:** Found in the Video Filter QuickTime bin, these tools have a sharpening effect and can also make a scene look more three-dimensional and give fuzzy or slightly out-of-focus elements more clarity. Instead of sliders, you adjust these filters by selecting values from a drop-down menu. You need to experiment with the extremes in the numbers here to see the possibilities for these filters. Used together, they can also produce dramatic, deliberately grainy results.

- ✔ **Emboss and Lens Flare:** Also in the QuickTime bin are several unusual tools for dramatically changing the look of a scene. Emboss mimics the Photoshop filter of the same name and turns the scene gray with hard edges. Lens Flare does just what it says: It gives you hundreds of possible lens flares like the rays and circles of light from the sun that sometimes appear on video or in photographs. You can select the size, shape, and color of the flare.

Blurring the Action

If you want shots to convey movement and speed, then you might want to add a little blur to the action. By using the Final Cut Express Blur filters, you can help create or enhance the sense of motion. Follow these steps to a blurry scene:

1. **Drag a clip from the Browser to a video track on the Timeline.**

2. **Position the Timeline playhead anywhere on the clip so you can see it previewed in the Canvas window.**

3. **Double-click the clip to open it in Viewer.**

4. **Click the Filters tab in the Viewer window.**

5. **Click the Effects tab in the Browser window.**

6. **Click the triangle next to the Video Filters bin to open it, and then do the same to open the Blur bin inside.**

7. **Drag each of the blur filters (Gaussian, Radial, Wind, and Zoom) to the Filters tab in the Viewer window.**

   Alternately, you could drag them onto the clip on the Timeline. Hey, you make the choice, but the results in the Filter tab should look like Figure 12-9.

8. **Start by selecting only the check box next to the Wind Blur filter.**

   You can see that the Wind Blur filter is checked in Figure 12-9.

9. **Move the wind direction indicator and the sliders until you get the desired effect.**

   The Canvas window shows the results. You can move the playhead around in the Canvas window to see what the results look like in other parts of the clip — but really, you can't judge this kind of effect well until you see it in motion.

10. **Try turning on the other blurring filters (by selecting the check boxes next to them) to exaggerate the blurring effect.**

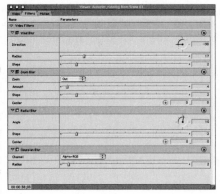

Figure 12-9:
Using a combination of blurring filters can create an illusion of motion.

11. **Select the clip on the Timeline and choose Sequence⇨Render Selection.**

12. **After Final Cut Express completes the rendering process, view the newly rendered effect on the Timeline.**

    Chances are, you'll want to make some tweaks to the blurs, so just go back to the Effects tab in the Viewer window, change some settings, and render again.

Saving and Applying Customized Filters

If you've taken the time to tweak the parameters of a video filter, you can save that tweaked filter as a Favorite so that you can easily apply it to other clips needing the same filter treatment. This saves you from having to apply the same filter again and again, and adjusting its settings each time it's applied. To do so, follow these steps:

1. **Open the Final Cut Express Effects tab.**

   You can click the Effects tab in the Browser window, or just choose Window⇨Effects to activate that tab in the Browser.

2. **Open an already-filtered video clip in the Viewer window, and click the Viewer Filters tab.**

3. **Click the name of the filter you want to save, and drag it to the Favorites bin in the Effects window (see Figure 12-10).**

Final Cut Express saves the filter to the Favorites bin, with all the unique parameters you set for it. You can now apply it to new clips just as you would any other filter (you might want to rename the customized filter while you're in the Browser window).

Technically, you can drag your filter anywhere in the Browser, but I recommend putting it in the Favorites bin where it's easy to find and is available to all of your projects. If you only want to make this customized filter available to your current project, then consider placing it in another bin within your project.

Figure 12-10:
A customized filter saved to the Favorites bin in the Effects window.

Chapter 13

Advanced Effects

· ·

· ·

Some projects call for you to do crazy things to your video clips, such as resize them, rotate them, reposition them, overlap them, change their opacity (to make them seem partially transparent), and more. You typically see these kind of effects in stylized montages featured in commercials, music videos, and the opening credits of TV news shows, sports programs, and even documentaries.

Creating these types of effects is the topic of this chapter. I cover how to manipulate video clips in all sorts of advanced ways. I also explain how to use handy tools called *keyframes* to add motion to these effects so that the effects happen over time.

If any of this sounds complicated, just relax. After you understand a few key concepts, you'll cruise through this stuff without breaking a sweat. The real challenge, in fact, is not grasping how these advanced effects work, but thinking of imaginative ways to combine them.

The skills that I describe in this chapter go hand in hand with topics covered in Chapter 12 and Chapter 14. I highly recommend checking out these chapters as well, to get the most from the unique Final Cut Express effects features.

Manipulating Images in Wireframe Mode

To tap into advanced Final Cut Express effects work, you want to shift into Wireframe mode, which then lets you change the size, rotation, position, and shape of any video clip in your project. To switch Express to Wireframe mode, make sure that either the Canvas or Timeline window is active, and then choose View➪Image+Wireframe.

If you didn't notice a change after switching to Wireframe mode, try selecting any video clip on the Timeline (move a clip there if necessary), and also make sure that you've positioned the Timeline playhead over the clip you've selected.

When you select the clip, you see the Canvas window display wireframe boundaries around your video clip, with a big X running through the image (see Figure 13-1). In this mode, the boundaries of video and still images appear as thin aqua lines that serve also as wire handles for the media. You tweak these handles to change the look and position of the imagery on-screen, as I explain in the next section.

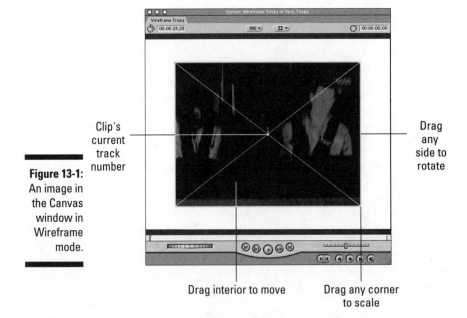

Clip's current track number

Drag any side to rotate

Figure 13-1:
An image in the Canvas window in Wireframe mode.

Drag interior to move

Drag any corner to scale

Scaling, rotating, and moving images

You can create some impressive video effects simply by scaling, rotating, and repositioning images on-screen. In fact, these straightforward tasks are the building blocks for most of the advanced effects you'll likely do in Express.

To start manipulating an image clip that's already on the Timeline, follow these easy steps:

1. **Make sure you're in Wireframe mode.**

   Remember, choose View⇨Image+Wireframe.

2. **Select the Final Cut Express Selection tool.**

   Remember, the Selection tool is the topmost tool in the Tool palette (it looks like an arrow).

3. **Select the clip on the Timeline, and make sure you can see it in the Canvas window.**

   You see the clip in the Canvas window when you position the Timeline playhead over it. But it's *also* very important to select the clip you want to work with on the Timeline. You need to select it to see its wireframe in the Canvas window.

4. **Click and drag the clip in various ways in the Canvas window (see Figure 13-2):**

   • **Scale:** To scale an image larger or smaller, click one of its four corners in the Canvas window, and drag the mouse pointer away from the center of the image to make it larger, or towards the center to make it smaller.

   • **Rotate:** To rotate an image, click the image in the Canvas anywhere on its wireframe border (but not the corners), and drag your mouse.

   • **Move:** To move an image (so it's off-center), move your mouse into the center of the image (anywhere away from its edges), and drag the image to a new spot in the Canvas window.

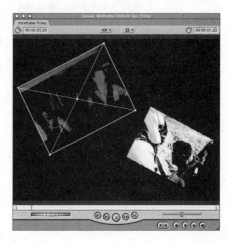

Figure 13-2: Two images, composited together on the Timeline, have been moved, scaled down, and rotated.

5. **Select the clip on the Timeline and choose Sequence➪Render Selection to render the clip, if necessary.**

   Depending on the changes you've made and whether Final Cut Express is in Real-Time mode (choose View➪Video to confirm your view mode and switch it if necessary), you may have to render before playing the clip from the Timeline.

Cropping or distorting an image

You can crop an image so that it ends at a point you choose. (I use cropping to create a quick and dirty wide-screen effect on video, cropping off the top and bottom portion of a video image.) You can also distort images, making them appear warped, stretched out, or compressed (see Figure 13-3).

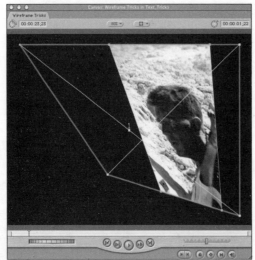

Figure 13-3: An image that's been cropped and distorted.

To crop or distort an image, follow the same steps used for scaling, rotating, and moving images (as described in the previous section), except instead of using the Final Cut Express standard Selection tool when manipulating an image in the Canvas window, use its custom Crop or Distort tools:

✔ **Crop:** Select the Crop tool from the Final Cut Express Tool palette (see Figure 13-4). Then crop any side of the image in the Canvas window by clicking and dragging the side of that image side inwards, towards the center of the Canvas window. When you crop at the corner of an image instead of its side, you crop two adjacent sides at once.

✔ **Distort:** Select the Distort tool from the Final Cut Express Tool palette (see Figure 13-4). Then click the tool on any corner of the wireframe that surrounds the image in the Canvas window, and drag your mouse to distort. **Note:** If you've cropped the image or scaled it, clicking the corners of the image itself won't work. You need to click the corners of its wireframe .

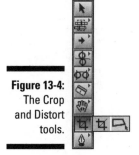

Figure 13-4:
The Crop
and Distort
tools.

If you hold down the Option key while you're using either the Crop or Distort tool, you can scale, move, and/or rotate an image by its wireframe, as if you were using the Final Cut Express standard Selection tool. This shortcut saves you the time from actually having to select the Selection tool.

Working in Wireframe mode in the Viewer

You can do all these manipulations to a clip (scaling, moving, cropping, rotating, and distorting) in the Viewer window too, not just in the Canvas window. I recommend doing it in the Canvas window after a clip is on the Timeline because the Canvas window simultaneously shows the clip you're trying to manipulate, as well as any other clips that happen to share the same sliver of time. (Final Cut Express places these clips on different tracks of the Timeline.) This way, as you manipulate a clip, you see how the changes affect the whole scene of your movie.

However, sometimes you may want to quickly manipulate a clip directly in the Final Cut Express Viewer without dragging the clip to the Timeline, and having to view it from the Canvas window. In this case, just open the clip in the Viewer (double-click it from the Browser window), and choose View➪ Image+Wireframe. Express then displays the same familiar wireframe outline on top of your clip, and you can make any manipulations you want, following the steps just covered.

Changing Images with the Motion Tab

Using Wireframe mode to manipulate images in the Canvas window is the most visual and intuitive way to move, scale, rotate, crop, and distort clips. However, you can accomplish the same thing by entering numerical values for a clip into the Viewer Motion tab. The Motion tab also offers a couple of new effects, such as a Drop Shadow and Blur, which you can apply to a clip.

I usually prefer the visual appeal of the Wireframe mode, but sometimes using the Motion tab is helpful (especially when you have to be very precise). For example, I recently used Final Cut Express to mock-up a Scenes menu for a DVD. I wanted four thumbnails of the DVD movie scenes to appear on the menu simultaneously. Of course, I wanted the thumbnails (which were just clips on the Express Timeline) to be the same size and to be perfectly aligned. Creating this menu was easier to do by entering the scale and position information for the clips in the Motion tab, rather than by using the Wireframe mode to try to arrange all the thumbnail clips visually in the Canvas window.

To alter a clip using the Viewer Motion tab, follow these steps:

1. **Place a clip on the Timeline.**

2. **Position the Timeline playhead over the clip to see it in the Canvas window.**

   This way, as you make changes to the clip in the Viewer Motion tab, you see the changes in the Canvas window.

3. **Double-click the clip on the Timeline to open it in the Viewer.**

4. **Click the Viewer Motion tab.**

   The Motion tab has all sorts of clip settings that you can adjust, including scale, rotation, and crop values (see Figure 13-5). The numeric values in the Motion tab reflect any adjustments you already made to this particular clip when it was in the Wireframe mode.

5. **Change the Scale, Rotation, and Center settings of the clip, and see the changes in the Canvas window:**

   • **Scale and Rotate:** To set the scale and rotation of a clip, drag the respective slider or dial, or type a numeric value into the respective field.

   • **Center:** To center the clip in a new position on-screen, click the cross-hair button in the Center area of the Motion tab, and the mouse pointer becomes a cross-hair symbol. Then click your mouse anywhere in the Canvas window to center the clip at that new point.

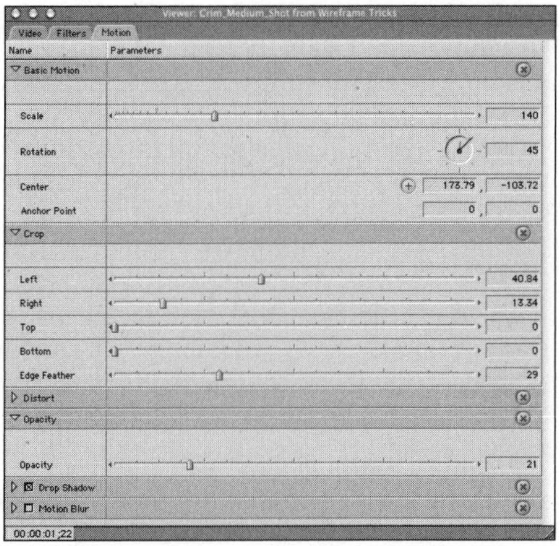

Figure 13-5:
Clip settings
in the
Viewer's
Motion tab.

6. **Either click the little triangle next to each control name or select a check box to turn the effects on to reveal theses other controls available in the Motion tab:**

   • **Crop:** You can set the number of pixels to crop off the side of an image. Even better, you can set a value to feather each side of an image so that its edges appear to gracefully fade away (a nice, sophisticated look).

   • **Distort:** You can define the position of each of the four corners of an image by X- and Y-coordinate, respectively. If you're thinking, "Wow! That's too many numbers to worry about," I agree wholeheartedly and recommend distorting an image visually in Wireframe mode (discussed earlier in this chapter).

   • **Opacity:** Remember, the less opacity you give to a clip, the more you can see through it to other clips that might be behind it (if you've stacked clips together on different Timeline tracks). Drag the Opacity slider or enter a value between 0 and 100. The higher the number, the less transparent the clip is.

   • **Drop Shadow:** Adding drop shadows to images create neat 3D effects (often making things feel more realistic). For instance, you can add drop shadows to text generators you place on the Timeline to make the text stand out. Another example: In making the DVD mock-up menu that I referred to earlier, I placed a drop shadow under each Scene thumbnail, making the thumbnails appear to float above the menu background. Anyway, Final Cut Express gives you lots of drop shadow control. The Offset value defines the number of pixels a drop shadow appears away from its subject. You can set the angle of a shadow from its subject, its color, opacity, and its softness (that is, how gracefully the edges of the shadow blend with whatever the shadow falls on).

- **Motion Blur:** You can create a stylized sense of motion by applying a Motion Blur to clips. You can control the power of the blur and the number of steps the blur uses. Leave some time to render out a few experiments before finding the right settings for this one.

If you tweak settings in the Motion tab, but then decide you don't like those tweaks and want to quickly reset the changes so that you can start over from scratch, just click the Reset button next to each value in the Motion tab (refer to Figure 13-5). This brings each setting back to the Final Cut Express default value.

7. **Select the clip on the Timeline and choose Sequence⇨Render Selection to render the clip.**

   You don't have to close the Motion tab. After playing the rendered clip on the Timeline, you can go right back to the open Motion tab and tweak the settings some more, but you'll need to render again to see your changes in action.

Using Keyframes to Change Motion Settings Over Time

The first half of this chapter outlined how to do all sorts of fancy things to your images, by using intuitive wireframes in the Canvas or by using the numerically precise approach of the Motion tab in the Viewer. These two methods may be enough for the projects you'll be tackling, but you can do more. In fact, considering the power of the Final Cut Express effects and compositing features, the rubber doesn't really meet the road until you combine the techniques described in the previous sections with the concept of keyframes, which let you *change* a clip's Motion settings (all the things you can control in the Motion tab) *over time*.

If this sounds kind of abstract, then consider this example: Using the skills you just acquired, you can scale a video clip to 50 percent of its original size. When that clip appears in your movie, Final Cut Express scales it to 50 percent, and you can *never* change that scaling size (or any other settings that define it, such as opacity, position, cropping, distortion, and so on). What if you want that clip to appear in your movie scaled at 50 percent, and then, after a second or so, begin scaling up so that after 3 or 4 seconds, it's 100 percent and dominates the scene? Well, the only way to change the Motion tab values such as Scale over time is by setting keyframes for them.

Keyframes are essentially marks you place in your movie that describe any Motion settings you want to give a clip. Final Cut Express notices the keyframes you place in your movie, and if the Motion values in those keyframes change over time, then Express smoothly changes the value between the two keyframes over time. For example, if the Scale value in Keyframe A is 50 percent and the Scale value in Keyframe B is 100 percent, Express continuously scales the clip up from 50 percent to 100 percent.

The speed of the changes between keyframes depends on how much time (in seconds, and even frames) lie between each keyframe you set. For example, if you set a keyframe at 5 seconds in your movie, and another at 10 seconds, then whatever values change between those keyframes will change over 5 seconds (the time between the two keyframes). To go back to the previous scaling example, the video clip gracefully scales from 50 percent to 100 percent over 5 seconds. However, if you set a keyframe at 5 seconds in your movie and set the next keyframe at 6 seconds, then the scaling effect takes place in only a split second, and the clip scales up very quickly. In other words, the more time between keyframes, the slower the transition (the more slowly a clip changes its scale, its opacity, its position, or any other value you may have changed between the keyframes).

Using keyframes to set clip opacity

If you read Chapter 12, then you're probably already comfortable with keyframes. (Chapter 12 covers how to use keyframes to change the volume level of clips over time to make some parts of a single clip soft and others louder.)

If you want to use keyframes to dynamically change the opacity level of a clip (so it appears to get more and less transparent over time), you can by placing keyframes on an Opacity *Overlay,* a fancy word for a line. This overlay appears on the clips on the Timeline, and you follow these steps to make changes:

1. **Place a clip on the Timeline.**

2. **Click the Clip Overlays button on the Timeline to toggle on the Opacity Overlay.**

   The Clip Overlays button is at the left corner of the Timeline (see Figure 13-6), and it toggles the overlays on and off. When it's on, you should see a thin black line that represents the opacity level appear at the top of all video clips on the Timeline.

   To better see the Opacity Overlay and the keyframes you're about to put on it, you may want to enlarge the view of the Timeline tracks. To do so quickly, click one of the taller vertical bars in the Timeline Track Height button, which is directly right of the Clip Overlays button.

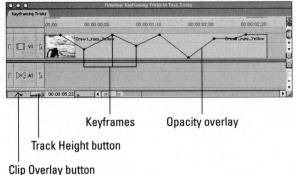

Figure 13-6:
Turn on clip
overlays to
view and set
keyframes.

Keyframes   Opacity overlay

Track Height button

Clip Overlay button

3. Select the Pen tool from the Tool palette.

The mouse cursor turns into the Pen symbol. The Pen tool lets you create keyframes in the Timeline window.

4. To place a keyframe, click the Pen tool on an Opacity Overlay.

You should place a keyframe wherever in time you want to set a new opacity level. When you place a keyframe, you see a little black diamond icon placed at that point on the Opacity Overlay.

5. Adjust the opacity level of the keyframe you just placed.

Move your mouse over the keyframe, and the pointer becomes a cross-hair symbol. Click and drag the Keyframe icon (the little diamond icon) up to increase the opacity level of the clip for that keyframe, or down to decrease the opacity (in other words, to make the clip more transparent). As you drag your mouse, a tiny pop-up box tells you the opacity level.

The change you make to the opacity level carries through for the rest of the clip unless you set another keyframe at a different opacity level.

6. Place another keyframe within that clip, and adjust its opacity level.

You're just repeating Steps 4 and 5 — with this exception: When you adjust the opacity level of the second clip, you should notice that the Opacity Overlay line moves from one keyframe to another over time (it begins to form what looks like a mountain range, as you can see if you refer to Figure 13-6). That's keyframing in action!

7. Place any other keyframes you might want within the clip.

The more keyframes you set now, the more practice you get free of charge.

8. Play the clip on the Timeline to see the opacity changes in action.

Editing existing keyframes

You can change the opacity setting for an existing keyframe, and you can also change where the keyframe is located in the clip (in other words, when in time the keyframe occurs). To make either change, just click and drag the keyframe (make sure you have the Pen tool selected), and drag the keyframe either left or right to move its location within the clip (so it plays earlier or later in time), or move it up or down to adjust its opacity level. To adjust the levels of adjacent keyframes simultaneously, hold down the ⌘ key, and drag the keyframe line between two keyframes up or down.

To delete an existing keyframe, make sure you have the Pen tool selected, hold down the Option key, and click on a keyframe. Final Cut Express then gives the keyframe the boot and adjusts its Opacity Overlay as if the keyframe was never there.

If you're doing quick and dirty keyframe adjustments (moving them in time or changing the level of their opacity), you can do so without selecting the Pen tool. With the standard Selection tool, just click on the keyframes and adjust them.

Using keyframes to set other motion values

The easiest way to change the opacity levels of a clip over time is by adding keyframes to its Opacity Overlay, as described in the section "Using keyframes to set clip opacity." If you want to create keyframes for other Motion settings — such as Scale, Origin, Rotation, Crop, Distort, and so on — then Final Cut Express requires you to use a different approach.

Now to be honest, the Final Cut Express approach to setting these other kind of keyframes is a bit clunky. It's fairly natural and intuitive to set keyframes on an overlay where you can visually see the values of each keyframe relative to each other and where each keyframe falls in time. It works well for setting Opacity Overlays, and this is how all keyframes work in Final Cut Pro (big brother to Express). However, I suppose Apple wanted to simplify the keyframe process for Express users and not put too much keyframe power into a $300 program.

The Express approach to setting most keyframes seems a little less intuitive and a bit less flexible (to me at least). It's still very easy to set keyframes, but it's a little tougher to go back and edit those keyframes later on (after you've rendered an effect and want to tweak keyframes to fine-tune the effect).

Anyway, you can use Motion keyframes to create a cool effect you see in a lot of Ken Burns documentaries by moving and scaling a large photograph around the screen (rather like zooming and panning). In fact, the Apple iMovie 3 does something like this effect and calls it the Ken Burns Effect no less, but Final Cut Express can do it with more control. And remember, if you're not interested in doing Ken Burns-style effects, you can still use these same principles and steps to make other Motion keyframes do practically whatever you can think of. Just follow these steps:

1. **Click and drag a still image from the Browser window to the Timeline.**

2. **Select the clip in the Timeline, and position the Timeline playhead over the clip so that you can see its image in the Canvas window.**

   You're going to watch the Canvas window to see how the Motion settings you'll soon be making affect the image. The results should look something like Figure 13-7.

Figure 13-7: Importing a still image and dropping it into the Timeline makes it look like a video clip in the Canvas window.

Some black areas appear around the edge of the image if the proportions of the image aren't exactly the same as the video frame. Don't worry: This is normal.

3. **Double-click the still clip on the Timeline to open it in the Viewer.**

   This step opens the clip in the Motion tab and activates the Motion tools for the clip.

4. **Click the Viewer Motion tab.**

   Ah, yes, the Motion tab. You should feel right at home here. If not, flip back a few pages to the section that explores this tab, "Changing Images with the Motion Tab."

5. **Position the playhead in the Timeline to the beginning of the clip.**

   You place the first keyframe at this position. Technically, you can place this keyframe anywhere in a clip, but this time you're starting at the beginning of a clip. By the way, having Snapping turned on (pressing N toggles it) helps snap the playhead to the edges of clips.

6. **Back in the Viewer Motion tab, set the clip starting values for settings such as Scale, Rotation, and Center.**

   For example, you can set the Scale at 100 percent (which, if the picture comes from a large scan or megapixel camera, makes the picture too large to fill the DV 720- x 480-pixel video frame). But this is often the idea; you might want to start off with just a small part of the picture filling the entire video frame.

   At any rate, you'll see the current state of the image in the Canvas window.

   Instead of making these adjustments in the Viewer Motion tab, you can also make the same kind of changes by clicking and dragging the image in the Canvas window, just as you did earlier in this chapter (see "Manipulating Images in Wireframe Mode"). Just make sure that you've set the Canvas window to Wireframe mode (choose View⇨Image+Wireframe) and that you've selected the clip you're working with on the Timeline. I often use both approaches to change images. I use my mouse in the Canvas window to make a general change and then use the Motion tab (with its numerical precision) for precision tuning.

7. **Click the Add Keyframe button in the Canvas window to place the first keyframe (refer to Figure 13-7).**

   By doing this, you're placing the first keyframe where the Timeline playhead happens to be and assigning the keyframe the values in the Motion tab at the time. But unlike setting opacity keyframes on an overlay (as in the last section), you won't actually see a cute little Keyframe icon show up anywhere. And that's what I meant when I said Final Cut Express handles keyframes a bit oddly — you'd expect to see something for all your effort, right? But . . . whatever. I live with it; so can you.

   Even though Express doesn't show a keyframe icon, you can create a makeshift icon yourself by placing a marker in the same exact spot as your invisible keyframe. After you place your keyframe, select your keyframed clip on the Timeline — but don't move the Timeline's playhead — and press M (for marker). Express places a marker in your clip at the playhead's position, which is the same position of your keyframe. You can now use this marker as visual reference to your invisible keyframes.

8. **Drag the Timeline playhead to the next place in the clip where you want to set a keyframe.**

   Remember, the more time between, the slower the changes when the clip plays.

9. **In the Viewer Motion tab, enter the values you want for this new keyframe so that Final Cut Express automatically places it.**

   If you've moved the Timeline playhead after setting the first keyframe (as you did in Step 8) and then you change one of the Motion settings, Final Cut Express guesses that it should just throw caution to the wind and places a keyframe for you. Handy, eh? But yet again, Express offers no icon or visual cue to represent the keyframe in the clip — you're flyin' blind here!

   Anyway, go ahead and change as many of the Motion values as you want. Two natural values to tweak would be Scale, to make the picture appear to zoom in or out, and perhaps also Center, which centers the picture in a different spot, making it appear to move or pan across the screen when your clip plays over time. These changes all become part of the keyframe you've just placed.

10. **If you want to set more keyframes in the clip, just repeat Steps 8 and 9.**

    Simpler animations and effects can get away with just two keyframes, but fancier ones can involve several keyframes.

11. **Select the freshly keyframed clip on the Timeline and choose Sequence⇨Render Selection to render it.**

    You're now ready to play it. Depending on the number and types of Motion values the keyframes call for and whether you're in the Final Cut Express Real-Time mode, you may not have to render. You can play a real-time preview directly from the Timeline. Lucky dog!

When you play your rendered clip, you see the motion you created. For example, an image can be made to scale from one size to another and move across the screen, as shown in Figure 13-8.

So that's how to set Motion keyframes in a clip. I oriented the example toward zooming and panning a still picture ala Ken Burns, but you can apply these steps to any other kind of motion effects you have in mind. Go crazy.

Editing motion keyframes

As you animate motion effects, you'll probably want to tweak keyframes a bit here or there to fine-tune your effects. However, remember, when you set motion keyframes, Final Cut Express leaves no icons to show where they went. So how do you tweak keyframes you can't even see?

Well, fortunately, you can use keyboard commands to jump the Timeline playhead to existing-but-invisible keyframes in a clip, and then use the Viewer Motion tab to review and possibly change the Motion values of each keyframe. Just follow these steps:

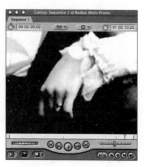

Figure 13-8: Animation is created on a still image with cropping, panning, and zooming.

1. **Double-click a keyframed clip on the Timeline to open it in the Viewer.**

2. **Click the Viewer Motion tab, which allows you to see the clip's current Motion settings.**

3. **Position the Timeline playhead near the clip you just opened in the Viewer.**

4. **Press Shift+K to move the Timeline playhead forward to the next keyframe in a clip, or press Option+K to move it back to the previous keyframe.**

   As the Timeline playhead jumps to the nearest invisible keyframe, the values in the Viewer Motion tab change to reflect the settings of each keyframe.

5. **To edit a keyframe, change its values in the Viewer Motion tab.**

   You don't have to reapply the keyframe. Just change its values.

6. **To edit more keyframes, repeat Steps 4 and 5.**

7. **Select the clip on the Timeline and choose Sequence⇨Render Selection to render the clip, if necessary.**

Want to delete a keyframe altogether? If you set it recently, you can always undo the keyframe by choosing Edit⇨Undo. But if undoing isn't an option, which is the case if, for example, you set the unwanted keyframes during another work session, then that's going to be a bit of a problem. Final Cut Express doesn't let you delete its hidden Motion keyframes. The most you can do is move the playhead to the keyframe you don't want there, and use the Viewer Motion tab to make its values match settings of the previous keyframe. However, that may still not give the results you want. If you really want the most flexibility, get in the habit of copying a clip (select it on the Timeline and choose Edit⇨Copy) and paste a backup version somewhere else on the Timeline before setting each keyframe. It's a pain, but doing so lets you go back to an earlier version of the clip that doesn't have the offending keyframe.

Chapter 14

Compositing

● ●

In This Chapter

▶ Choosing a composite mode

▶ Understanding alpha channels

▶ Use a matte to hide parts of a video clip

▶ Creating a key for green and blue screen effects

● ●

*T*his chapter presents *compositing,* the merging of two or more different images into one. An example of compositing is the old trick of making an actor appear in front of a background he or she was never in. First, you film the actor in front of a solid color background. Later, you remove the background and film the actor in front of a beach, an exploding building, or something else. Another miracle of compositing is the collage of images and text — all moving and fading in and out gracefully — that you typically see at the beginning of a news or sports program or a documentary. (This kind of work utilizes the skills described in Chapter 13 for scaling and moving images around and changing their opacity.)

In this chapter, I cover how to do compositing as well as discuss some related compositing topics such as *mattes,* which let you selectively crop out parts of an image. When you combine the information in this chapter with the details in Chapters 12 and 13, you can create some very impressive visual work!

If you expect people to watch your finished movie on a TV, make sure you preview all your compositing work on a TV beforehand! Composited images can appear subtly different in the way colors interact or in the sharpness of an image's edges when they are displayed on your Mac's screen versus a TV.

Get ready to render! If you don't like to sit around waiting for clips to render, well, I hate to break the news, but this chapter isn't for you! The kind of advanced effects work that I do in this chapter requires you to render your clips with every tweak you make. The good news is that when you're willing to put in a little extra time, you achieve some very cool results!

Choosing a Composite Mode

In effect, *composite modes* allow you to set how the colors of one clip mix into the colors of the second clip. Final Cut Express has many composite modes that I loosely group in two categories: practical and artistic.

The Multiply composite mode, which eliminates white pixels from an image, is an example of the practical mode. You may want to use it if, for example, you have a still image you want to separate from a white background. The Screen composite mode is similar, but it drops out black pixels.

Artistic composite modes, on the other hand, are good for creating a pretty, colorful picture based on the interaction of the colors in the two clips. For example, the Difference mode subtracts the color values of a clip from a clip in the Timeline track above it. Figure 14-1 shows the results of two clips when combined with a Difference mode. As you can see, the Difference mode is best reserved for moments when you want to play the artist and achieve fantasy effects.

Figure 14-1:
The clip on the left was placed on top of the middle clip, and the Difference mode was applied to create the clip on the right.

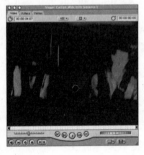

Final Cut Express offers 13 composite modes. I explain what effect each mode has on your images. If you can't grasp what these modes do by reading, don't worry about it too much. Even the most experienced composite mode users don't go by mathematical descriptions of pixel behavior when it comes to choosing composite modes. Most just try out a few until they like what they see. You can do the same.

When talking about compositing, I use the term *layer* a lot. By layer, I simply mean a video clip that's on its own Timeline track. Compositing involves merging clips together, and each clip is considered a layer in the overall composited effect. (Other programs, such as Photoshop, use the concept of layers, and the concept here is the same: A layer is an element that's merged with another.) When I use the terms bottom or top clips, I'm referring to how Final Cut Express stacks clips together on different tracks on the Timeline. A bottom clip might be on Track V1 on the Timeline, and a top clip on Track V2.

The following list provides a brief explanation of each composite mode effect:

- ✔ **Normal:** This is the default mode for all clips that are edited into the Timeline. The Normal mode shows the clip on the topmost Timeline track, without any modifications.

- ✔ **Add:** This mode combines the values of the color pixels of the top clip with those of the bottom clip and creates a final image that is brighter than the two combined.

- ✔ **Subtract:** This mode subtracts the values of the color pixels of the top clip from those of the bottom clip. The final image is darker than the original two.

- ✔ **Difference:** Difference mode subtracts the color values of the bottom clip from those of the top clip. This mode can give you some artistically interesting combinations, depending on the colors of the two clips.

- ✔ **Multiply:** This mode compares the color values of the pixels of the top clip with those of the clip below it and then multiplies the two values together. If the image is dark, this mode has little effect. This mode darkens a light image. Multiply, commonly used to drop out white backgrounds from stills and other images, is one of the more useful modes. For example, if someone gives you a Photoshop still with a logo against a white background, you can use the Multiply mode to drop out the white and place the logo over the video layer of your choice (hopefully, the logo won't have any white in it because that will be lost too!).

- ✔ **Screen:** This mode is another one of those useful modes than can save the day in a pinch. The Screen mode, in effect, drops out the black pixels of a clip. If you have a video clip or a still that has an element you want to save over a black background, you can apply this mode to the clip to eliminate the black pixels. If you find it hard to live without the mathematical explanation of this mode, here it is: Screen mode compares the color values of the pixels in the top clip to those of the bottom clip and multiplies the inverse of each. So now you know!

- ✔ **Overlay:** The Overlay mode combines the color values between the two layers and maintains the highlights and the shadows. You can use this mode to combine images together so that they appear to merge into one another.

- ✔ **Hard Light:** The Hard Light mode multiplies the colors, depending on the color values of the clip. This mode often creates a slightly dramatic, colorful look to the final composite. Again, the result depends on the colors you have in the layers, and experimenting can produce quite a pleasing effect.

- ✔ **Soft Light:** This mode darkens or lightens the layers. The colors that result from this compositing mode depend on the original layer color.

- ✔ **Darken:** Darken compares the color values of two composited clips and displays the darker of the two.

- ✔ **Lighten:** The opposite of Darken, this mode compares the color values of the two composited clips and displays the lighter of the two.

- ✔ **Travel Matte-Alpha:** This mode applies a matte to the top clip, using information from the bottom clip. You can use travel mattes to create halos or cutout borders that combine the two layered clips. The Alpha option of this mode ignores the RGB channels and looks only for the alpha channel — if one is present. I talk about alpha channels in a moment, but they define colors intended to be transparent and you can create them using Adobe Photoshop or other such photo-editing applications.

- ✔ **Travel Matte-Luma:** This mode works just like the preceding one except that instead of the alpha channel, it uses luminance values (black and white values) to create the final matte. The advantage here is that you don't need an alpha channel in an image beforehand. Anything black in the image is invisible (transparent), whereas anything white in the image is visible (or opaque).

For readers who have worked in the Adobe Photoshop or After Effects applications, keep in mind that the 13 Final Cut Express composite modes behave exactly as they do in the Adobe applications.

Applying a Composite Mode

You use composite modes on layered clips in the Timeline (that is, clips that are stacked together on different tracks). To apply a composite mode, you must first add two clips to the Timeline, right on top of one another. (See Chapter 6 if you need a refresher on how to do so.) Figure 14-2 shows how these layered clips appear in the Timeline.

After you place the two clips on different tracks, on top of each other, follow these steps:

1. **Select the top clip.**

2. **Choose Modify⇨Composite Mode and choose one of the composite modes you see in the submenu, as shown in Figure 14-3.**

   Final Cut Express applies the composite mode to the topmost clip on the Timeline.

Figure 14-2:
Composite
modes are
applied to
the topmost
clip in a
layered
setting.

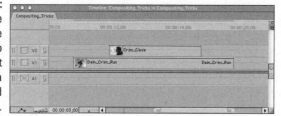

Note that composite modes create an effect between two layers, working
downwards. In essence, the layer (that is, the clip) that has the composite
mode needs another layer (clip) beneath it to show an effect. You *can* technically apply the composite mode to the bottom layer, but it will not show any
changes because it has no layer beneath it.

Figure 14-3:
Choosing a
composite
mode.

Understanding Alpha Channels

Channels are nothing more than layers that, combined together, create a
final image. Most video clips have three channels of color: red, green, and blue.
These color channels combine to create all the other colors you see in the clip.
However, you can create some video and still images with a fourth channel, the
alpha channel. This alpha channel contains information that pertains to the
transparency of the clip. Alpha channels tell Final Cut Express which parts of
the image to make visible and which parts to make invisible.

For example, maybe you're working with an artist who's using the Adobe After Effects program to create a movie of an animated logo against an alpha channel background. You can import this movie (assuming it's saved in the QuickTime format, of course) into Final Cut Express and layer it above an existing video track. Express recognizes the animation's alpha channel background and makes it transparent, while the logo remains visible and composites cleanly over your video track. If the artist had created this animation without an alpha channel background (for example, with a solid black background), then you'd have a tougher time compositing the logo with your video in Express. (In truth, you can use a different compositing mode to knock out the logo's background, as discussed earlier, but that is more complicated and can lead to some problems.) The point is that by building artwork with built-in, alpha-channel backgrounds, you make it very easy to composite that art with your Express video.

In some situations, Final Cut Express may misinterpret the alpha channel that's built into some artwork you're trying to use. This problem may be obvious in some artifacts such as edge-fringing or halos around your final composited image. These artifacts make your final composite look grungy and rough at the edges. If you have these problems, select the clip in the Timeline and choose Modify⇨Alpha Type and choose a different type of alpha from the submenu. Experiment with different alpha types: The problem disappears and the edges appear smooth when you choose the correct type.

Compositing with Mattes and Keys

Mattes and keys are common in software programs devoted to compositing and creating special effects. Even though Final Cut Express is mainly a nifty editing program, it fortunately has many features and functions built into it that allow you to create these kind of interesting composting effects:

- **Mattes:** *Mattes* are nothing more than still images used to create various cutout effects. In fact, you can think of mattes as cardboard cutouts (imagine a cardboard sheet with a circle cut out in the middle, revealing any imagery behind it). In fact, digital mattes get their name from the old-fashioned mattes that surround a professionally framed art print or photograph. Of course, mattes in the digital world are much more versatile than cardboard mattes are. In Final Cut Express, you can fill the inside or the outside of the matte with different video or stills. You see this in effect in the next section.

- **Keys:** *Keys,* on the other hand, eliminate certain color or luminance values from an image to create transparency. You use keys to create, among other things, the "weatherperson effect" on your local news: A meteorologist is photographed in front of a blue or green background and later that particular color is keyed out (made transparent) so that the image of a satellite weather map can appear behind the meteorologist.

Creating a simple matte

You can apply simple mattes to your clips very easily in Final Cut Express. This section discusses how to apply a quick and dirty matte, such as the one shown in Figure 14-4, just to get your feet wet. As an extension of these steps, I explain how to composite your matted clip over another image, so you can see how the two different clips interact together. Just follow these steps:

1. **Drag a video clip from the Browser to the Timeline.**

2. **Position the Timeline playhead over the clip so you can see it in Canvas window.**

3. **Select the clip on the Timeline, and choose Effects⇨Video Filters⇨Matte⇨Mask Shape.**

   Notice that an invisible rectangular matte automatically crops your clip, as seen in the Canvas window. You can adjust the shape of the matte in just a moment.

   By the way, you'll find all the Final Cut Express Matte related filters by choosing Effects⇨Video Filters⇨Matte, but I am sticking with the Mask Shape filter because it illustrates the basics of a matte so well.

Figure 14-4:
An oval matte applied to a video clip.

You can also apply a filter to your clip by opening the Final Cut Express Effects window (choose Window⇨Effects), opening the Matte bin, and dragging the Mask Shape filter onto the Timeline clip.

4. **Double-click the video clip on the Timeline to open it in the Viewer.**

5. **Click the Viewer Filters tab.**

   Remember, you can use the Filters tab in the Viewer to tweak any filter you apply to a clip.

6. **From the Viewer Filters tab, adjust the matte settings (see Figure 14-5):**

   - **Shape:** Adjust the matte shape by clicking the Shape pop-up menu (you can change it to an oval, round, rectangle, or diamond shape).

   - **Size:** Change the matte size by tweaking its Horizontal and Vertical scale values (you can drag the respective sliders or type a value up to 200).

   - **Center:** To center the matte in a new position on-screen, click the cross-hair button in the Center area of the Mask Shape filter (the mouse pointer becomes a cross-hair symbol). Then click your mouse anywhere in the Canvas window to center the matte at that new point.

   - **Invert:** You can invert a matte (swapping the areas of the clip that the matte hides and reveals) by selecting the Invert check box.

   When you position the Timeline playhead over the clip, you see the changes made in the Canvas window.

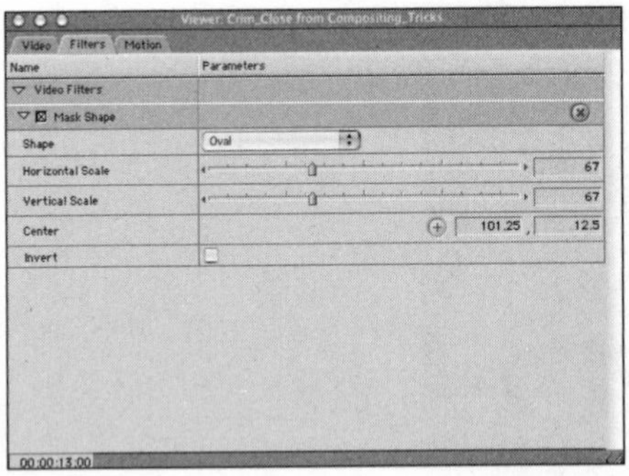

Figure 14-5:
Tweak these Filter settings to customize the matte.

Softening the edges of your matte.

By default, the edges of a matte are *hard,* meaning it looks like they've been cut with a very sharp knife, creating very well defined lines. But you can soften those edges so that your video clip seems to gracefully fade into the edges of the matte, as shown in Figure 14-6. This option is especially handy when you want to composite the matted clip with another image (which I explain how to do in a moment).

You can easily soften the edges of a matte you've already applied to a clip, using these steps:

1. **Position the Timeline playhead over the matted clip whose edges you want to soften.**

   This way, you can see the clip displayed in the Canvas window.

2. **Select the clip on the Timeline, and choose Effects⇨Video Filters⇨Matte⇨Mask Feather.**

   When you apply the Mask Feather filter to a matted clip, you notice a subtle softening of the matte edges. You can increase this effect.

3. **Double-click the video clip on the Timeline to open it in the Viewer.**

4. **Click the Viewer Filters tab.**

5. **From the Viewers Filters tab, adjust the Soft settings of the matte.**

   Drag the filter slider or type a number as high as a 100. The greater the Soft number, the softer the edges of the matte become.

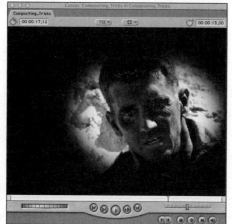

Figure 14-6:
The matte,
softened
up with
the Mask
Feather
filter.

Compositing your matted video clip with another clip

Now that you've applied a matte to a video clip (effectively hiding some areas of the clip behind the matte), you can composite this matted clip with another video clip so that the areas hidden by the matte reveal the second clip behind it, as shown in Figure 14-7. Just follow these steps:

1. **Place the second, new clip on the Timeline.**

2. **On the Timeline, drag the matted clip onto the track directly above the new clip.**

   In other words, if the new clip is on Track V1, drag the matted clip onto Track V2 so Final Cut Express stacks the two clips together.

Final Cut Express then composites (combines) your matted clip with the new clip. Remember, the clip that's on a higher track number appears first, but the clip matte is transparent, so you can see through to the new clip below!

Figure 14-7:
The matted clip composited with a new clip.

Using intricate mattes

As you can see, the Final Cut Express filter tools let you create mattes with simple shapes. If you want to create a more sophisticated matte design — such as a design featuring rows of vertical columns, something that resembles Venetian blinds, or a matte featuring lots of random cutouts — you can use a graphics program like Adobe Photoshop to create the matte (in black and white, typically), save it as a Photoshop file (or even a TIFF or JPEG), and then import the graphic into Express. Then, on the Express Timeline, you can stack the matte on top of another video clip, select the matte, and then choose Modify⇨Composite Mode⇨Travel Matte-Luma. If you created the matte using an alpha channel in Photoshop, try Modify⇨Composite Mode⇨Travel Matte-Alpha.

Compositing with keys

Another way of creating composites is by using keys. You create a *key* by using a clip in which the subject is filmed against a blue or green background (green backgrounds tend to be the color of choice these days, but blue can have advantages too). You later replace the colored background with another background element, such as a computer-generated scene. (Nearly all recent Star Wars or Matrix movies would not be possible without the use of keys.)

This process may sound simple, but creating a good clean key is quite a bit of work. Many companies, such as Ultimatte and others, specialize in creating high-end software that has the sole purpose of creating clean color keys. The Final Cut Express tools aren't nearly as sophisticated as some on the market, but they're not a bad place to start. Use the Final Cut Express tools by giving Toby the cat a little cameo appearance in the sci-fi action pic, *Radius*.

To create a key, follow these steps:

1. **Drag the foreground and background shots from the Browser and stack them on different tracks on the Timeline.**

   Place the key (the subject shot against a green or blue background) on the top track, and place the background you want to insert on the bottom video track.

   For the example, I filmed our key, a cat, against a green screen, and the background is a scene from *Radius*. The two elements are shown in Figure 14-8.

2. **Position the Timeline playhead over the stacked clips so you can see them in the Canvas window.**

   This way, you can use the Canvas window to preview the clips as you tweak them.

Toby the cat

Gun-toting soldier

Figure 14-8: Toby the cat, filmed against a green screen, is keyed into a shot from *Radius*. From a story standpoint, you can see how they should be together, yes?

3. **Select the green screen layer (in this case, Toby the cat) by clicking it and then choosing Effects⇨Video Filters⇨Key⇨Blue and Green Screen.**

   Final Cut Express applies the Blue and Green Screen filter to the top clip.

4. **To adjust filter settings, double-click the green screen key layer to open it into the Viewer window.**

5. **Click the Filters tab, as shown in Figure 14-9.**

   The settings for the Blue and Green Screen filter appear.

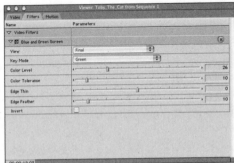

Figure 14-9:
The Blue and Green screen filter settings.

6. **From the Key Mode drop-down list, select Blue or Green, depending on the color of the background of the video.**

   See the sidebar "Shooting for green or blue screens" for more about the blue versus green debate.

7. **Keeping an eye on the image in the Canvas window, click and drag the Color Level slider to a lower setting until the color or the blue or green screen disappears.**

   Drag the slider slowly so that you can see the green color in the video drop out bit by bit. You may have to tweak this to your satisfaction. The slider defaults to 100.

8. **Click and drag the sliders to adjust Edge Thin and Edge Feather and tweak your work:**

   • **Edge Thin:** The Edge Thin creates a choking in or out of the outer boundaries of your subject.

   • **Edge Feather:** The Edge Feather creates a slight feather to an edge.

   In this case, I also scaled Toby the cat a bit and moved him to one side to better fit the scene (I describe how to scale and move images in Chapter 13), although between you and me, Toby probably has no business in an action movie anyway. Figure 14-10 shows the final results.

Figure 14-10:
No cats were harmed in the making of this *For Dummies* book.

Tips for getting clean keys

The basic key filters in Final Cut Express are just the first step in getting a clean key. You can use many other tools on the Effects➪Video Filters➪Key menu to help you clean up the key. The following list gives a brief rundown of a few of them:

- ✔ **Luma Key:** The Luma Key filter allows a key based on luminance values (such as black and white) as opposed to color values (green or blue). For example, if you shot an all-white element against a solid black background, you may want to use this key to drop out the blacks and retain the white element.

- ✔ **Difference Matte:** This type of key compares two layers and eliminates what they have in common. You need to prepare for using this matte when you're in the shooting phase. The Difference Matte requires that you film a shot twice: once with the subject in front of the background, and the second time with just the background and without the subject. Ideally, these shots are exactly the same (except for the presence of the subject of course — in other words, not even a slight difference in the camera position, angle, and so on (that's why it's important to use a good tripod). The final results compare the two layers and eliminate the background while retaining the subject.

  The main advantage to the Difference Matte method is that the background doesn't have to be blue or green. It can be anything, as long as it doesn't change.

- ✔ **Spill Suppressors:** In many cases, when you finish filming the green or blue screen shots, you may notice that your subjects often have a little of the screen color reflected on them (this is called *spill*). Final Cut

Express has two filters that can help correct this spill — one for green and one for blue. These suppressors eliminate color spills, which are otherwise quite difficult to get rid of using a simple key. To apply a suppressor, click your clip in the Timeline to select it, and then choose Effects⇨Video Filters⇨Key⇨Spill Suppressor - Green or Blue.

✔ **Use the matte tools:** You can find numerous matte tools that are useful for creating clean keys. For example:

• **8-Point and 4-Point Garbage mattes:** Garbage mattes are rough mattes that eliminate parts of the image that won't be used in the final key. For example, in some keying work, you may notice a black line at the edge of your video frame. By using a Garbage matte, you can quickly mask out the areas around your subject and simply get rid of the distracting edges on the frame.

To apply the Garbage mattes, select a clip on the Timeline, and then choose Effect⇨Video Filters⇨Matte menu. After you apply the 4-point or 8-point Garbage mattes, double-click the Timeline clip to open it in the Viewer. In the Viewer Video tab, you should see each point that the filter controls labeled clearly with a number, as shown in Figure 14-11. (You can adjust these points to crop out offending parts of a frame; my example is exaggerated to illustrate the point). Drag the Viewer Video tab outside the Viewer, and then click the Viewer Filters tab (this way you can adjust the filter while seeing its results at the same time in the Video tab). The Filters tab displays coordinates for four or eight points (clearly labeled). You can move these points by clicking the cross hair in the Filter setting and clicking different portions of the image in the Viewer Video tab to create a new matte shape.

Figure 14-11:
An 8-point Garbage matte as seen in the Viewer Video tab.

- **Matte Choker:** The Matte Choker is the ideal substitute for the Edge Thin slider found in some of the Final Cut Express key filters. *Edge thinning* is the process of removing the outer edges of your subject. The Edge Thin sliders in the Express key filters often produce a harsh edge. Use the Matte Choker instead to slightly *choke* (move the matte inward around the subject) the matte in to cut out some of the green or blue fringes that may appear around the edges. You apply the Matte Choker by selecting a clip on the Timeline, and then choosing Effect➪Video Filters➪Matte➪Matte Choker. Slider settings allow you to decide how much edge thinning you want to do and also to be able to feather or soften the edge.

Shooting for green or blue screens

If you're struggling to create a good green or blue screen effect, remember this adage from the pros of keying: Most of the work for green screening is already done by the time the video ends up in your hands. That means that the real trick to getting a good, clean key is to shoot your video right in the first place.

Filming actors or other elements in front of a green screen is an art and a science. Some of the best directors in Hollywood call on companies and professionals who specialize in shooting green screen, but I have some guidelines you can apply for best results:

- **Green or blue?** The general rule is that if a lot of flesh tone is in the shots, use a green color (one of the reasons why green screens have become fairly popular these days). But consider the colors your subject will feature as well. If an actor is wearing a loud, neon-green shirt, you don't want to film them in front of a green screen because removing the green screen color without taking out part of your actor's shirt may be difficult.

- **Use the right color grade:** The blue or green you may see in the green screening shots is not just any green or blue. These paints are

a standard color and should be obtained from a photo supply or specialty paint store (in other words, don't start using that old house paint in your garage). Many photo supply shops also sell background cloth with the right shade of blue or green. This hanging cloth saves you the trouble of painting for hours.

- **Light and paint the background evenly:** It's absolutely crucial to light and paint the screen evenly so that no part is lighter or darker than the rest. Uneven areas make it very hard for Final Cut Express to key out, because it's ideally looking for a single color to separate, and it won't interpret uneven areas (such as a light green and dark green) as a single color.

- **Keep your distance:** Maintain a distance of at least 10 feet between your subjects and the green or blue screen background. The distance prevents the color of the screen from reflecting subtly onto your subjects, which will complicate your efforts to get a proper key later and make your subjects look as if they have strange skin conditions!

Part V
Outputting Your Masterpiece

In this part . . .

*W*hen you're finished editing and adding any transitions, titles, effects, and so on, you're ready for Part V, which focuses on outputting your Final Cut Express movie to its final destination. I cover how to record your finished masterpiece back to DV videotape (for tape duplication or broadcast) and how also to save your finished movie to a QuickTime digital file, which you can later burn to a DVD or CD-ROM, or broadcast over the Internet.

Chapter 15

Recording to Tape

• •

• •

*O*ne of the last stages of working on a project in Final Cut Express is to record your edited, polished movie from a sequence back to DV video-tape (or maybe even old fashioned VHS). Recording your final edited project to tape is a common method for delivering your project to a broadcast house or to a client. It's also a popular option for archiving all those home movies you may be editing.

As with anything else in Final Cut Express, you have a couple of choices available to you at this stage. Make your final choice based on your equipment and the needs of your clients or whomever is awaiting the delivery of the final master tape.

Setting Up for Recording

Before you record your edited project to tape, you need to set up your equipment for recording back to tape, and verify some settings in Final Cut Express:

1. **Connect your DV equipment.**

   Just connect your DV camera or deck directly to your Mac FireWire port with a FireWire cable. This process is exactly the same, simple setup you used to capture DV video, so you don't have to worry about new tricks.

   If you're recording to a VHS, flip ahead to the section "Recording to VHS" for more information.

2. **Set the DV camera or deck into VCR or VTR mode.**

   Make sure that your DV deck or camera is in VCR mode. Sometimes the VCR mode is also labeled VTR (Video Tape Recorder) or Playback. Final Cut Express doesn't record to your DV device when it is set to Camera mode.

   If, by any chance, your DV device (such as a DV deck) has multiple inputs (often labeled Video 1 or Video 2 or Line 1 or Line 2), check that you're using the right input. Video decks often have an Input button that switches the inputs to the deck or the camera. The indicators for the Input selected appear either on the front panel of the deck or inside the viewfinder of the camera.

   Still have questions about setting up your equipment? The best thing to do is dig up your owner's manual. (You did save it, didn't you?)

   You may also want to check the recording prevention tab on your DV tape to be sure that it isn't in the Save setting. DV s have a small tab on one side that switches between Record (meaning you can erase over the tape) and Save, which means you cannot record over your tape.

3. **Check the Final Cut Express settings.**

   You need to make Final Cut Express aware of the DV camera or deck that you've just hooked up (if it's not aware of it already). You know a camera is aware when it can display video from your Timeline on its little LCD viewfinder. The easiest way to make Express aware of your camera or deck is by using the Easy Setup dialog box.

4. **Choose Final Cut Express⇨Easy Setup.**

   In the Easy Setup dialog box, make sure that the External Video For Playback field shows Apple FireWire and the External Video for Recording field shows Same as Playback, as shown in Figure 15-1. This setting indicates that you're ready to output via FireWire, so just click the Setup button to lock in that setting.

   When you click the Setup button, it causes Final Cut Express to make a connection with your camera/deck. At this point, you should be able to see the video from your Timeline displayed on your DV camera or the TV hooked into your DV deck. If not, choose View⇨Video, and make sure you have the FireWire option selected.

Figure 15-1:
Check the
Easy Setup
dialog box
before
recording
to tape.

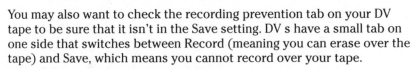

5. To render your sequence, choose Sequence⇨Render All.

You may not need to render, depending on your project, but it's better to be on the safe side. This step ensures that Final Cut Express has properly rendered all items. Without rendering, some of the items, such as effects, may not play at all in your sequence.

6. Choose Sequence⇨Mixdown Audio.

This step renders all the audio in a sequence. If you don't follow this step, your sequence may drop frames during playback or have hiccups in the audio.

Looking out for dropped frames

Many other editing systems come with high-powered video cards that perform most of the processing tasks otherwise done by the computer, but not Final Cut Express. Instead, Express relies almost entirely on the hardware muscle built into your Mac. In some cases, if the requirements of the video are too taxing for the CPU or hard drive, Express *drops* some video frames, meaning it won't record all your frames back to tape (resulting in jittery playback and hiccups in your video — not at all desirable).

To be sure that Final Cut Express notifies you when it drops frames as you record to tape, choose Final Cut Express⇨Preferences and, within the General tab, make sure that you have selected the Report Dropped Frames During Playback option, as shown in Figure 15-2.

Check here to report dropped frames

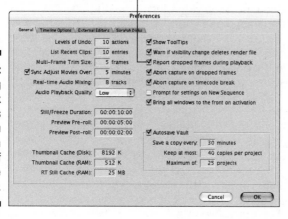

Figure 15-2:
Selecting this check box ensures that you receive a warning if frames are dropped.

Selecting this option assures that Final Cut Express warns you about any dropped frames that may occur during recording to tape. When you do get this warning, you can take steps to prevent frames from being dropped, such as closing all other applications, suspending any network tasks that may be taking place, and speeding up your hard drive (see Chapter 3 for more about dropped frames related to hard drive issues). Then restart your computer and attempt to record to tape again.

Recording to VHS

VHS remains one of the most common video formats around, and you may want to record your Final Cut Express movies back to VHS, rather than DV tape. Fortunately, Express offers a quick and easy way to do this, as long as you have a DV camera or deck as well (I refer to DV cameras from now on). See, most DV cameras have analog video and audio output connectors, which are there so you can play your camera signal *out* to a TV set. But instead of hooking up a TV to your DV camera, you can hook up a VHS VCR, and use it to record the video/audio signal coming from your camera to a VHS tape. The DV camera effectively works as a middleman between your Mac and the VHS deck: The camera receives a DV video signal from your Mac through its FireWire cable, converts that signal to analogue, and then sends it over to the VHS deck for final recording.

The connectors used to connect a DV camera to a VCR look very much like the stereo RCA-type connections found on the back of your home stereo, as shown in Figure 15-3. Most VHS decks have RCA-type video and audio inputs. (These inputs should be on the back of your VCR. Usually, the video input is yellow, and the audio inputs are red and white — one carries the left channel of stereo audio and the other carries the right.) All you need is a pair of RCA-type connectors to connect the video and audio outputs of your DV device to the video and audio inputs of your VHS deck. Your DV camera may have shipped with the cables you need already — a common cable these days has with three RCA connectors on one end (yellow, red, and white), and a single, small connector at the other, which connects to your DV camera. If you don't have these connectors, you can get them from Radio Shack or any other store that sells stereos.

If your DV camera *and* your VHS VCR both have S-Video connectors, then you may want to consider using an S-Video cable to connect the two devices. S-Video is desirable because its signal quality is better than that of RCA connectors, and this increased quality results in a better looking video image being transferred from your camera to the VHS tape (not significantly better, but a little sharper to the discerning eye). S-Video only carries a video signal, though, so you'll still need to attach two RCA connectors between your camera and VCR to transfer stereo audio (one connector for your stereo audio's left channel, and one connector for its right channel).

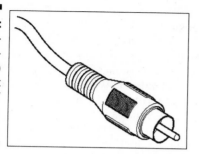

Figure 15-3:
Use RCA-
type con-
nectors to
connect
your DV
camera to a
VHS deck.

To connect your equipment using RCA connectors, follow these steps:

1. **Connect your RCA cables to the video/audio inputs on your VCR deck.**

   You need to connect three cables to your deck: one for video, and two for audio.

   If you opt to use an S-Video cable to transfer video, connect that to the S-Video input on your VHS deck.

2. **Attach the other ends of your RCA cables to your DV camera's audio/video input connector.**

   Many DV cameras — particularly small ones — have only one connector port for both RCA video and audio, and provide you with a special cable that has three RCA connectors at one end (these go to your VCR in Step 1), and one single connector at the other (this goes into your camera).

   Again, if you opt to use S-Video, connect this cable to your DV camera's S-Video connector.

3. **Be sure to hook up the output of your VHS deck to a television so that you can see if the recording is proceeding successfully.**

   That's it. You should be ready to record your DV camera signal to a VHS tape.

Just because you attach a VCR to your DV camera doesn't mean that recording works. Some VHS decks have multiple inputs (sometimes labeled Line 1 and Line 2), which means they can have more than one device attached to their inputs at a time. These VCRs have to know which input to record a signal from, so you may need to tell your VCR to record the signal from a different input (there's usually a button on the VCR or remote control that lets you switch from one input source to another). To make sure your VCR is getting a signal from your DV camera, you should be able to see and hear your Final Cut Express project via the TV that's hooked to your VCR, which shows that the DV signal is making it into the VCR. To be sure, do a test recording and then play your VHS tape to see that the DV camera signal made it to the tape.

If you don't have a DV camera or deck, but need to record your Final Cut Express video to a VHS VCR (or any other analog device, actually), then you have one last resort: You can get a media converter box (a small little device made by Sony and some other companies) that hooks into your Mac via a FireWire cable and converts the DV signal coming through the FireWire cable to an analog signal VHS decks can understand. By attaching a VHS deck to the RCA connectors on the media converter, the media converter box fills the same middleman role as a DV camera would have.

While having the option of recording DV video to VHS tape is nice, keep in mind that the quality of video recorded to VHS loses a little quality. First of all, VHS is a notoriously low-quality format (that's why so many people prefer to watch movies on DVDs). Secondly, converting a signal from one format to another (DV to analog) tends to deteriorate the signal a little bit, resulting in a lower quality. On the other hand, you may not even notice this loss of quality, or it may be acceptable given your purposes.

Recording Back to Tape

Make sure that you've hooked up your DV camera to your Mac, and verify that the camera's getting a video signal from Final Cut Express (you should be able to see the video in your Timeline play on the camera LCD screen). Now you're ready to record your show back to tape, using two options:

- ✔ Playing back from the Timeline
- ✔ Printing to video

Each method has some advantages as well as some disadvantages, which I discuss in the following sections.

Recording directly from the Timeline

Recording doesn't get any easier than this: Just press the Record button on your DV camera and play your Timeline in Final Cut Express (you can play from any point, and even stop and start playback). If the Express settings are correct and you have set up all your hardware correctly (see the earlier section "Setting Up for Recording" to verify proper setup), your Timeline records back to tape.

- ✔ **Pros:** The most obvious pro is that this method is fast and easy. You don't have to bother with any dialog boxes and struggle with additional settings.

✔ **Cons:** The main disadvantage of this method is that you cannot specify any "leader" elements, such as color bars or slates, to go before your show (unless you build them directly into your timeline sequence). If you want color bars and other elements in the beginning of your tape (which is required for some formal projects that may be meant for broadcast), see the Print to Video option described in the "Printing to video" section.

To record directly from the Timeline, use the following steps:

1. **Open your Timeline sequence and render all items by choosing Sequence⇨Render All or by pressing the ⌘+R shortcut.**

   Before you record to tape, you must make sure that all items have been properly rendered. This step ensures that all effects and other items have been rendered and are now ready to go to tape. Without rendering, some effects may not play.

2. **Choose Sequence⇨Mixdown Audio to mix (in other words, render) your audio tracks.**

   This step is critical to avoid dropping frames during your recording. When you have a lot of audio tracks, your Mac may have a hard time playing them all in real time if it doesn't have the chance to render them first. Mixing down your audio turns them into a single file that Final Cut Express plays during the playback and avoids any on-the-fly recalculations that can lead to dropped frames.

3. **Position the Timeline playhead where you want to start recording.**

   Note that you should place your playhead on a blank area of the Timeline just before your project starts. Final Cut Express records whatever is under the playhead to your tape, so placing the playhead just before your movie starts prevents a weird beginning (such as a frame that appears to be frozen for a few seconds).

4. **Press Record on your deck or camera.**

   Wait a few seconds after you press Record. Some decks take a few seconds to get up to speed, and you don't want your project to start the moment your tape plays. After a few seconds, you're ready to play your Timeline.

5. **Press the space bar to play your Timeline.**

6. **Press the space bar to stop playback.**

   You can also press Stop on your deck to stop recording.

If you like, instead of pressing the space bar for playback, you can choose other playback options from the Mark⇨Play submenu. You have options such as Play In to Out, which plays only from the In to Out points you may have marked in your Timeline sequence, and Reverse, which plays backwards from the current position. Handy, eh?

The steps I've just described apply if your DV camera works the way Apple expects it to. A large number of cameras fall into this camp, but there are a few exceptions. If these steps don't seem to work for your camera, you can consult your owner's manual (look for information on how to record a DV signal from another source, such as a computer). You can also visit Apple's online support for Final Cut Express. Try www.apple.com/support.

Printing to video

Another option you have to record your sequence is the Print to Video option. Taking this approach lets you add industry standard color bars, countdowns, and slates to the beginning and end of the tape.

- ✔ **Pros:** A simple dialog box allows you to add color bars, a slate, and other options to your edited movie without adding them into your Timeline sequence itself. You can also loop your sequence, so it's recorded again and again, which may be important in some situations (Venues such as video kiosks and convention booths often require videos to be looped for playback throughout the shows.)

- ✔ **Cons:** If you don't need to display colors bars and other stuff at the beginning of your sequence, you don't need to take this extra step!

To print to video, do the following:

1. **Render all the items on your Timeline by choosing Sequence⇨ Render All.**

2. **Choose File⇨Print to Video.**

   The Print to Video dialog box appears, as shown in Figure 15-4.

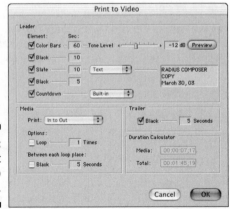

Figure 15-4: The Print to Video dialog box.

3. **Select the appropriate options in the Print to Video dialog box.**

   The Print to Video dialog box contains Leader, Media, Trailer, and Duration Calculator sections:

   - **Leader and Trailer:** Leader options are elements that appear before your movie, whereas the Trailer options follow your movie. For example, in the Leader area, you can select the Color Bars option and then specify how many seconds of color bars you want. You can also use these sections to add a few seconds of black at the end or beginning of your tape to avoid an abrupt start or stop of your movie (highly recommended). Finally, the sections have options for adding a simple text card (you can provide the name of your production, and maybe a recording date), and add an industry-standard, 8-second countdown, with an audio pop at the 2-second mark (if you're working with a composer or sound effects person, they may request this countdown at the beginning of your program).

   - **Duration Calculator:** The Duration Calculator shows the final length of the media you have selected when printing to tape. The Media box shows the total length of all your media clips; the Total box displays the Media length plus the length of all extra elements you may have added, such as color bars or black (helpful if you're worried about fitting your program onto a 60-minute DV tape).

   - **Media:** The options in the Media section allow you to loop a sequence and the media you want printed to tape. For example, you can print the sequence from the In point to the Out point, or loop it ten times.

4. **Click OK when you're finished with your selections.**

5. **When Final Cut Express displays a message that it is OK to start recording, then start recording with your DV camera or deck, and click OK in Express.**

   Depending on your options in the Print to Video dialog box, Final Cut Express may take some time to render some of these elements, such as color bars. Also, after you get a message to start recording, press Record on your deck, but wait a few seconds before clicking OK to close the dialog box (giving your camera time to spin up to speed). Express responds by taking over the screen, and playing your program from start to finish. If you want to abort at any time, you can press Escape.

6. **When your movie stops playing, stop recording on your DV camera.**

   You know the show is over when you see your standard Final Cut Express work area. Rewind your DV tape and play through it, to make sure that recording went okay.

Chapter 16

Exporting Your Movie to a Digital File

*I*nstead of recording your finished movie to DV tape, you can export it to a QuickTime digital file, which is a great way to distribute your movie to other people. For example, you can post QuickTime files on the Internet so that anyone with an Internet connection can download them. You also can place them on a CD-ROM or DVD (with a the help of a program such as iDVD) so that you can easily hand a sleek, shiny disk to family, friends, and business associates.

Anyone who has the QuickTime Player software on a computer can play QuickTime files that Final Cut Express exports. Practically every Mac working today has QuickTime installed, and a large number of PCs do as well. If PC users don't have QuickTime, they can easily download the free player from www.apple.com/quicktime. Beware of this one catch, though: The movies you export from Express (depending on their settings) play only with version 6 of the QuickTime player. If someone can't play your movie but has the QuickTime player, he or she probably doesn't have the latest version.

Understanding the Variation in Digital Files

Not all digital files are created equal! When you decide to export your movie as a digital file, you'll want to be very specific about the kind of file you export. Base your decision about the type of digital file you export on how you want to use the movie.

Some of the factors that can set one digital file apart from another are the kind of video and audio compression the file uses, the size of its image, its frame rate, data rate, and more. In the end, these factors are all important in determining the balance your digital file strikes between its video and audio quality and its file size. For example, a movie that's 720 x 480 pixels, at 30 frames a second, and using a high data rate looks and sounds better than a movie that's 320 x 200 pixels, at only 15 frames a second, using a low data rate. That better-looking movie also uses a lot more digital data to describe it, which means it's going to be a larger file on your hard drive than a lower-quality version.

In some situations, you don't care about movie file size at all (for example, if you're burning it to a DVD). However, if you're posting your movie to the Internet where your audience has to download the movie through relatively slow connections such as standard 56 kilobytes per second (Kbps) modems or even relatively fast DSL connections, then file size becomes more important. You don't want your audience to spend a whole day downloading your movie! (In fact, many people simply lose interest in waiting for movies that take forever to download.)

Choosing a QuickTime Format

When you're ready to export your Final Cut Express movie as a digital file, you have to choose how you are going to export your file:

> ✔ **As a QuickTime DV Movie.** Remember, DV is the native format of Final Cut Express. Your movie is already in the DV format, which is defined by a frame size of 720 x 480 pixels and a frame rate of 29.97 frames per second. If you want to keep that format, then this is the option to choose. You may decide to export your movie as a DV Movie for a couple reasons:
>
> > • Export your movie in DV if you want the option to edit it again in Final Cut Express, because Express will treat it as any other DV clip.

- Keep your exported movie in DV if you plan to import it into
  another program, and you want to preserve the movie's high quality. For example, if you are burning your movie to a DVD (maybe
  using the Apple iDVD software), you'll want to keep the movie in
  its original, high-quality form.

✔ **In a different QuickTime format.** As I said, if you want to distribute
your exported movie on the Internet or burn it to CD-ROM, keeping it in
DV is not be practical because DV movies are typically too large to fit on
most CD-ROMs and certainly too large to download. By exporting in a
different QuickTime format, you can reduce movie file size considerably
while still maintaining pretty good image and sound quality. (However,
striking this balance between file size and quality can take some tweaking and patience.)

Exporting a sequence as a DV Movie

Follow these steps to export a Timeline sequence (your finished movie) as a
QuickTime DV file:

1. **Open the Timeline sequence you want to export so that it's active on
   the Timeline.**

   You can make sure the sequence is active (in case you have multiple
   sequences open), by clicking its tab on the Timeline.

2. **If you want to export only a portion of the movie, define that segment
   on the Timeline by setting In and Out points.**

   Place the Timeline playhead on the frame to be the first in your
   exported movie, and press the I key to set an In point. Then move the
   Timeline playhead to the frame to be the last in your exported movie,
   and press the O key to set an Out point.

3. **Choose File⇨Export⇨Final Cut Movie.**

   The Save dialog box appears, as shown in Figure 16-1.

4. **In the Where drop-down menu, indicate where you want to save the
   exported file and then type a name for the movie in the Save As text
   box.**

5. **From the Include drop-down menu, select the Audio and Video
   option.**

   Alternatively, you can choose to export only your movie's video or its
   audio. Exporting one or the other, and not both, makes the movie file size
   smaller, but use this approach only if you really want just one of the two.

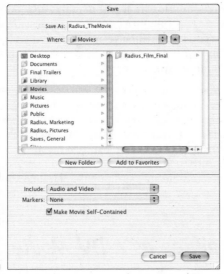

Figure 16-1:
Saving a
Final Cut
Movie in the
DV format.

6. **From the Markers drop-down menu, select any marker types (if any) that you want to embed in the exported movie.**

   This step only applies if you've already set chapter or compression markers, which can be read by other programs such as DVD Studio Pro when they are exported. See Chapter 7 for more about these markers.

   To export both compression and chapter markers, choose the DVD Studio Pro Markers option. To export only one marker or the other, choose either Chapter Markers or Compression Markers.

   If you choose to export compression markers, Express exports all the compression markers you set yourself, but it also places additional compression markers on every cut (between clips), transition, and gap in your Timeline sequence. (If this explanation means nothing to you, then you probably don't need compression markers in the first place.)

7. **Decide whether to select the Make Movie Self-Contained check box:**

   • **Self-contained:** Making your exported movie self-contained means that the exported file contains all the video and audio media for your movie, built right into the file. The advantage to making an exported movie self-contained is that the file is now a permanent, stand-alone archive of your movie. If you want to clear some space from your hard drives, you can now delete your project's original media, much of which is probably unused by the finished sequence.

   On the other hand, when you export a self-contained movie, Final Cut Express needs more time to export your file, because it has to write each frame of video and audio again to your hard drive. Also, you can wind up with a huge exported file. (*Remember:* DV video uses about 1 gigabyte for every 4.5 minutes.)

• **Not self-contained:** If you don't make your movie self-contained, the exported file simply includes a bunch of pointers to your movie's original media, which is on your hard drive. (This is the media you captured from video tape or imported from other sources when you started your project).

An exported move that's not self-contained is called a *reference movie*. You may want to export a reference movie when you want to bring the finished sequence into another program, such as iDVD (to burn it to a DVD disk), or maybe Cleaner 6, which is great for converting movies to all sorts of different formats (more on this later). In this case, you don't need to make yet another copy of your movie media, which is essentially what making the movie self-contained does. Just export a reference movie with pointers to the original media already on your hard drives, and that file will work great when you import it into other programs — as long as the original media stays on your hard drives. If you delete or move the media, your reference movie becomes useless, because it will point to media it can no longer find on your hard drives.

8. **Click Save to export away!**

Exporting can take time (especially if your movie is self-contained), so Final Cut reports its progress in a status bar. You can cancel the export any time by clicking the Cancel button on the status bar.

After you export the movie, you can import it into another program (such as iDVD), or open it in the QuickTime Player by dragging the file to the QuickTime player icon in the OS X Dock. When you double-click your exported movie icon from the Finder, the movie opens as a DV clip in Final Cut Express, and you can edit it like any other clip.

Exporting for the Internet or CD-ROM

If you want to distribute your exported movie over the Internet or burn it to CD-ROM, then you have to export it in a QuickTime format other than DV because DV video files are typically too large for these mediums. However, as I said earlier, if you're going to export your movie in something other than DV, you can use many different many formats.

You can export your movie with different frame sizes, frame rates, data rates, and compression technologies — all of which affect your exported movie's image and audio quality and file size. Figuring out the best blend of all these characteristics can be very time-consuming (not to mention a bit frustrating!), Fortunately, Final Cut Express offers some predetermined settings that make exporting movies for the Internet pretty easy.

The methods people use to connect to the Internet work at many different speeds. Some use antiquated 56 Kbps modems that really belong in the Smithsonian, and they download movie files (any files, really) at a snail's pace. Others use faster cable and DSL modems, but these often run at different rates. For example, my home DSL connection can download data at around 1000 Kbps (about 18 times faster than a modem), but a friend of mine has a cable connection that runs at only 500 Kbps (still, pretty fast). As a result of the variety of Internet connections that people have, you want to plan on exporting multiple versions of your movie. You want to design each version for common Internet connections, such as a 56 Kbps modem, and a variety of cable/DSL connections that people might have. This way, you'll have a movie to offer modem users (so they don't have to wait very long to download your video), and also cable/DSL users (who can enjoy a movie that uses more data and therefore looks and sounds better).

To export as a QuickTime file for the Internet, follow these steps:

1. **Open the Timeline sequence you want to export, and make it active on the Timeline.**

   You can double-click the sequence from the Final Cut Express Browser window. You can make sure the sequence is active (in case you have multiple sequences open), by clicking its tab on the Timeline.

2. **If you want to export only a portion of your movie, define that segment on the Timeline by setting In and Out points.**

   Place the Timeline playhead on the frame to be the first in your exported movie, and press the I key to set an In point. Then move the Timeline playhead to the frame to be the last in your exported movie, and press the O key to set an Out point.

3. **Choose File⇨Export⇨QuickTime.**

   The Save dialog box appears, as shown in Figure 16-2.

4. **In the Where drop-down list, indicate where you want to save the exported file and then type a name for your movie in the Save As text box.**

5. **In the Format drop-down list, select QuickTime Movie.**

   This option tells Final Cut Express to export the movie to the QuickTime Movie file format. (Express probably selected this option by default.) As you can see from the list, you can also export to audio formats such as AIFF or WAV, or DV Streams (which can be imported into iMovie).

6. **From the Use drop-down list, select the option that best matches the Internet connection your audience will use:**

   • **Modem:** To export a movie intended for modem users (in other words, small file size for quicker downloads, but pretty mediocre image quality), then select Modem or Modem – Audio Only if you're just exporting sound.

- **DSL or Cable modem:** To export a movie better suited for down-loading on a DSL or Cable modem, select the Low, Medium or High options for these connections. The Low version anticipates a slower cable or DSL connection, so your exported movie file size is smaller (to compensate for downloading over a slower DSL/Cable connection) and image quality suffers a bit.

- **Local Area Network:** To export a movie to be downloaded over a Local Area Network (such as one in your office or home), select the LAN option. This option also works if you're exporting a movie for use on a CD-ROM.

7. **Click Save to export away!**

   Exporting can take time, so Final Cut Express reports its progress in a status bar. You can cancel the export anytime by clicking the Cancel button on the status bar.

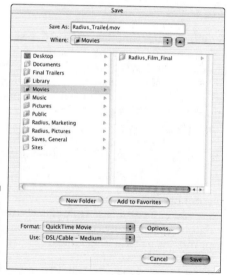

Figure 16-2:
Exporting
as a Quick-
Time file.

Find your exported movie file using your Mac Finder (it should be in the folder you specified in the Where drop-down list), and open the movie in the QuickTime Player by double-clicking it. Play it to see how your audio/video quality held up in the export.

To see how large your file is, you can select it on the Mac desktop, and choose File⇨Get Info.

If your movie seems choppy when it plays or if it appears in a window that's too small for your tastes, it is because of the Final Cut Express predetermined settings. You can tweak those settings to get better results, but changing these settings inevitably causes the file size of your exported movies to grow, meaning they take longer to download. Nothing's ever easy, is it?

Optimizing Movie Quality

Before you look at how to customize the settings of movies you export in Final Cut Express, you need to understand a few basic concepts that will help you get better results. Many factors can affect the quality and file size of your exported movie, as I describe in the following sections.

Compression codecs

Remember: Pure, raw video requires a huge amount of data to describe it (almost a gigabyte per minute!) and requires expensive hardware to work with it. Clever engineers have figured out how to compress video into smaller, much more manageable file sizes while still preserving a great deal of quality in the compressed images and audio. However, compression technologies have different purposes. Some compression technologies don't compress video very much; for example, the DV video that you work with in Final Cut Express features only 5x compression (meaning a DV clip uses ⅕th the data that raw, uncompressed video would). Other compressors can squeeze video dozens of times.

These different compression technologies are called *codecs,* which stands for compressor/decompressor, and you can compress QuickTime video using a wide variety of codecs. Fortunately, you're likely to care about only three codecs if you're exporting your movies as QuickTime files:

- ✔ **MPEG-4:** By default, Final Cut Express exports QuickTime movies using this codec. MPEG-4 delivers nice image quality but packs it into fairly small file sizes that you can put on the Internet or on a CD-ROM. MPEG-4 works pretty quickly too, so you don't have to wait forever as your movie is being exported.

- ✔ **Sorenson 3 Pro:** This is the best codec you can use for compressing high-quality video into small file sizes (and it's not to be confused with the standard Sorenson 3 codec included free with QuickTime). Sorenson 3 Pro can compress video into very small file sizes, just as MPEG-4 can, but your image quality keeps more detail and looks sharper. In fact, if you ever watch movie trailers posted on the Apple Web site (www.apple.com/trailers), or other movie studio sites, they're likely to all be encoded with Sorenson 3 Pro. Unfortunately, good things don't come cheaply. You have to buy this codec, and it sells for $299 (try www.sorenson.com).

✔ **MPEG-2:** This is a codec used to compress any video that ends up on a DVD (like commercial DVDs you rent or buy). When you bring your exported Final Cut movie into iDVD, it compresses your video with MPEG-2 automatically. Or, if you're using the more sophisticated DVD Studio Pro to author your DVDs, you can export your Express movies directly as MPEG-2 files. (However, DVD Studio Pro must have installed the MPEG-2 codec on your Mac beforehand.)

Data rate

Codecs compress video and audio at a certain data rate, which has a huge impact on whether it looks and sounds good. *Data rate* refers to how much data the codec uses to describe video and audio, and it's usually measured in either kilobits or kilobytes per second (Kbps). (A kilobyte has 8 kilobits, if you ever want to convert between the two.) Naturally, the higher a movie data rate, the better it looks and sounds, because more data is there to describe the media. If you have a very low data rate (such as 5 Kbps), well, you just don't have enough data per second to create a sharp, detailed picture and clear audio. You can increase this quality by setting your data rate higher — maybe to something like 120 Kbps or so.

Of course, when you increase the data rate of your movie, you're increasing its overall file size. (You can multiply the movie's per-second data rate by the number of seconds in the entire movie to see how large your movie will be.) Increased file size means your viewers wait longer while downloading your movie. On the other hand, it's not the end of the world if your viewers have to wait a little longer to complete the download. In fact, they'll probably appreciate the movie's higher quality, even if they have to wait a bit more for it. The last thing you want to do is leave someone with the impression that your movie looks like a low-budget student film!

How do you figure out where to set your movie's data rate? Well, Table 16-1 lists data rate bandwidths of common Internet connections, but be aware that these can always vary from case to case. If your data rate matches these bandwidths (or falls just below them, to account for some other data overhead), then it probably plays in real time as it downloads, with no delays.

If the movie's data rate is higher than the bandwidth rates listed in the table, your movie pauses before it starts initially playing. During this pause, your Mac buffers all the data it needs so that when the movie *does* start playing, it can play through from start to finish. (If you've downloaded a QuickTime movie trailer, you've probably noticed a thin gray bar filling in across the QuickTime Player's scrubber bar. This bar represents data received over your connection, and it usually fills up by a third or more before the movie trailer begins to play.)

Table 16-1	Data Rates for Real-Time Play on Common Internet Connections	
Connection Type	Data Rate in Kilobits per Second	Data Rate in Kilobytes per Second
28.8 Kbps Modem	20 Kbps	2.5 KBps
56.6 Kbps Modem	40 Kbps	5 KBps
ISDN Modem	96 Kbps	12 KBps
DSL/Cable (Low)	384 Kbps	48 KBps
DSL/Cable (Medium)	512 Kbps	64 KBps
DSL/Cable (High)	768-1024 Kbps	96-128 KBps
T1 line	1500 Kbps (1.5 Mbps)	188 KBps

Frame size and frame rate

Adjusting your exported movie frame rate and frame size also affect the video quality — sometimes for the good and sometimes not. For example, if you want to increase your movie frame size (perhaps from 320 x 240 pixels to 480 x 360 pixels), you may actually *decrease* your picture quality. Why? Because your movie now has to create images that use more pixels, but it has the same data rate to describe all the details those pixels are supposed to create. An easy way to avoid this problem is to increase your data rate.

Conversely, say you're trying to keep your data rate as low as possible because you want your movie to be easily downloaded by someone using a 56 Kbps modem. If you're concerned that your data rate isn't high enough to ensure sharp, clean imagery, you can decrease your frame rate (perhaps in half, from 29.97 frames per second, to 15). Then your data rate has to describe only half as many frames of video as before, which means that each existing frame gets more data devoted to it, thereby boosting image quality.

The QuickTime Player can show you a ton of important details about a QuickTime movie, including the compression codec it uses, its data rate, frame rate, and frame size (see Figure 16-3). To get this info, open a QuickTime movie in the Player (double-click the file icon from the Mac desktop), and then choose Window⇨Show Movie Info.

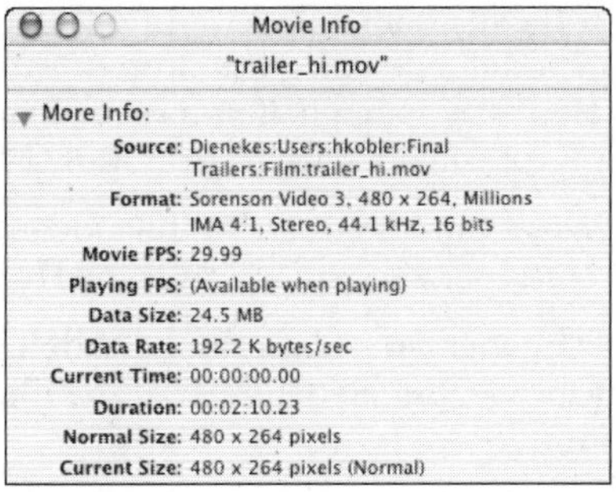

Figure 16-3:
The Quick-
Time Player
Movie Info
window.

The Movie Info window content:

```
Movie Info
"trailer_hi.mov"
▼ More Info:
       Source: Dienekes:Users:hkobler:Final
               Trailers:Film:trailer_hi.mov
       Format: Sorenson Video 3, 480 x 264, Millions
               IMA 4:1, Stereo, 44.1 kHz, 16 bits
    Movie FPS: 29.99
  Playing FPS: (Available when playing)
    Data Size: 24.5 MB
    Data Rate: 192.2 K bytes/sec
 Current Time: 00:00:00.00
     Duration: 00:02:10.23
  Normal Size: 480 x 264 pixels
 Current Size: 480 x 264 pixels (Normal)
```

Customizing Your Export Settings

Now that you have a few key concepts under your belt, you're ready to customize the Final Cut Express predetermined settings to improve the quality of your exported QuickTime movies. However, keep in mind that finding the settings that work for you definitely takes some trial and error. Follow these steps:

1. **Open the sequence you want to export, and make it active on the Timeline.**

2. **If you want to export only a portion of the movie, define that segment on the Timeline by setting In and Out points.**

3. **Choose File➪Export➪QuickTime.**

4. **In the Where drop-down list, indicate where you want to save the exported file and then type a name for the movie in the Save As text box.**

5. **In the Format drop-down list, select QuickTime Movie.**

6. **From the Use drop-down list, select the option that best matches the Internet connection your audience will use.**

   You use one of these settings as a departure point for the custom stuff you want to do.

7. **Click the Options button.**

   The Movie Settings dialog box appears, as shown in Figure 16-4. It shows all the settings that define the quality and file size of your exported movie.

8. **Click the Settings button in Video to adjust the video compression settings.**

   This brings up the Compression Settings dialog box, as shown in Figure 16-5, in which you can customize the following:

- **Compression codec:** You can change the compression codec used to compress your exported movie using the drop-down list at the top of the dialog box. Honestly, though, if you're exporting movies directly from Final Cut Express, it's hard to beat MPEG-4 quality.

- **Frame rate:** You can change the frame rate of the movie, but don't go higher than 29.97 frames per second, which is the DV native rate.

- **Data rate:** You can also change your data rate, which increases the picture quality of your movie, but also increases the file size (leading to longer downloads).

- **Quality and keyframes:** I recommend leaving the Quality slider at Best and not adjusting the number of keyframes. Keyframes have a very subtle effect on video quality. You can always tweak them later if you like, but keep your focus on the big fish now.

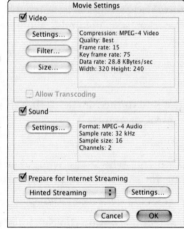

Figure 16-4:
The Movie Settings dialog box shows you all the settings that will define the exported movie.

9. **Click OK in the Compression Settings dialog box to lock in your changes.**

10. **Click the Size button in Video to adjust the frame size of the movie.**

    This brings up the Export Size Settings dialog box, shown in Figure 16-6. Select the Use Custom Size radio button, and then type pixel values for the new width and height of the frame size. Just make sure you stick to using a 4:3 ratio of width to height, which is the same ratio used by the original DV media in your movie. For instance, 400 x 400 pixel dimensions distorts your video (that's a 1:1 ratio), but 480 x 360 pixels and 640 x 480 pixels work.

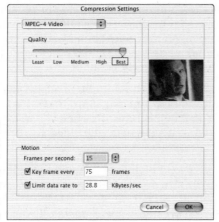

Figure 16-5:
The Compr-
ession
Settings
dialog box.

11. **Click OK in the Export Size dialog box to lock in the changes.**

I don't recommend setting a frame size larger than 480 x 360 pixels for Internet video. Anything bigger looks good only with a very high data rate, and yet that high data rate creates long download times for even fast DSL modems. Most people are used to downloading video at smaller frame sizes anyway.

Figure 16-6:
The Export
Size Settings
dialog box
lets you
scale your
movie so it
plays in a
larger or
smaller
window.

12. **Click Settings in the Sound section of the Movie Settings dialog box to adjust your sound settings.**

The Sound Settings dialog box appears (shown in Figure 16-7), in which you can adjust these settings:

- **Audio codec:** Click the Compressor button to change the audio codec used to compress the audio. For example, you may have good results, depending on the audio content, with a codec such as IMA 4:1, or Qualcomm Purevoice. On the other hand, the standard MPEG-4 Audio codec is pretty good too.

- **Rate:** Chances are, you'll want to set audio to a fairly high rate, such as 44.1 kHz, and 16 bits. You can afford to do this because audio doesn't take too much bandwidth when you're exporting a movie for the Internet — it's the data-rich video you usually have to worry about.

- **Stereo or mono:** If you want high quality audio but still want to keep your exported file size down as much as possible, consider switching your exported audio from Stereo to Mono. This change plays audio equally on two stereo speakers, but if your soundtrack didn't use stereo to great effect, you might not be missing much. You also cut the Audio data rate in half.

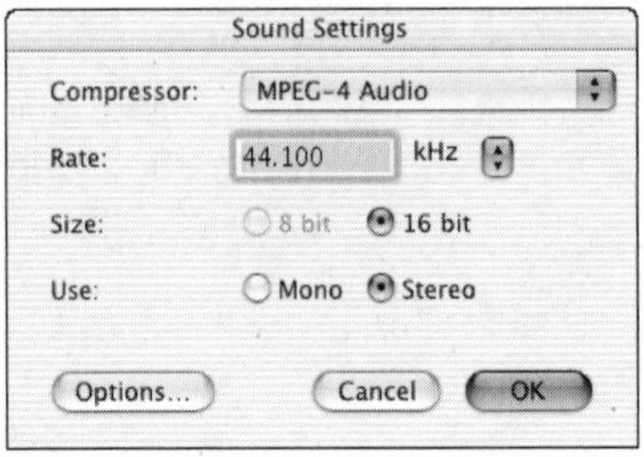

Figure 16-7:
The Sound
Settings
dialog box.

> Sound Settings
>
> Compressor: MPEG-4 Audio
> Rate: 44.100 kHz
> Size: ○ 8 bit ● 16 bit
> Use: ○ Mono ● Stereo
>
> Options... Cancel OK

13. **Click OK in the Sound Settings dialog box to lock in the changes.**

14. *Optional:* **From the Movie Settings dialog box (refer to Figure 16-4), select Prepare For Internet Streaming and choose Fast Start from the drop-down menu.**

    You don't have to worry about this step if your QuickTime file won't be downloaded via the Internet, which would be the case if you're creating this file for CD-ROM distribution.

15. **When you finish your tweaks, click OK in the Movie Settings dialog box.**

16. **Click Save in the Save dialog box to export your movie.**

17. **Review your movie to make sure it looks and sounds good.**

    Use your Mac's Finder to navigate to your newly created movie. Double-click the Quicktime file and view the movie beginning to end to confirm it came out the way you thought it should.

Part VI
The Part of Tens

The 5th Wave — By Rich Tennant

©RICHTENNANT

"Of course graphics are important to your project, Eddy, but I think it would've been better to scan a _picture_ of your worm collection."

In this part . . .

*I*n this part, I offer some ten-odd tips on how to make your Final Cut Express editing experience easier and more enjoyable, so you can focus on the fun, creative stuff (you get lots of project management advice here). I also serve up ten simple things you can do to become a more capable Express editor, from honing your creative and technical know-how to upgrading your current Mac setup.

Chapter 17

Ten Tips for Making Your Editing Easier

*E*diting can be challenging (and of course, rewarding!) work, but you can make it much easier by developing some simple habits to keep your media well organized and your workflow flowing.

Keep Your Media Organized

After you import your media into the Browser, Final Cut Express remembers where on your hard drives each clip of media really is — that is, you only have to find a clip in the Browser to work with it rather than fish through lots of folders on your hard drive for the right file. That's a nice feature, but it doesn't mean you should get lazy or careless about where you store the original media clips on your hard drive — that is, clips shouldn't be strewn in all sorts of random folders on your drive (or on multiple drives) because at some point, you'll probably need to find those media files outside of Express. For instance, you may need to clear off some space on your hard drive — if the media is stored in a variety of folders and mixed in with unrelated media or files, figuring out what files can stay or go is a lot harder (while accidentally deleting some media gets easier). I have a couple of tips for organizing the media files on your drive:

- ✔ **Keep media files for different projects in different folders:** Don't capture media for Video A into the Video B project folder. (You can target these media folders when you capture — see Chapter 3.)

- ✔ **Divide media logically between multiple drives:** Keeping your media on a single hard drive is always nice, but if you have too much media, try to organize the drives in a logical way — for instance, keep Scenes 1–50 on Drive A, 51–100 on Drive B, and so on.

Keeping your source DV tapes on hand and organized is also a good idea. Just because you've captured video and audio from your original DV tapes doesn't mean that you should let those tapes out of your sight. You may need them in case you lose some of your captured media. For instance, you may have deleted media intentionally to temporarily clear some space on your hard drive. Or you may have lost media unintentionally, by accidentally deleting the wrong folder, or perhaps some QuickTime files become corrupted (it happens occasionally), or your hard drive crashes. To make life easier on yourself, keep your source tapes clearly labeled, label any timecode breaks that occur within a tape (see Chapter 3 for more about timecode breaks), and store them in a safe secure place that you can easily get to.

Use Bins, Lotsa Bins!

When you're importing media clips, don't let them clutter up the Browser window — the more clips you have there, the harder it gets to find any particular one (check out Figure 17-1). Instead, create bins (folders) for each of your project's scenes (for instance, Scene 1, Scene 2, Scene 3, and so on) and store the video and audio clips in the appropriate bins. (If your video doesn't have traditional scenes, figure out some other themes you can use for organizing clips.) If you're dealing with lots of clips per scene, you may even create sub-bins within Scene bins — say, for video, music, dialogue, and sound effects.

You can drag files and folders directly from your Mac desktop to the bin of your choice in the Browser.

You can capture video clips from DV tape directly into the bin of your choice, by making it the logging bin for your project. (See Chapter 3 for more information.) You can also import a clip directly into the bin of your choice, rather than import it straight to the Browser and *then* drag the clip into a bin. Just double-click a bin to open it in its own window; then choose File⇨Import to send a clip right into that window.

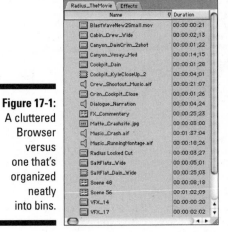

Figure 17-1:
A cluttered
Browser
versus
one that's
organized
neatly
into bins.

Keep Your Clip Names Informative

This is very important: When importing or capturing media, try to
name clips in a way that says as much as possible about them in a consistent, systematic way. When you're disciplined about doing this, you make
finding a given clip much easier because a quick look at its name can tell you
a lot about it. For instance, don't just name one clip Dan's Close-up at
the Dinner Table, another clip Everyone at the Dinner Table, and a
third clip Medium shot of Pam. Instead, use DinnerTable_Dan_Closeup,
DinnerTable_Group_Wideshot, and DinnerTable_Pam_Medium. Naming
the clips with this kind of systematic approach (you're free to use your own
systems, of course) makes spotting media, either in the Browser or after it's
on the Timeline, easy.

Document Your Clips

Besides naming clips, Final Cut Express lets you thoroughly document each
clip with an FBI-like dossier — for example, you can detail a clip scene and
its take, describe its contents, add several additional comment lines, apply
labels to it (best take, alternate shot, and so on), and more. You get your first
opportunity to add this kind of info when you capture a clip from DV tape,
in which case the Capture window features all the necessary data fields (see
Chapter 3 for more information), but you can also add these helpful details to
clips later on. To do so, just select the clip in the Browser, choose Edit⇨Item
Properties, and click the Logging Info tab (as shown in Figure 17-2).

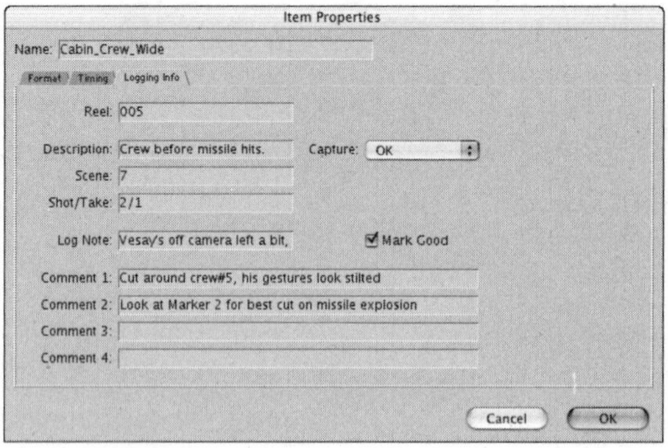

Figure 17-2:
Use the Item
Properties
dialog box
to document
important
clips.

Of course, I'm the first to admit that documenting clips to this extent is a bit of a pain (you're an editor, not a librarian!), and I wouldn't blame you if you didn't go all out. But the fact is, doing a little advance legwork here can save you a lot of time when you're sifting through hundreds of clips, looking for just the right one: For instance, you can quickly organize the Browser to show clips by their labels or find clips (using the Final Cut Express Find feature) by looking for keywords in the description or comments. See Chapter 5 for more about labeling and documenting clips.

Use the Find Feature

The Final Cut Express Find feature is incredibly powerful and can pull the proverbial needle out of a haystack when you're looking for a particular clip, or group of clips, without sifting through a sea of endless bins and unrelated clips (something any editor who works on long projects can definitely appreciate).

To search for media, just make sure the Browser window is active and then choose Edit➪Find. The Find dialog box, shown in Figure 17-3, lets you specify tons of different search criteria — you can search for keywords in a media clip name, description, or comments (another reason why you should carefully name and document your clips!), or by labels you've applied, or by the clip's scene, log tape, or any number of other criteria (even the compression codec the clip uses or its frame size). You can also combine different search results — for example, finding only the clips in scenes 48 and 56 that you labeled as best or good takes and that feature the actress called Pam.

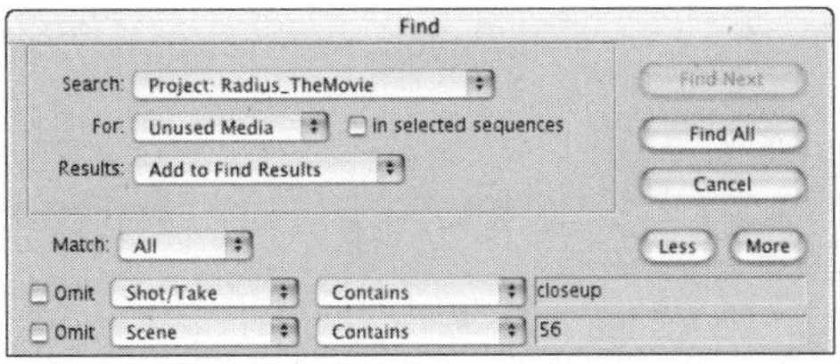

Figure 17-3:
The Final
Cut Express
Find dialog
box.

Stay Oriented with Markers

You can place markers to highlight important moments in either your individual clips or Timeline sequences. Using markers makes finding these moments easier when you're in a hurry.

You can set two kinds of markers. The first variety is a Timeline marker, which you place in a Timeline sequence (maybe at the beginning of a new scene on the Timeline or at some notable event within a scene), as shown in Figure 17-4. The second variety is a clip marker, which you set within a single clip. Clip markers are especially handy for breaking up long clips into more manageable morsels — for instance, when you set markers within a clip, each marker becomes a subclip of the master clip, and you can open a subclip individually by clicking it in the Browser (as shown in Figure 17-5) or move it exclusively to the Timeline.

You'll set Timeline markers in the Timeline window and clip markers while looking at a clip in the Viewer window. Just position the playhead for either window at a frame you'd like to mark and then press M on your keyboard. (You see a marker symbol appear at that point, as shown in Figure 17-4.) To give the marker a name, choose Mark⇨Markers⇨Edit. To search for Timeline markers, hold down the Control key, click the timecode box (refer to Figure 17-4), choose the marker you want from the pop-up menu that appears, and Final Cut Express jumps to that marker. To search for clip markers, you can use the Express Find feature. Make the Timeline window active and choose Edit⇨Find to search for markers in clips already on the Timeline, or make the Browser window active and choose Edit⇨Find to search through all your project clips.

So much for your crash course in markers. To learn more about these handy little tools, check out Chapter 8.

Figure 17-4:
Sequence
markers on
the Timeline.

Markers in the Browser

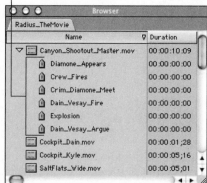

Figure 17-5:
A clip's
markers are
recognized
in the
Browser.

Break Scenes into Sequences and Nest the Sequences

If you're working on a long project — anything more than 30 minutes, really — don't edit it all together in a single Timeline sequence. You'll find yourself getting disoriented easily when you're staring at an endless string of clips on the Timeline; also, the longer the sequence is, the more scrolling and zooming in and out you'll do.

Instead, break down a big video into smaller scenes (or acts, or some other kind of division) and build each of those smaller morsels in its own Timeline sequence. Then, when you want to watch your whole video, you can easily assemble it together by creating yet another sequence (this will be the master sequence) and nesting all the scene sequences into the new one — check out Figure 17-6. In other words, just drag the scene sequences from the Browser window into the master sequence (as if they were individual media clips) and arrange them on the Timeline in the order you'd like them to play. See Chapter 8 for more details.

Figure 17-6:
Nested
sequences,
with a clip
of back-
ground
music
running
beneath.

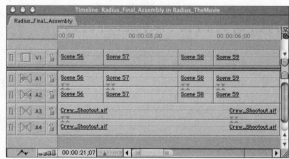

Master Your Rendering

Rendering is the process Final Cut Express uses to calculate how a media clip should look or sound before you can play it into your movie. (A clip that needs rendering is usually a non-DV video clip or a DV clip that you've changed by applying a filter or other effect.) When Express renders media, it writes its calculations out as an entirely new clip, called a *render cache file,* which is saved to your hard drive and gives the clip a name like `Scene 56-FIN-00000005`. The following sections cover some helpful tips and tricks for dealing with renders.

Avoiding rendering by using real-time previews

Sometimes, rendering is inevitable, but Final Cut Express can show you temporary previews of many transitions and motion effects (such as scales and repositions) that you apply to clips, which would ordinarily require rendering. Thanks to these real-time previews, your clips play normally on the Timeline, without any rendering required. A preview can be a great time-saver when you're experimenting with different effects settings, but watch out for these catches:

✔ You need a G4 processor in your Mac (the G4 has the muscle power to generate mini-renders in real time).

✔ You have to watch these rendered previews on your Mac screen, not on a TV hooked up through a DV camera or deck (via a FireWire cable to your Mac). If you have a DV camera or deck hooked up to Final Cut Express, you can stop it from sending its signal to a TV by choosing View➪Video➪ Real-Time. If you ever want to disable real-time previews so you can see your imagery on a TV again, then choose View➪Video➪FireWire.

✔ Real-time previews work only with certain transitions and effects (for instance, the Cross Dissolve transition previews in real time but not the Spin3D transition). You'll know that a transition works in real time because Final Cut Express displays its name using bold type in its menus and in the Effects window. Some motion effects, such as scales and opacity and crops, also allow previews, but some don't, such as rotations.

✔ When you finally want to record your finished movie back to tape or export it as a digital Quicktime file, you still need to do an old-fashioned render of all the real-time effects. But at least you haven't had to render them as you experimented with them and tweaked their settings.

Understanding rendering status

You probably already know that the Final Cut Express Timeline displays a thin red line above any clip that needs rendering. This line appears in what's called a Render status bar, as shown in Figure 17-7.

The Timeline also gives you more information about a clip's rendering status. For starters, the Timeline actually features two Render status bars, just over the timecode ruler (they're so thin they may appear as one at first glance). The upper status bar is for video clips and the lower one for audio. What's more, the colors you see in these bars show the rendering status of any clips below on the Timeline.

Figure 17-7:
The video and audio Render status bars.

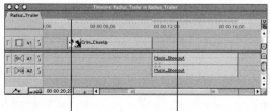

Video render status bar   Audio render statur bar

This list describes what each color means:

- ✔ **Red:** This one's probably familiar. The clip needs to be rendered. Sorry, hang out and relax.

- ✔ **Dark gray:** No need to render. You see this color for DV clips you've imported or captured, since DV is the Final Cut Express native language, and it plays these clips without any fuss.

- ✔ **Green:** This color is for effects that don't need rendering and can be played in real time. You see this color if you're lucky enough to meet the criteria noted in the previous section, "Avoiding rendering by using real-time previews".

- ✔ **Yellow:** Good news: Yellow indicates that Final Cut Express can show a real-time approximation of the final effect during playback (you see this color when you apply motion effects to a clip, like a scale or change of opacity). Bad news: When you're finished with your project and ready to record it to tape or a Quicktime file, you'll need to render these preview effects. Also, these preview renders are only approximations, like rough sketches. They don't look as good as a true render would, so if you want to see how the effects look at their best, you'll have to render them.

- ✔ **Light gray:** The clip has already been rendered! No need to worry about it!

Avoiding repeated rendering

If you've already rendered a clip on the Timeline, you sometimes can accidentally trick Final Cut Express into thinking that the clip needs rendering again, even though you're happy with the render as it is (and dread the idea of sitting around waiting for yet another render). The easiest way to create this rendering headache is by dragging some other clip to another Timeline track, directly above the rendered clip (or vice versa: dragging the rendered clip to another track directly below some other clip). Or, you can mess up the existing renders by temporarily turning off a Timeline track that contains any rendered clips (see Chapter 7). Either way, if you try either of these operations and find that Express suddenly demands to re-render your perfectly fine clips, then choose Edit⇨Undo, and figure out another approach to whatever you're trying to do (if possible).

Locating and moving rendered files

You don't have to know where the computer saves renders during the course of a project, but it can be helpful to track them down at the end of a project, when you want to delete old renders from your hard drive. (You'll be surprised by the amount of disk space old renders you've forgotten about can tie up over time). To find where Final Cut Express is saving the renders, choose Final Cut Express⇨Preferences and click the Scratch Disks tab in the Preferences dialog box. In the Scratch Disks tab, you can set up several potential scratch disks for your project, but Express saves renders (audio and video separately) to whichever disk has its check box turned on (see Figure 17-8). To the right of those check boxes, you'll see the path name that shows where, on a particular disk drive, the renders are ending up. (Express puts them in a folder called Render Files, and within that folder are folders that contain the render files for all the Express projects you've created.)

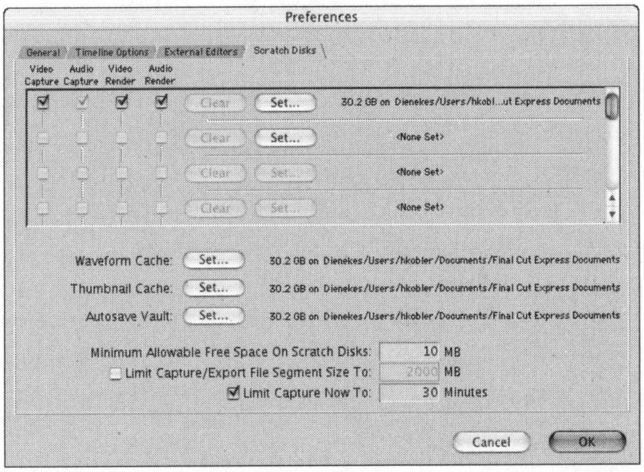

Figure 17-8:
The Scratch
Disks tab
in Prefer-
ences.

Why would you want to save audio and video renders to different places, as Final Cut Express allows? This feature is really a holdover from Final Cut Pro — some Pro projects can have very demanding rendering needs, and they separate renders to different hard disks largely to ensure speedy access to renders without dropping frames. But when working with DV video in Express, you really have no good reason to split renders between multiple drives or locations.

If you ever want to change the location where render files are going, just click the Set button that corresponds to the check boxes for Audio and Video renders, and then choose a new folder (or even a new hard drive, if you have multiple drives attached) in the Choose a Folder dialog box that comes up.

Chapter 18

Ten Tips for Becoming a Better Editor

*A*fter you've gotten your feet wet with Final Cut Express, you can do plenty of things to nurture your abilities as an editor. This chapter outlines a few tips to bring your skills to the next level.

Try Out the Final Cut Tutorials

Final Cut Express includes a DVD featuring a nice set of tutorials that take you through the basics of using all aspects of the program. These videos aren't detailed enough to take you through features step by step, but they can help give you a quick, visual overview of some of the Express meat-and-potatoes features. (You can then fill in all the important details by opening up this book!) I especially recommend taking a look at the tutorials for effects work, since those topics lend themselves to video.

If you don't have a DVD player, chances are your Mac CD-ROM drive also plays DVDs.

Study (Don't Just Watch) Movies and Commercials

A great way to improve your picture-editing instincts is to carefully study all the professional editing work on television and in movies. Record a bunch of videos, commercials, and music videos and watch them carefully — in fact, a good tactic is to watch with your TV volume turned off, so you can focus solely on how shots move from one to another. You'll see an infinite number of editing styles (fast and slow, or super-stylized and very subtle), and you can refine your own tastes from there. Finally, when you start to see the conscious design behind movie shots — that is, how the editor uses shots in a particular order to communicate information and set a mood — you'll also start seeing a payoff in your own work.

Practice on Someone Else's Real-World Footage

The best way to improve your editing skills is to edit as much as possible, and I heartily recommend that you come up with practice projects to cut together, so you can keep honing your skills. That being said, it's hard to constantly come up with new footage to edit. For instance, I used to record my own practice scenes on a video camera (using friends as placeholder actors), but eventually ran out of fresh ideas for new footage and grew frustrated with the raw (that is, *ugly*) look of the video (it was too time-consuming to shoot practice video that had a lot of polish).

I eventually discovered a great alternative: borrowing real-world, professional footage from working editors. For instance, I found an editing company that loaned me the source footage for real-world commercials its pro editors had worked with. It was a perfect solution: I worked with professionally shot footage that looked great and offered lots of angles and perspectives to choose from (called *coverage*). When I had edited this footage together, I compared my work against the final version the editing company had produced (a great learning tool).

If you're looking for good practice material, approach established editors to see whether they'll let you work with some of their finished projects. Chances are, you can find someone willing to lend an editor-in-training a hand.

Go Online and Find a Community

I recommend two great Web sites for expanding your technical grasp of Final Cut Express as well as your general editorial knowledge:

- ✔ **2-Pop.com** (`www.2-pop.com`): This world-class site focuses on all things Final Cut. Most of the emphasis is on Final Cut Pro, but Final Cut Express is similar to Pro in so many ways that you'll find plenty of useful stuff: news of Final Cut-related products, how-to tutorials, and most importantly, a variety of message forums where fellow users can answer just about any Final Cut question you can conjure up. (2-Pop has a couple of forums dedicated to other digital media topics as well.)

- ✔ **EditorsNet** (`www.editorsnet.com`): This great site has daily news about the editing business and new products, but it really shines for its interviews with pro editors (film and television editors usually) about their latest projects. These interviews and other articles give you a great perspective on both the art and the craft of real-world editing.

Join a Final Cut User Group

You can join (or just drop in on) a growing handful of user groups just for Final Cut editors. Their members typically meet monthly for product demos and helpful Q&A sessions. Some of the most active groups can be found in the following locations:

- ✔ Boston (`www.bosfcpug.org`)
- ✔ Los Angeles (`www.lafcpug.org`)
- ✔ San Francisco (`www.sfcutters.org`)

To see if a Final Cut user group is near you (or a general Mac user group that has some active Final Cut users), go to the Apple site at `www.apple.com/usergroups/contact.html`.

Upgrade Your Hardware

Even if your hardware can technically handle Final Cut Express, you can add a few items to enhance your editing experience. I have a couple of suggestions, in no particular order:

✔ **Speakers or headphones:** A nice pair of speakers or headphones can help you can pick up the subtle details in your audio.

✔ **Television monitor:** Get a TV monitor (any decent TV will do) so that you don't have to watch media clips in the Final Cut Express smallish Viewer or Canvas window.

✔ **RAM:** If your Mac has 256 or 384MB of RAM, boosting it to 512 or 640MB makes Final Cut Express run a little faster overall. You won't see major speed gains, but you will see the OS X spinning cursor less.

✔ **Programmable mouse or trackball:** A programmable mouse or trackball sports extra buttons, which you can program to invoke Final Cut Express features that you use a lot. Taking advantage of these features means you don't have to spend so much time moving your mouse around the screen or reaching for some keyboard shortcuts.

Upgrade Your Software

You can use several software packages along with Final Cut Express, depending on what type of video you're working with and what you do with the final product. After you become more experienced with Express and more sure of what you want to do with your projects, you may want to buy additional software. The following software packages are ones you may want to consider:

✔ **Sorenson 3 Professional Edition:** If you export a lot of projects as QuickTime movies (for CD-ROM or the Internet), you probably export them using the Sorenson 3 compression codec. This codec squeezes video into small file sizes but still maintains pretty good image quality — the mark of a great codec. However, you can get much better results (better-looking images at even smaller file sizes) if you buy the Professional Edition of the Sorenson 3 codec. At $299, Sorenson Pro is a bit on the expensive side but gives your exported movies a polish that sets them apart. (Most movie trailers you find online are compressed with the Sorenson professional edition.) Check out `www.sorenson.com` for more information.

✔ **Cleaner 6:** If you export a lot of projects as QuickTime movies (for DVD, CD-ROM, or the Internet), Cleaner gives you much better control over that process than Final Cut Express ever can. For starters, Cleaner lets you encode movies by the batch, automatically creating several compressed versions of the same movie. (For example, you can make low-, medium-, and high-bandwidth versions of a movie trailer, each using settings that you customize ahead of time.) Cleaner saves time by letting you preview how encoded video will look after compression and also lets you adjust image settings for your encodes (such as brightness and contrast, gamma correction, and much more). Finally, if you want to save your Express movies in other video architectures, such as RealVideo or Windows Media (both popular on the PC), Cleaner can handle that, too.

The only catch is that Cleaner costs $599 (and that's not including the Sorenson Pro codec mentioned before), but if you prepare a lot of video in a lot of different digital formats, Cleaner can be well worth its price. Check out www.discreet.com for more.

Curl Up with a Good Book

A couple of good books can help bring your editing skills and general post-production knowledge to the next level:

✔ ***In the Blink of an Eye: A Perspective on Film Editing,*** by Walter Murch (Silman-James Press): If you read just one book on editing theory, make it this one. It's short and informal and has hardly any technical stuff in it. Instead, Murch focuses on editing from a creative standpoint, with an emphasis on telling a story and setting emotion through editing. The book also has a nice section on digital editing and its effect on the aesthetics of editing. Murch knows a thing or two about editing, by the way, with editing credits on such movies as *American Graffiti; Apocalypse Now; The Godfather (Parts 2 and 3); Ghost; The English Patient;* and *The Talented Mr. Ripley.* Plus, he's a big Final Cut fan. In fact, he's the first pro editor to use Final Cut on a major motion picture (*Cold Mountain,* due in the fall of 2003).

✔ ***When the Shooting Stops, the Cutting Begins: A Film Editor's Story,*** by Ralph Rosenblum and Robert Karen (Da Capo Press): This book is another little gem about the aesthetics of editing and the flow of the editing process, as a film goes from raw dailies to final cut. Rosenblum did most of his cutting in the '60s and '70s and talks in depth about his experiences on classic movies like *The Pawnbroker* and *Annie Hall.* (I recommend renting these at a video store to get the most out of the book.)

✔ ***Understanding Comics,*** by Scott McCloud (Kitchen Sink Press): Okay, the book is not about editing per se, but it's still surprisingly helpful for filmmakers (directors, storyboard artists, and especially editors). Written in comic book form, *Understanding Comics* explains how comics are composed, read, and understood. As you read it (it's a quick read), you realize that the principles behind comic design actually apply to visual language in general — and what is video if not a visual language? Give it a try; you won't regret it.

✔ ***Practical Art of Motion Picture Sound,*** by David Lewis Yewdall (Focal Press): If you find yourself editing and affecting audio quite a bit, check out this volume. It's a great introduction to post-production audio topics from both a technical and artistic standpoint. Topics include planning an audio strategy for production and post-production, tips for recording better production audio (something a lot of all-in-one-filmmakers using Final Cut can appreciate), making preliminary versions of your score, recording sound effects, and dialogue editing.

Step Up to Final Cut Pro

If you've mastered Final Cut Express and you have some spare change lying around (er, $1,000 worth of spare change, that is), consider graduating to Final Cut Pro. It can open all your Express projects, and it uses the same interface windows (Viewer, Canvas, Timeline, and Browser), menu commands, and keyboard shortcuts as Final Cut Express. Final Cut Pro has exactly the same editing tools that Express has, so everything you learned about Express in Chapters 6 through 8 apply to Pro as well, and you get some new features to boot. Some of the benefits of working with Pro that you don't have with Express are

✔ **More flexibility in media formats:** You can work with video in any format (not just DV). That means you can create movies that use uncompressed standard definition video, or high-def video (HD), which are necessary for some top-tier broadcast work (you'll also need an expensive capture card and speedy new disk drives to handle all that high-quality video). And if you want your movie to eventually be projected on a movie screen, Pro can generate all the data that a film negative cutter needs to physically cut your film negative together, based on your digital edit.

✔ **More advanced use of keyframes:** Final Cut Pro offers all the same video and audio filters that Final Cut Express offers, but you can use keyframes to change them within a single clip. (***Remember:*** Express uses keyframes only for setting volume levels, opacity levels, and Motion tab values — not all filters). Being able to use keyframes for anything (see Figure 18-1) can be very handy (or essential) when you're doing lots of complicated effects work.

✔ **Logging and batch capture:** When capturing video, you can log it first (that is, review a tape and note all the clips you want to capture), and then tell Final Cut Pro to batch capture all the clips you want, while you go grab a latte (or do something else more productive . . . but wouldn't you rather have a latte?). Final Cut Express makes you manually capture each clip before moving on to the next one. If you have lots of video tape to review, the manual approach can be time-consuming.

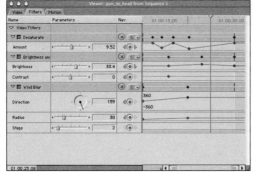

Figure 18-1:
Final Cut
Pro lets
you apply
keyframes
to filters
(seen here
in the
Viewer
window).

✔ **Media management:** Final Cut Pro has great media-management tools for consolidating and archiving projects (or select sequences within a project) when they're done, or when you just have to free up some hard drive space. For example, as you work on a project, you import and capture a lot of media that you won't end up using in your finished edit. Before you know it, your hard drive may be bursting at the seams and you'll want to free up some of that space. With Final Cut Pro, you can easily resave your project, using only the media that your movie actually uses (for instance, a project that originally hogs up 10 gigs of media could suddenly slim down to only 2 gigabytes!). The Media Manager, shown in Figure 18-2, accomplishes this mean feat. You can then continue working with this meaner, leaner project (and some welcomed free space on your hard drive), or archive the project to a backup hard drive or DVD disk, so you can still open it (and all its media) at a later date.

✔ **Offline RT:** Final Cut Pro lets you capture media in a unique compression codec called Offline RT (as opposed to a codec like DV, which you're already very familiar with). The beauty of Offline RT is that it stores video in very small file sizes — 1 gigabyte of drive space per hour of video instead of the DV rate of 13 gigabytes per hour! So even if you have a small hard drive (like those typically found in laptops), you can still store a boatload of video (a nice luxury, especially when you're working on longer projects, such as a 2-hour feature). The only catch is that Offline RT video doesn't look as good as DV video (or other formats you might work with), but that's okay, because you're just using it for editing purposes. When you finish your edit and are ready to record your final movie back to videotape or a QuickTime digital file, you can quickly recapture only the media your finished project needs, in a better codec such as DV or whatever else you want.

Final Cut Pro features lots of other enhancements — such as improved color-correction tools, the capability to work with high-end video decks, and more. You can learn more about Pro in all its splendor by checking out `www.apple.com/finalcutpro`.

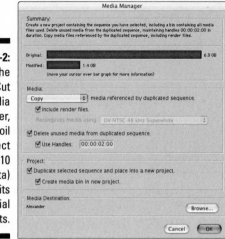

Figure 18-2:
Using the
Final Cut
Pro Media
Manager,
you can boil
a big project
(using 10
gigs of data)
down to its
essential
parts.

The Final Cut Pro $999 retail price is daunting, no doubt. But if you're a student (no, not a "student of life", but one who actually attends an accredited college), you can probably get it at a steep discount. At UCLA, in my neck of the woods, it currently sells for only $299!

Index

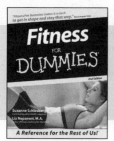

FOR DUMMIES®

A world of resources to help you grow

HOME, GARDEN & HOBBIES

0-7645-5295-3

0-7645-5130-2

0-7645-5106-X

Also available:

Auto Repair For Dummies
(0-7645-5089-6)

Chess For Dummies
(0-7645-5003-9)

Home Maintenance For Dummies
(0-7645-5215-5)

Organizing For Dummies
(0-7645-5300-3)

Piano For Dummies
(0-7645-5105-1)

Poker For Dummies
(0-7645-5232-5)

Quilting For Dummies
(0-7645-5118-3)

Rock Guitar For Dummies
(0-7645-5356-9)

Roses For Dummies
(0-7645-5202-3)

Sewing For Dummies
(0-7645-5137-X)

FOOD & WINE

0-7645-5250-3

0-7645-5390-9

0-7645-5114-0

Also available:

Bartending For Dummies
(0-7645-5051-9)

Chinese Cooking For Dummies
(0-7645-5247-3)

Christmas Cooking For Dummies
(0-7645-5407-7)

Diabetes Cookbook For Dummies
(0-7645-5230-9)

Grilling For Dummies
(0-7645-5076-4)

Low-Fat Cooking For Dummies
(0-7645-5035-7)

Slow Cookers For Dummies
(0-7645-5240-6)

TRAVEL

0-7645-5453-0

0-7645-5438-7

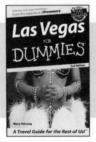

0-7645-5448-4

Also available:

America's National Parks For Dummies
(0-7645-6204-5)

Caribbean For Dummies
(0-7645-5445-X)

Cruise Vacations For Dummies 2003
(0-7645-5459-X)

Europe For Dummies
(0-7645-5456-5)

Ireland For Dummies
(0-7645-6199-5)

France For Dummies
(0-7645-6292-4)

London For Dummies
(0-7645-5416-6)

Mexico's Beach Resorts For Dummies
(0-7645-6262-2)

Paris For Dummies
(0-7645-5494-8)

RV Vacations For Dummies
(0-7645-5443-3)

Walt Disney World & Orlando For Dummies
(0-7645-5444-1)

Available wherever books are sold. Go to www.dummies.com or call 1-877-762-2974 to order direct.

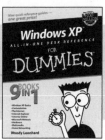

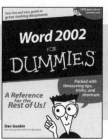

FOR DUMMIES®

Helping you expand your horizons and realize your potential

INTERNET

0-7645-0894-6

0-7645-1659-0

0-7645-1642-6

Also available:

America Online 7.0 For Dummies
(0-7645-1624-8)

Genealogy Online For Dummies
(0-7645-0807-5)

The Internet All-in-One Desk Reference For Dummies
(0-7645-1659-0)

Internet Explorer 6 For Dummies
(0-7645-1344-3)

The Internet For Dummies Quick Reference
(0-7645-1645-0)

Internet Privacy For Dummies
(0-7645-0846-6)

Researching Online For Dummies
(0-7645-0546-7)

Starting an Online Business For Dummies
(0-7645-1655-8)

DIGITAL MEDIA

0-7645-1664-7

0-7645-1675-2

0-7645-0806-7

Also available:

CD and DVD Recording For Dummies
(0-7645-1627-2)

Digital Photography All-in-One Desk Reference For Dummies
(0-7645-1800-3)

Digital Photography For Dummies Quick Reference
(0-7645-0750-8)

Home Recording for Musicians For Dummies
(0-7645-1634-5)

MP3 For Dummies
(0-7645-0858-X)

Paint Shop Pro "X" For Dummies
(0-7645-2440-2)

Photo Retouching & Restoration For Dummies
(0-7645-1662-0)

Scanners For Dummies
(0-7645-0783-4)

GRAPHICS

0-7645-0817-2

0-7645-1651-5

0-7645-0895-4

Also available:

Adobe Acrobat 5 PDF For Dummies
(0-7645-1652-3)

Fireworks 4 For Dummies
(0-7645-0804-0)

Illustrator 10 For Dummies
(0-7645-3636-2)

QuarkXPress 5 For Dummies
(0-7645-0643-9)

Visio 2000 For Dummies
(0-7645-0635-8)

Available wherever books are sold. Go to www.dummies.com or call 1-877-762-2974 to order direct.

FOR DUMMIES®

The advice and explanations you need to succeed

SELF-HELP, SPIRITUALITY & RELIGION

0-7645-5302-X

0-7645-5418-2

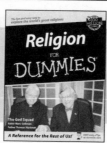

0-7645-5264-3

Also available:

The Bible For Dummies
(0-7645-5296-1)

Buddhism For Dummies
(0-7645-5359-3)

Christian Prayer For Dummies
(0-7645-5500-6)

Dating For Dummies
(0-7645-5072-1)

Judaism For Dummies
(0-7645-5299-6)

Potty Training For Dummies
(0-7645-5417-4)

Pregnancy For Dummies
(0-7645-5074-8)

Rekindling Romance For Dummies
(0-7645-5303-8)

Spirituality For Dummies
(0-7645-5298-8)

Weddings For Dummies
(0-7645-5055-1)

PETS

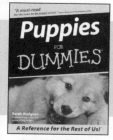

0-7645-5255-4

0-7645-5286-4

0-7645-5275-9

Also available:

Labrador Retrievers For Dummies
(0-7645-5281-3)

Aquariums For Dummies
(0-7645-5156-6)

Birds For Dummies
(0-7645-5139-6)

Dogs For Dummies
(0-7645-5274-0)

Ferrets For Dummies
(0-7645-5259-7)

German Shepherds For Dummies
(0-7645-5280-5)

Golden Retrievers For Dummies
(0-7645-5267-8)

Horses For Dummies
(0-7645-5138-8)

Jack Russell Terriers For Dummies
(0-7645-5268-6)

Puppies Raising & Training Diary For Dummies
(0-7645-0876-8)

EDUCATION & TEST PREPARATION

0-7645-5194-9

0-7645-5325-9

0-7645-5210-4

Also available:

Chemistry For Dummies
(0-7645-5430-1)

English Grammar For Dummies
(0-7645-5322-4)

French For Dummies
(0-7645-5193-0)

The GMAT For Dummies
(0-7645-5251-1)

Inglés Para Dummies
(0-7645-5427-1)

Italian For Dummies
(0-7645-5196-5)

Research Papers For Dummies
(0-7645-5426-3)

The SAT I For Dummies
(0-7645-5472-7)

U.S. History For Dummies
(0-7645-5249-X)

World History For Dummies
(0-7645-5242-2)

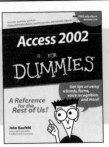